Accounting and Recordkeeping Made Easy for the Self-Employed

Accounting and Recordkeeping Made Easy for the Self-Employed

JACK FOX

JOHN WILEY & SONS, INC.
New York • Chichester • Brisbane • Toronto • Singapore

Copyright © 1995 by John Wiley & Sons Inc.
Published by John Wiley & Sons, Inc.

This publication is designed to provide accurate and authoritative information in regard to the subject matter covered. It is sold with the understanding that the publisher is not engaged in rendering legal, accounting, or other professional services. If legal advice or other expert assistance is required, the services of a competent professional person should be sought.

Library of Congress Cataloging in Publication Data:
Fox, Jack.
    Accounting and recordkeeping made easy for the self-employed/ Jack Fox.
      p. cm.
    Includes index.
    ISBN 0-471-03216-6 (cloth). -- ISBN 0-471-03217-4 (paper)
    1. Small business--Accounting. 2. Financial statements.
3. Accounting--Data processing. 4. Self-employed--Accounting.
I. Title.
HF5657.F65   1995
657'.91--dc20   94-16687
                                           CIP

DEDICATION

This book is dedicated to the countless entrepreneurs who built this great country of ours.

It is also dedicated to the memory of the six million Jewish victims of the Holocaust who were prevented from living their lives and dreams. May that memory stay in focus forever so that the world may never again experience such a horror.

ACKNOWLEDGMENTS

I would like to acknowledge and express my gratitude to a number of people who contributed to this project and to my life:

Benjamin Fox, my beloved father, who demonstrated that one did not require a formal education to have a thorough grasp of business. Rebecca Fox, my wonderful mother, who literally taught me the rudiments of writing and penmanship. Mrs. Lichtman, my sixth grade teacher at P.S. 177 in Brooklyn, New York, who instilled a love for journalism and responsible writing and introduced me to *The New York Times*. Professor John Bauer at Baruch College of the City University of New York, for sharing and caring. Robert T. Porter, M.D., for contributing so much to my putting it all together. Midge Longley, effective and caring mentor at *The New York Times*. Ronald Fieve, M.D., who provided the answers and the solutions at a critical time in my life. Tracy King, my editor at John Wiley, for her enthusiasm and invaluable suggestions throughout the writing of this book.

Finally, I thank my wife, Carole Olafson Fox, a patient and helpful listener. I am fortunate to have her as a partner.

Contents

CONTENTS

CONTENTS

CONTENTS

CONTENTS

CONTENTS

CONTENTS

CONTENTS

Come now and let us reason together.

Bible, Isaiah 1:17

Preface

Once upon a time, businesses did not require keeping records, elaborate accounting systems, governmental reporting burdens, onerous tax preparation and filings, permits, and regulations on everything from environmental concerns to sexual harassment.

During that time of "once upon a time," business had achieved the phenomenon much sought after by today's business establishment—the "paperless" society. Today, the businessperson faces stacks of newspapers, magazines, important documents, bills, forms, research reports, bank statements, letters to read and answer, competitive intelligence, invitations, to-do lists, vacation schedules, newsletters, have-to lists, appointments, checks from customers, want-to lists, and internal memos. To make matters worse, some of the aforementioned arrives almost daily, threatening to drown the businessperson—especially if he or she is self-employed—under the deluge of paper.

If the thought of accounting brings up memories of your struggle with Accounting 101 in college or the fact that you opted to avoid accounting courses altogether, this book is for you. A great many people like you who undertake a business venture or are contemplating self-employment are fearful of attempting their own accounting. Some cringe at the idea of tackling anything even remotely connected with mathematics. Others are further intimidated by the jargon of the accounting professionals. Even when accountants use terms we think we understand, such as "cash basis," to refer to the accounting system, we often find, utlimately, that the words do not mean what we think they mean.

But help is on the way! Accounting software is now readily available and affordable. Such software products can serve the needs of the self-employed and are described and evaluated in this book. You, as a self-employed businessperson, will be able to know at all times how you are doing in terms of costs and profits, because the computer is posting and balancing the books. It is no longer necessary for you to be an accountant, or even a bookkeeper, to keep your own accounts; you don't even have to know how to calculate percentages or subtract line 6c from line 6b.

Aside from whether you can or cannot do it yourself, there is the important and often overlooked question of why you need to use accounting in your venture. Why must you keep records? The answer to that question bears most strongly on the issue of doing it yourself. If the accounting system fails to provide the proper information in a timely manner, the self-employed businessperson may miss important opportunities. Inadequacy of accounting information is a fatal weakness because it conceals the true state of the business and thus misleads you, the owner. In many cases, a business loses money for a long period of time before the self-employed owner becomes aware of the situation. By the time the losses become clearly apparent, even with proper feedback, it is often too late to save the venture.

The basic goal of this book is to assist the businessperson in learning more effective ways of managing the financial and clerical aspects of a business. This book differs from typical how-to books on self-employment, in that it covers the newest in technology, highlighting real breakthroughs in computer software. Those of you who are actually engaged in self-employment as well as those who are thinking of and preparing for self-employment will find the material of great interest. This book will educate the reader as to the benefits of learning and applying accounting theory and practice to proper recordkeeping and information retrieval. The various chapters address head-on such vitally important topics as how to understand accounting and how to manage the paper flow of business. It is important for almost everyone in business to gain these insights.

The typical book on self-employment offers this kind of information only indirectly. Such books generally do precisely what they caution readers not to do. They focus on selecting business advisors rather than on understanding and mastering the analytical and financial accounting dynamics that will mean the most to a business's success. Self-employment, from the perspective of the business owner, has been explored, analyzed, ruminated on, and written about, almost to excess, but how to understand accounting, perform vital financial exercises, and master the paper chase—understanding what is necessary—has rarely been explored other than superficially and in passing.

I write only on subjects of which I have some reasonable amount of personal knowledge. Although I have written two other books on business topics, they addressed specifically the professional advisors to small business, rather than focused directly on the self-employed person per se. However, the idea for this book was inspired primarily by my experiences in presenting seminars at universities, community colleges, and professional groups. Calls and letters from many readers and seminar participants have confirmed and reinforced the belief that this book is wanted and needed.

You will find that following somewhat revolutionary ideas about fundamental principles and practices of accounting and recordkeeping (e.g., that accounting can be fun), and especially the eye-opening methods used dramatize the concepts, command special attention, can provide you with new insights into what makes the front office, and the back office, really work.

Your new and more cogent insight into accounting and record-keeping will allow you to grasp and accept the rationale as to what accounting really is, or should be. A completely fresh and infinitely more useful perspective on the books and records of a business can replace the stale and never very helpful accounting-is-accounting-is-accounting approach, so beloved of many financial gurus.

I wish you well and godspeed on your self-employment path. For me it has been worth all the effort. There is no substitute for being in charge of your own business future. The promise of rewards is always present, as is an awareness that the extra effort is directly beneficial to you and your family. There is no more exciting activity in the marketplace than working for yourself.

Jack Fox, M.B.A.
San Diego, California

TRADEMARKS, REGISTERED TRADEMARKS, AND SERVICEMARKS

America Online is a registered trademark of America Online, Inc.

Apple, Macintosh are registered trademarks of Apple Computer, Inc.

Apple II, Quadra, and *TrueType* are trademarks of Apple Computer, Inc.

Computer Buyer's Guide and Handbook is a trademark of Bedford Communications, Inc.

Borland Paradox and *Paradox* are trademarks of Borland International, Inc.

OnTime is a registered trademark of Campbell Services, Inc.

DEC is a registered trademark of Digital Equipment Corporation.

M.Y.O.B. Accounting Software is a trademark of Best!Ware Inc.

CompuServe is a registered trademark of CompuServe Incorporated.

Simply Accounting is a trademark of Computer Associates International, Inc.

DacEasy is a registered trademark of DacEasy, Inc.

Delrina is a trademark of Delrina Technology Inc.

Dialog is a servicemark of Dialog Information Services, Inc.

GEnie is a trademark of General Electric Company.

Delphi is a trademark of General VideoText Corporation.

HP is a registered trademark of the Hewlett-Packard Company.

ClientWorks is a trademark of IMS, Information Management Services.

Intel, FaxBack are registered trademarks and *Intel 486, i386, i486* and *Pentium* are trademarks of Intel Corporation.

IBM, OS/2 are registered trademarks and *Power PC* is a trademark of International Business Machines Corporation.

PC World is a trademark owned by International Data Group and used under license by PC World Communications, Inc.

Quicken is a registered trademark and *QuickBooks* is a trademark of Intuit.

Lotus, Lotus 1-2-3, Ami Pro and *Approach* are registered trademarks and *Lotus Notes, Organizer, cc:Mail, Improv, Smarticon, In-Call* are trademarks of Lotus Development Corporation.

BusinessWorks and *BusinessWorks Accounting for Windows* are registered trademarks of Manzanita Software Systems.

Microsoft, Microsoft Access, and *MS-DOS* are registered trademarks and *Microsoft Excel, Word, Microsoft Profit, Windows, Fox-Base,* and *FoxPro* are trademarks of Microsoft Corporation.

Motorola is a trademark of Motorola, Inc.

Mondial, Pacioli 2000, and *CashBiz* are trademarks of M-USA Business Systems, Inc.

One-Write Plus is a registered trademark and *NEBS Software, NEBS,* and *New England Business Service* are trademarks of New England Business Service.

SQL°Text Retrieval is a trademark of Oracle Corporation.

Peachtree Accounting is a trademark of Peachtree Software, Inc.

Polaris PackRat, Action Bar, Action Buttons, Instant Options, PackRatBasic, and *SmartStart* are trademarks of Polaris Software, Inc.

Prodigy is a registered trademark of Prodigy Services Company.

Rolodex is a registered trademark of Rolodex Corporation.

SourceMate and *AccountMate* are registered trademarks of SourceMate Information Systems, Inc.

By Design Portfolio is a trademark of Streetwise Software, Inc. *Symantic Q & A* is a trademark of Symantic Corporation.

Post-it is a trademark of the 3M Company.

Timeslips and *Time$heet Professional* are registered trademarks and *TAL Timeslips Accounting Link, TSRemote, TSSpeller, LapTrack, Timeslips Navigator, TimeView,* and *TSTimer* are trademarks of Timeslips Corporation.

Unix is a registered trademark of Unix System Laboratories, Inc.

DataPerfect, LetterPerfect, WordPerfect, Grammatik and *PlanPerfect* are registered trademarks and *WordPerfect InForms, Quick Finder, WordPerfect Office, TamperSeal, Button Bar* and *WordPerfect Intellitag* are trademarks of WordPerfect Corporation.

PC Computing and *PC Magazine* are registered trademarks of Ziff-Davis Publishing Company, L.P.

Other products not specifically cited as trademarks are the trademarks of their respective owners.

> Opportunities are usually disguised as hard work, so most people don't recognize them.
>
> Ann Landers

Chapter 1

Getting Organized

The personal face of business is all too familiar. Most people have, at one time or another, suffered from the underlying anxiety or have borne the burden of seeing colleagues and associates suffering from it. The signs are clear even if the malaise is not: an edgy feeling that there are not enough hours in the day to do it all; the multiplying stacks of papers; the constant interruptions; the seemingly incompetent staff; and the loss of confidence. Instance by instance, basic skills are compromised by what appears to be an inability to organize the business environment.

SUCCESS STARTS WITH ORGANIZATION

The process of regaining or establishing control by getting organized is often difficult. The most common assumptions equate a business environment with order—rows of neat desks, organized shelves, and clean counters. The precept is that orderliness is next to godliness. Any sign of disorganization indicates weakness and lack of moral fiber.

Other paragons of business management consider sloppiness and disorderliness to be signs of creativity. They believe disorganization is their manifest destiny. Some business leaders believe that organization requires an inflexible regimen. They feel instinctively that organization is bureaucratic, related to nitpicking, and generally unworthy of people like themselves who are capable of thinking on a grander scale.

And other businessowners think that a secretary should be able to organize everything for them.

Not only are none of the foregoing true, but these persistent misconceptions often get in the way of genuine organization and the benefits such organization can bring to your business. Neatness and organization do not necessarily go together. It is purely a matter of style.

As far as entrusting your secretary with the role of organizing for you, forget it! Your secretary has the potential to be a key organizing aide, yes, but only you, however, can define the needs and set the policies that organizing requires.

Essentially, the ability to organize is a learned skill. It requires a set of methods and tools with which to arrange your time and work load so as to meet your goals.

Being organized is not an end in itself, though it is a vehicle to take you from where you are to where you want to be. A good system expresses the organization of your mind within in the environment. You can achieve your goals through skillful management of time, data, paper, and people.

One of the prime motives for reading this book is that you want your business to be successful. Why, therefore, should you be concerned about effective accounting and management of record-keeping in your business? So you and your business can be more successful.

Success means different things to different people. For some, success is the additional money to be earned with a prosperous business. For others, success means the opportunity to expand the business and the recognition that goes with it. For many, success means more personal time for golf, traveling, or playing on the beach. For still others, success means the increase in prestige, money, or fame that comes with a reputation for always getting results.

Regardless of what motivates you to develop the necessary abilities, the end result is always the same: using your time and skills better leads to greater success, however success is defined. People who become successful earn their success. However, not everyone who wants to be successful will actually achieve it.

CREATING A BALANCED, REWARDING LIFE

Of the many entrepreneurs I have known and interviewed, not one said that hard work wasn't involved—hard work, long hours, and putting their resources on the line. Very few, however, reported regretting the effort, and fewer still would go back to work for someone else if that were possible.

Despite the long hours demanded by self-employment, well-organized entrepreneurs have greater control over their time, and certainly over their activities, and a better balance in their lives than they had when they worked for someone else. Although it can't be proven scientifically, it seems that the self-employed are more interested in achievements than in amassing wealth. They tend to maximize their options rather than their income, and the result is, for them, a balanced life.

In 1900 nearly half of all working Americans were self-employed. The proportion dropped steadily, reaching a low of 7 percent in 1970, rebounding to 9 percent in 1985, and expected to reach 15 percent by 1995, according to the Newhouse News Service. Working without a safety net poses many risks, and most new businesses fail. However, the courageous minority will continue to move or to be pushed in that direction, drawn by the possibility of the many benefits, including the potential for a balanced, rewarding life.

THE FIVE BASIC INGREDIENTS OF SUCCESS

Success in any type of endeavor requires at least five basic ingredients:

1. Positive attitude;
2. Sufficient time;
3. Necessary skills;
4. Effective tools; and
5. Consistent maintenance.

Maintain a positive attitude and realize that you can and will develop a system for your business and yourself (with the help of this book) that will meet your needs and suit your temperament. You will find a sense of relief when you realize how much simpler your recordkeeping can become and how you can use your computer to manage records and data so that you can manage your business more efficiently. There is no perfect universal way to maintain an accounting and recordkeeping system. Your system must be designed around your individual needs. There are many effective ways to meet those needs. As you set up and use your system, you will continue to find all sorts of ways to streamline and improve upon it. Various systems and computer software are discussed in subsequent chapters, but don't fall into the trap of being concerned about how other people or businesses work. Concentrate on the methods and software that work for you. Keep in mind that any system you develop is only a tool to enable you to do what you want or need to do. Make sure that the system is your servant, rather than the other way around. Managing your recordkeeping system is a lot like exercise. Most people hate exercise, but they love having exercised. Few businesspeople, if any, enjoy recordkeeping and accounting, but taking the time to set up a system that works for their business means less time searching for items and shuffling paper, and more time reaping the benefits and achieving satisfying results.

PROCRASTINATION EQUALS FAILURE

Procrastination costs money. In some cases it can lead to the failure of your business. Nobody likes to bring up the matter of business mortality, especially in books dealing with better and more effective ways to run your business. Capitalization and management skill, as well as other factors, are the primary determinants of success or failure. Procrastination is surely among the "other factors."

Here is a list of the best and the worst small business performers as compiled by the Small Business Administration in terms of success or failure rates over the past twenty years:

Business	Success Rate (%)
Skilled nursing homes	96.4
Veterinarians	96.3
Vocational schools	94.1
Portrait studios	93.8
Dentists	93.4
Physicians	92.5
Optometrists	91.3
Petroleum bulk stations	89.3
Petroleum wholesale	88.4
Bowling alleys	87.3
Chiropractors	86.5
Radio stations	85.9
Funeral directors	85.5
Hotels/motels	84.2
Auto repair; miscellaneous	82.8
Water transport	81.9
Legal services	80.7
Auto painting	79.6
Mail order houses	79.3
Health care, miscellaneous	79.2
Drug stores	79.0
Accountants	78.6
Laundries	78.5
Photo Labs	78.5
Architects	77.6
Gas stations	77.1

Business	Failure rate (%)
Masonry contractors	68.8
Radio/TV repair	58.6
Men's stores	56.1
Wood furniture upholsters	55.4
Single-family residential builders	54.3
Music stores	53.7
Taxicabs	53.5
Women's stores	51.8
Sporting goods, wholesale	50.0
Plasterer/drywaller	48.9
Wood furniture	48.4
Meat and fish market	48.1
Trucking, long distance	47.9
Trucking, local	47.4
Industrial builder	46.9
Highway construction contracting	46.6
Family clothes store	46.5
Used car dealers	46.3

DIGGING OUT FROM UNDER THAT MOUNTAIN OF PAPER CALLED "MAIL"

Whatever your business, whether you are a self-employed sole proprietor working alone or own an enterprise with many employees, you are, or will be, deluged with paper. There are stacks of bills, advertising material, product solicitations, catalogs, junk mail and, it is hoped, checks all over your desk or kitchen table, which seem to multiply before your eyes.

You might feel that the situation is out of control. You can, however, stop the pattern with an effective paper management system. *Paper management*—or, more broadly, *records management*, to encompass the electronic data in your computer—will assist you in managing the information that is important to you.

With any type of business you confront a large mass of mail that arrives daily, demanding various types of response. The computer age was heralded as the advent of the "paperless society," but the result was the creation of even more paper forms and increasingly sophisiticated direct mail which is segmented, targeted, personalized, and delivered to your business. Perhaps your business uses a computer in this way or perhaps you will soon join the ranks of businesses using the computer for marketing and other purposes. The way to deal effectively with and profit from the deluge of information generated and facilitated by computers is to use your own computer to become part of the solution.

Just deciding what to do with the various pieces of mail can become a major issue. Remember, what you do with each piece of mail is not nearly as important as doing it consistently.

GOOD RECORDKEEPING—A KEY TO SUCCESS

Each year in the United States more than 600,000 new businesses are launched by independent men and women eager to make their own decisions, express their own ideas, and be their own boss. All hope to attain the personal satisfaction that comes from the successful operation of one's own business. Yet the reality of economic business life is very harsh. More than half of the businesses that fail each year are in their first five years of operation. More than 85 percent of the businesses that start each year will fail within five years. A good portion of this failure is more than likely due to poor recordkeeping and paper management.

Start by Sorting Data into Four Categories

There is a simple business axiom regarding recordkeeping: Data clutter, both paper and electronic, is the result of uncompleted decisions; effective management is making decisions and acting upon them.

There are only four questions to ask about any item of data:

1. Do I really need to retain this?
2. Where should I keep it?

3. How long should I or must I keep it?

4. How can I find it when I need it?

Also, there are only four basic things you can do with any one item of data. Understand this concept and you can sort your data into four categories:

1. To do;

2. To pay;

3. To read; and

4. To file.

The rest of the mountain of data litter is not important at this time. What is important is not to get sidetracked with concerns about the process. You are only sorting now, so don't start reading the latest correspondence from your most important supplier or pause to wonder why you didn't answer that important letter from the subscription service, which might cost you your entry in the $10 million sweepstakes. You are just sorting, so keep on sorting.

To Do.   Once you have sorted the entire pile, piles, or boxes, go through each category again. Begin with the papers in the to-do pile, and ask yourself these questions:

- Do I really need to do this? If not, dump it in the trash or file it as necessary.
- Is it too late to do this? If it is too late, file it or dump it.
- Do I really want to do this? If the answer is no, delegate it or dump it.
- Does anybody care whether I do this? If the answer is no, then why should you? Dump it or file it.

The rest of your to-do data should be only those matters that you must do something about.

To Pay.   Ask yourself these questions:

- Has this already been paid? Check your computerized accounting system. If it has, mark it paid and file it. Often suppliers send duplicate bills without indicating "Duplicate" on the invoice. A bill may also have been sent by the creditor shortly before it was paid by your business, and hence it is a duplicate bill. Follow the accounting system and you will not pay a bill twice.
- Is there a problem with this bill that needs to be researched? If the answer is yes, move the bill into the to-do category so the problem can be straightened out before it is paid erroneously.

All matters pertaining to accounting should be directed to the accounting area of the business. A separate department or room is not necessary. Keep all financial papers, invoices, checks, statements, tax returns, and related correspondence in a segregated area for entry into the accounting system.

To Read.   Whatever you do as you go through this category, do not succumb to the temptation to read the magazines, journals, or catalogs. Quickly scan the table of contents and ask yourself these questions:

- Is there a worthwhile reason that I must read this? If there isn't, dump it.
- Do I have time to read this? If negative, dump it.
- Is this out of date? If the material has been updated, contains outdated information, or has been replaced with a new edition, dump it.
- Do I have more than three months' worth of issues? If you have magazines backed up more than three months, consider canceling your subscription (you usually get a refund on unmailed issues) and eliminate at least the earliest month.

Once you have gone through the materials and discarded as many magazines, trade publications, and journals as you can bear to part with, review the remaining materials and cut out any articles that you need to read and staple them together. Throw away the rest of the magazine, journal, or other material and put the articles in the to-read bin. Carry a file of these articles in your briefcase so that you can read from them when waiting for appointments, during a commute (if you are not driving), or during breaks.

To File. Eighty percent of everything you file you will never look at again. Consider how expensive it is to use space for paper storage and how much time is expended to actually file the materials. You have three filing options:

1. File in archival files;
2. File in current files; or
3. File in circular files.

Archival files are usually kept in cardboard file boxes available in both letter and legal sizes at office supply stores and warehouse club-type stores. They may be stored in a garage, off-site storage unit, closet, or warehouse. Materials that should be kept and stored are those that you are required by law to keep for a specified period of time. There are a few concrete rules about how long documents must be kept. To determine which of your important records need to be kept and for how long, check with your accountant, your attorney, or the IRS. Generally, you must keep your records as long as they are important for any federal tax law. You should keep records that support an item of income or a deduction on your return at least until the *period of limitations* expires for that return. (A period of limitations is the limited period of time after which no legal action can be brought.) Usually this is three years from the date you file the return or two years from the date you pay the tax, whichever is later. The IRS treats returns filed before the due date as filed on the due date.

If you do not report income that you should report, and it is more than 25 percent of the income shown on your return, the period of limitations does not expire until six years after you file the return. If a return is false or fraudulent, or if no return is filed, an action can generally be brought at any time.

There are instances when you should keep your records longer than the period of limitations. For example, you should keep records relating to the basis of property you own as long as they are needed to figure the basis of the original or replacement property.

To verify the nontaxable part of distributions from your IRA, keep a copy of Form 8606 (Nondeductible IRA Contributions, Distributions, and Basis). Also keep copies of the following forms and records until all distributions are made from your IRA(s).

- Forms 1040 filed for each year you made a nondeductible contribution;
- Forms 5498 or similar statements you received showing the value of your IRA(s) for each year you received a distribution; and
- Forms 1099-R received for each year you received a distribution.

Moreover, new laws may provide tax benefits to taxpayers who can prove from their records from previous years that they are entitled to such benefits.

Good records will help you if the IRS selects your personal or business tax return(s) for examination. The examination of a return usually occurs one to three years after the return has been filed. If you have good records, you should be able to clear up any questionable items and determine the correct tax with a minimum of effort. If you have not kept good records, you may have to spend a considerable amount of time getting statements and receipts from various sources. You may also have to pay more in taxes because you cannot prove expenses deducted or the basis of property sold.

An important consideration to keep in mind is that the storage area for your archival records must be clean, dry, and free of vermin that could eventually ruin your records.

Current files contain materials that are used as a resource on a regular basis, including current financial, business, and legal documents.

Circular files are also known as the trash! The best part of this classification is that you don't have to spend time and money to set up files before you put the papers into a trash can or plastic garbage bag. All you have to do is dump it in and cart it out.

YOUR OFFICE SHOULD BE "USER FRIENDLY"

A paperless office is as likely as a paperless bathroom. It may be diffiicult to accept the fact that you are disorganized, unless you are one of the very few who are well organized. If you find that your work habits have slowly eroded and now affect your bottom line, that is a sure sign of disorganization. If bills are past due, receivables are late, and hot leads are turning cold, that's further evidence of disorganization. The worst sign is that you are avoiding your office.

As you establish an organized data processing center (often known as your office), carefully consider the furniture and equipment you should buy in order to make information processing (paper pushing) as painless as possible.

Before arranging your office, take stock of your physical surroundings. It may seem insignificant, but even something like a poorly insulated window can cause enormous problems later. Plan your work space carefully; once you get your office furniture and equipment in place, you'll find it difficult to shift it around. The best thing to do is set aside an entire room for your office. That way you'll have a space where you won't be interrupted and you can close the door on your work at the end of the day.

Start With That Mess You Call a Desk

Take a good look at your desk. Chances are you'll find an abundance of paper. Because you are striving to build a successful business, you must try to keep up with the latest developments and breakthroughs that affect your business. You routinely sift through huge stacks of data looking for the information you need, which is buried under tons of information you don't need. Clear your desk and make room for the essentials.

Your desk, or the desk arrangement you designate for your work center, is very important to your business success and satisfaction. The desk has to work for you. It must be functional and "user friendly."

Clean the Floors, Rearrange Furniture, and Sort Your In-Box

First, tackle the floors. Eliminate the stacks from the floor so that you can open and close the closet door. After the floor has been completely cleared, rearrange the office furniture, and end the session by sorting through the wire rack of overflowing papers that is your in-box, chores that have dominated your thoughts for weeks.

Create a Filing System to Eliminate Clutter

The next task is to create a filing system. Write a list of the main categories of your business activities. Justify the files to force yourself to think about how necessary they are to your business. Discard any unnecessary paper.

Many people are so emotionally involved with everything in their office that when they try to organize, they get distracted from the project at hand. Check your daily action files, which you probably have not used for some time. Action files are those which should be used on a daily basis. One file "Call Today" would contain materials, letters, seminar announcements or anything that you receive in the mail that you want to call that day. It is more than a "to do" list since it contains more information and paper than you can attach to a list. "Irons in the Fire" is a folder that contains bits and pieces of various projects or projects in the making that have not yet progressed to their own individual file. "Letters to Write" is another folder to be reckoned with on a daily basis as is "Follow Up" which implies just what it says. You can utilize your own personalized action files but keep in mind that you can overdo it. Work with the minimum necessary to keep track of activities. Do not try to over-compartmentalize your files as it could have a negative influence on anxiety. Action files should be recycled frequently and not used as storage.

Relabel your files to match a new color-coded system, for instance, red for Accounts Payable, green for Accounts Receivable, blue for Projects, yellow for General Information, and white for other categories. Assign one file drawer to each color. When checking folders, throw away duplicate information and merge related files.

Clean Out Your Closet

Organize your closet (if you have one) by assigning a specific purpose or task to each shelf. For instance, product display baskets could go on the top shelf, literature about products on the next, and accounting and recordkeeping software and materials on the third shelf. Cartons of materials could go on the bottom, but the contents must be necessary; the cartons should not be just a storage place for materials you don't feel like going through.

Sort Your Computer Files

Rearrange the computer files to conform with the nomenclature of the physical files, treating major directories as if they were file cabinets, second-level directories as file drawers, and subordinate directories as file folders.

DON'T THINK SMALL!

Don't think small just because your business isn't one of the Fortune 500. Here are some pointers on setting up a home or small business office that makes the most of the latest technologies—without breaking your budget.

Take Advantage of the Waldo Revolution

Office automation isn't just for big companies with big budgets. Whether you work in a home office in a spare bedroom or in your basement, or in a small office in a commercial district or in an executive office setup, you can still take advantage of the latest technologies to work more productively. Hardware and software prices continue to drop, so now is the perfect time to get a faster, more powerful system or to add a network (if you need it) and phone and fax equipment to your office system.

Office automation is one of those mysterious terms that seems to say a lot without saying anything specific. But office automation is not so nebulous after all. It just means taking advantage of the *waldo revolution*.

Robert Heinlein coined the term "waldo" in his 1942 novella to describe the devices people in the not-too-distant future would be using to work from home, controlling machines in factories hundreds of miles away. Do waldoes exist today? Absolutely. The proliferation of inexpensive personal computers (PCs) and improvements in communications technology have turned the PC into a waldo of sorts, enabling a growing number of people to take work home at night from their "real" offices, spend part of their workweek at home, or even work entirely at home.

Choose the Right Equipment for Your Office

A full-time home office or small business office requires much the same equipment as a conventional one. Whether you have a small conventional office downtown or an office at home, your equipment needs are going to be much the same. Wherever you set up shop, you'll have one or more PCs, possibly a network, a printer, phone and fax equipment, a copier, and a few other bits and pieces of hardware. You'll also need software to make all that wonderful technology work.

PC Requirements. Thinking about your PC requirements is a good starting point. For a conventional office, the logical conclusion

15

might be to buy one PC for each person who could use one. But because PCs are among the most expensive pieces of equipment you'll need, it may make sense to consider a different approach. We will discuss the specifics of hardware and software requirements in later chapters.

Take a look at how the people in your office will probably make use of computer resources. If their needs are such that they would use a system only half the time and it's possible to stagger their work load, then install PCs on a time-sharing basis. Give each user access to a shared system for a certain number of hours during the day. If possible, add an extra PC to allow for work overflow, but take care that it isn't monopolized by any one person. See whether you can have work done by associates or independent contractors who would work out of their own offices and use their own equipment. Work can be transmitted by modem, allowing you to avoid the expense of the additional equipment. In addition, there is the benefit of not having to pay the employment taxes of regular employees.

If you're setting up a home office, your PC requirements will be somewhat different. Assuming that you are the only person who is going to be working in your office, it might seem reasonable to conclude that you need only one PC. But have you considered the computer needs of your spouse, housemate, or children? If your spouse will also be bringing work home, two systems might make more sense.

Setting up two systems, however, doesn't have to cost you twice as much as one. You can load up one system with plenty of disk space and CPU (central processing unit) power, use a minimum configuration for the other system, and connect the two with a peer-to-peer network for sharing disk and printer resources. Having two systems also gives you the benefit of a backup system in the event something terrible happens to one of the systems in the middle of a crucial project.

When you've decided how many PCs you need and can afford, what type should you buy? Although any Windows-ready PC will serve your needs, you must pay special attention to features such as expandability, size of the case, and upgradability. The same goes for peripherals, which must frequently duplicate the functionality of voice-mail, fax, and modem; copier and scanner; filing cabinets and data backups. The good news is that with the proliferation of multifunction peripherals, getting up and running can be fairly easy and not too expensive.

You can never work too smartly or too efficiently. A little extra forethought and planning as to how you'll run your operation pays off later in time and money.

Keep it simple. Many self-employed individuals get carried away with software for letterheads, business cards, and faxes. DTP (desktop publishing) and graphics applications only make it worse, allowing you to customize every font and pull in any image you want—there's a danger of doing it merely because you can. Stick to templates whenever possible; they'll keep your output looking professional, rather than overdone or amateurish.

The Advantages and Disadvantages of a Notebook. A major consideration in regard to your computer needs is whether or not to buy a notebook PC. Although you are limited in the devices you can install in a notebook, it offers a versatility that a nonportable system just can't match. For example, you can use the computer in the back seat of your minivan while your spouse drives the family to the shore for a working vacation.

The notebook may also give you more flexibility at home. When it gets hot in your office in the afternoon, you can pick up the PC and cordless phone and move to the basement, where it's cool. When the weather is nice, you can work out on the deck (working at home does have its perks).

If you're setting up an office outside your home and face the possibility of having to take work home with you, a notebook makes even more sense. If you own a notebook, you don't have to copy your work onto a disk and take the files home to a second system. Instead, just unplug the notebook and take the whole thing home with you. The same benefits apply when you're traveling.

As versatile as they are, however, notebooks aren't the best option for some situations, primarily because of a lack of expandability in today's notebooks. This drawback may be solved by the time you are reading this book—you might even be reading it on a notebook computer. If your work requires special-purpose hardware that can't be connected externally to the notebook via SCSI, parallel or serial interfaces, you may be limited to a desktop system. SCSI are the initials for Small Computer Systems Interface and is pronounced Scuzzy by much of the computer community. A system-level inter-faces that provide what is essentially a complete expansion bus into which to plug peripherals.

Nevertheless, you can connect many devices to a notebook system. CD-ROM drives, scanners, modems, network adapters, and many other devices can be installed in the notebook's PCMCIA slots or connected to special port adapters, depending on the device. Expect audio adapters and other special-purpose devices to evolve over the next year or two to serve an emerging notebook market. PCMCIA stands for Personal Computer Memory Card Industry Association, Standard. It is far more than a simple set of physical specifications for card dimensions. The standard also describes file formats and data structures, a method through which a card can convey its configuration and capabilities to a host, a device-independent means of accessing card hardware and software links independent of operating systems and currently remains the only standard for the expansion of notebooks and smaller PCs.

Many notebooks can work in tandem with a docking station to overcome this drawback. A docking station sits on your desk and the notebook plugs, or docks, into the station. Many docking stations enable you to install standard ISA bus adapters and disk drives in them, so it doesn't matter that you can't install these devices in the notebook itself. Docking stations also simplify the process of con-necting to your printer, network, or other peripherals when you use the notebook in the office. The peripherals remain connected to the docking station, and you simply unplug the notebook and go. Notebook PCs can also be connected to a full-sized monitor. ISA (Industry Standard Architecture) bus adapters are a facility for transferring data between several devices located between two end points, only one device being able to transmit at a given moment. The bus is governed by rules that dictate which signals flow when and where. These rules determine how fast and successful information passes across the bus, what resources are available to expansion boards, and whether the overall computer works.

SUMMARY

Organization is a key to success in any venture, but it is imperative for all small businessowners. Although the techniques we discussed in this chapter can be painful to implement, the results will be reward enough. Organize and you will stay organized and successful. Disorganization leads to failure.

> The art of living lies less in eliminating our troubles than in growing with them.
>
> Bernard M. Baruch

Chapter 2

Understanding Accounting Basics

The typical self-employed person has no desire to ever become an expert accountant, or any type of accountant for that matter. Yet with a basic understanding of accounting and how it relates to your business, you can get the information you need quickly and easily, keep track of your activities, and print out the reports that your accountant (the one who is supposed to enjoy being an accountant) can use expeditiously, thereby shortening the time necessary to do the work and resulting in a lower professional accounting services fee. Proper accounting and recordkeeping will minimize both your accounting and legal fees.

The accounting software solutions explored in depth in this book may not make accounting fun, but they offer an easy and painless way to keep your books and records in order. If you're more interested in running your own business than in becoming an accountant, there are great software programs available to enable you to do just that.

"ACCOUNTING" DEFINED

Accounting is defined in many different ways. By combining these definitions we arrive at the following definition: *Accounting* is the process of providing quantitative information about economic entities to aid users in making decisions concerning the allocation of economic resources.

The process of providing such information necessitates a series of activities leading up to and including the communication of accounting information. These activities are:

1. Identifying the information;
2. Measuring;
3. Recording;
4. Retaining; and
5. Communicating it.

Quantitative means that this information is communicated by using numbers. In accounting, "numbers" are numbers of dollars. *Economic entities* means not only all types of businesses, but also hospitals, charitable organizations, churches and synagogues, municipalities, governments, and other organizations whether for-profit or not-for-profit. Accounting, as defined here, applies to all of these.

Decisions concerning the allocation of economic resources include, among others, whether to buy, sell, or hold investments, whether to extend credit, and whether to manufacture and sell a particular product.

The term *accounting theory* is commonly used, but it has no unified, standardized definition. Very closely related to the realm of accounting theory is the area of measurement. *Measurement* is concerned with the process of assigning numbers to the attributes or characteristics of the elements being measured.

Accounting information has been useful for hundreds of years. The double-entry framework was first described in a book written by Luca Pacioli, a fifteenth-century Italian monk and mathematician, although its origins can be traced back another 300 years. The formal structure for processing financial transactions is at least 700 years old.

In addition to accounting, *accountancy* has emerged as a profession, alongside the professions of medicine and law. The study and practice of accountancy requires a broad understanding of concepts in such areas as economics, sociology, psychology, and public administration, as well as in-depth knowledge of specialized accounting areas. The three main fields of accountancy include:

1. Public accounting;
2. Managerial accounting; and
3. Governmental and quasi-governmental accounting.

Each of these fields has several accounting specialty and subspecialty areas.

Accounting has been called the language of business. Throughout our early education we learned the vocabulary and other basic elements of the English language, or another language, so that we would be able to communicate effectively. The purpose is the same for accounting. Most of you will not become accountants. You may be self-employed or employed by others in a business (a manager, banker, or investor) and will use accounting information, whether you know it or not. In order to understand and to use accounting information most effectively, you must have a solid grounding in its fundamentals. Rather than going through the rigors of college Accounting 101 and Accounting 102 courses which each last a semester, you can master the basics of accounting with the material in this book. The finer points of accounting are things that you will probably never encounter in your business transactions, but you will know how to read those important financial statements and how to effectively use the material that will emanate from your computerized financial system.

Let's begin our discussion of accounting practices with a few of the basics (i.e., types of businesses, financial statements, income statements, etc.).

TYPES OF BUSINESS ORGANIZATIONS

A business may be organized in three ways:

1. A sole proprietorship;
2. A partnership; or
3. A corporation.

A *sole proprietorship* is a business owned by one individual who is the sole investor of money in the business. The money invested is called *capital*. Usually, the sole owner (self-employed) also acts as the manager of the business.

A *partnership* is a business owned by two or more individuals who each invest capital. The individuals are called *partners*, and their responsibilities, obligations, and benefits are usually described in a contract called a *partnership agreement*.

A *corporation* is a business incorporated as a separate legal entity according to the laws of the state in which it is based. Shares of capital stock are issued to owners—called *stockholders*—as evidence of their investment of capital in the corporation; these shares usually are easily transferable.

Individuals may own several types of businesses, including sole proprietorships, partnerships, and corporations. One individual may own all or part of several businesses. From an accounting standpoint, each business is treated as a separate economic entity. An *entity* is considered to be separate from its owners and from any other business.

UNDERSTANDING FINANCIAL STATEMENTS

Businesses operate to achieve various goals. To meet these goals a business must achieve two primary objectives:

1. To earn a satisfactory profit; and
2. To remain solvent (be able to pay its debts).

If a business fails to meet either of these primary objectives, it will not be able to survive in the long run.

Financial statements are accounting reports used to summarize and communicate financial information about a business. Three major financial statements—the *income statement*, the *statement of changes in financial position*, and the *balance sheet*—are used to report information about the business's primary objectives. These financial statements are the end result of the accounting process. Each of them summarizes certain information that has been identified, measured, recorded, and retained during the accounting process.

The Income Statement

An income statement is a financial statement summarizing the results of a business's earnings activities for a specific period of time. It shows the revenues, expenses, and net income (or net loss) of the business for this period. Revenues are the prices charged to the business's customers for goods and services provided. Expenses are the costs of providing the goods or services. The net income is the excess of revenues over expenses; a net loss arises when expenses are greater than revenues.

The Statement of Changes in Financial Position

A statement of changes in financial position is a financial statement summarizing the results of a business's financing and investing activities for a specific time period. The results of the business's financing activities are shown in a "Sources" section of the statement; this section includes sources from operations and other sources. For example, profits from operations and additional investment by the owner(s) or proceeds from loans (Borrowing from a bank or others). The results of the business's investing activities are shown in a "Uses" section of the statement.

The Balance Sheet

A balance sheet summarizes a business's financial position on a given date. It is alternatively called a *statement of financial position*. A balance sheet lists the business's assets, liabilities, and owner's equity.

Assets. Assets are the economic resources of a business that are expected to provide future benefits to the business. A business may own many assets, some of which are physical in nature, such as land, buildings, supplies to be used in the business, and goods (inventory) that the business expects to sell to its customers. Other assets do not possess physical characteristics, but are economic resources because of the legal rights they convey to the business. These assets include amounts owed by customers to the business (accounts receivable), the right to insurance protection (prepaid insurance), and investments made in other businesses.

Liabilities. Liabilities are the economic obligations (debts) of a business. The external parties to whom the economic obligations are owed are referred to as the creditors of the business. Usually, although not exclusively, legal documents serve as evidence of liabilities. These documents establish a claim (equity) by the creditors (the creditors' equity) against the assets of the business. Liabilities include such items as amounts owed to suppliers (accounts payable), amounts owed to employees for wages (wages payable), taxes payable, and mortgages owed on the business's property. A business may also borrow money from a bank on a short- or long-term basis by signing a legal document called a *note*, which specifies the terms of the loan. Amounts of such loans would be listed as notes payable.

Owner's Equity. The owner's equity of a business is the owner's current investment in the assets of the business. For a partnership, the owner's equity might be referred to as the *partners' equity*; for a corporation, *stockholders' equity*. The owner's equity is affected by the capital invested in the business by the owner, by the business's earnings from its operations, and by withdrawals of capital by the owner of the business. For a sole proprietorship, the owner's equity is shown by listing the owner's name, the word "Capital," and the amount of the current investment. Owner's equity is sometimes referred to as *residual equity*, because the creditors have first legal claim to a business's assets. Once the creditors' claims have been satisfied, the owner is entitled to the *remainder* (residual) of the assets.

BECOME FAMILIAR WITH ACCOUNTING PRACTICES AND PRINCIPLES

To understand the structure of accounting, you must realize that, prior to 1930, accounting in the United States was largely unregulated. The accounting practices and procedures used by accounting firms were generally considered confidential. In practice, one accountant had little knowledge of the procedures followed by other accountants. There was a considerable lack of uniformity in accounting practices among accountants and their client businesses. The only real direction provided in accounting practices was established by bankers and other creditors, because they were the primary users of financial reports. Bank and creditor pressure was aimed primarily at the disclosure of cash and near-cash resources that could be used for the repayment of debt.

Accounting principles may be classified into two broad types:

1. Input-oriented; and
2. Output-oriented.

Input-oriented principles are concerned with general approaches or rules for specifying the method of preparing financial statements and their content, including any necessary supplementary disclosures. *Output-oriented principles* are concerned with the comparability of financial statements of different businesses.

Input-Oriented Principles and General Rules of Operation

Input-oriented principles may be further classified. Principles concerned with general underlying rules of operation are involved with broad approaches to revenue and expense recognition. These principles point out the primary orientation of historical cost accounting toward income measurement rather than asset and liability valuation.

Output-Oriented Principles and Recognition of Revenue

The *output* of a business is listed in terms of its product(s) and/or service(s). This definition says nothing about the receipt or inflow of assets arising as a result of revenue performance. Defining *revenue* in conjunction with what it gives rise to can lead to problems in terms of when to recognize revenue as being earned.

The most prevalent *revenue recognition point* is the point of sale. The assets to be received from the performance of the revenue function are realized or realizable. The performance of the revenue function must be substantially accomplished. The prevailing concept of revenue recognition has its roots in the historical costs approach. The terms *realized* and *realizable* refer to the conversion or ready convertibility of the business's product or service into cash or claims to cash. "Realized" means that the business's product or service has been converted to cash or claims to cash, and "realizable" has been defined as the ability to convert assets already received or held into amounts of cash or claims to cash. Realization has often been used as a synonym for *recognition*.

Matching Expenses

Matching expenses are defined as costs that expire as a result of generating revenues. Expenses are necessary to the production of revenues. If all expenses could be directly identified with either specific revenues or specific time periods, expense measurement would be fairly simple. Unfortunately for the business owner, but more advantageous for the accountant, many significant expenses cannot be specifically identified with particular revenues, and they also bring benefits to more than one time period.

The various methods used for recognizing *cost expiration* (expense incurred) for categories such as depreciation, cost of goods sold, interest, and deferred charges are called *matching*. "Matching" implies that expenses are being recognized on a fair and equitable basis relative to the recognition of revenues.

Constraining Principles

Constraining principles either impose limitations on financial statements, as in the case of conservatism, or provide checks on them, as in the case of materiality and disclosure.

Conservatism holds an extremely important place in the ethos of accountants. It has even been called the *dominant principle of accounting*. A classic example of conservatism is the lower-of-cost-or-market valuation for inventories and marketable securities, the selection of *generally accepted accounting methods* that will result in any of the following:

1. Slower revenue recognition;
2. Faster expense recognition;
3. Lower asset valuation; or
4. Higher liability valuation.

Disclosure

Disclosure refers to relevant financial information both inside and outside the main body of the financial statements themselves, including mention of methods employed in financial statements where more than one choice exists or an unusual or innovative selection of methods is used.

Materiality

Materiality refers to the degree of importance of an item (or group of items) to users in terms of its relevance to evaluation or decision making. It can also be viewed as the other side of the disclosure coin, because what is disclosed should be material.

Objectivity

Objectivity is concerned with the quality or verifiability of evidence underlying transactions that are eventually summarized and organized in the form of financial statements.

Comparability

Comparability has often been described as accounting for like events in a similar manner, but this definition is too simplistic to be useful. Comparability refers to the degree of reliability users should find in financial statements when evaluating, on an interbusiness basis, financial condition or the results of operations or predicting income or cash flows.

Consistency

Consistency refers to the use of the same accounting methods over consecutive time periods by a given business. Consistency is necessary if predictions or evaluations stemming from a business's financial statements over more than one time period are to be reliable. Should change occur because of the adoption of a more relevant or objective method, full disclosure must be made to users and the auditor's opinion must be appropriately qualified.

Uniformity

Uniformity includes a uniform set of principles for all businesses, with interpretation and application left up to the individual entity. Similar accounting treatment is required in broadly similar situations, ignoring possibly different circumstances (rigid uniformity). Similar accounting treatment takes into account different economic circumstances (finite uniformity).

Proprietary Theory

The *proprietary theory* assumes that the owners and the business are virtually identical. The theory, which goes back at least as far as the early eighteenth century, is quite descriptive of economies largely made up of small owner-operated businesses. Under proprietary theory, the assets belong to the business's owners and the liabilities are their obligations. Ownership equities accrue to the owners. The balance sheet equation would be:

$$\text{Assets} - \text{Liabilities} = \text{Owners' Equities}$$

Expenses include deductions for labor costs, taxes, and interest, but not for preferred or common dividends. Income represents the owners' increase in both net assets (assets minus liabilities) and owners' equities arising from operations during the period. The essentials of the proprietary approach largely coincide with the components of the income statement.

RECORDING AND REPORTING ACCOUNTING INFORMATION

An *account* is a business document that is used to record and retain the monetary information emanating from business transactions. Separate accounts are used for each asset, liability, and owner's equity item. The number, types, and names of the accounts for each business depend on the particular business's operations, whether it is a sole proprietorship or corporation, and the type of assets it owns and liabilities it has incurred. A *general ledger* is the entire set of accounts for a business. For this reason, accounts are sometimes referred to as *general ledger accounts*.

An account can take several physical forms. It might be a location on a computer disk or a standardized business paper in a loose-leaf binder containing all the accounts of a manual system. Regardless of the physical form, all accounts are used for recording and retaining accounting information. In any form, the same logical format is used throughout for recording and retaining accounting information in the accounts. This format is easiest to understand in a manual system. A simple format for the accounts in a manual system is called a *T-account* because it looks like the capital letter "T." As shown in Figure 2-1, each T-account has three basic parts:

1. A place at the top for the particular asset, liability, or owner's equity title;
2. A left side, called the *debit side*; and
3. A right side, called the *credit side*.

The title of each account describes the nature of the account (e.g., notes payable). The left (debit) and the right (credit) sides of each account are used for recording and retaining the monetary information from business transactions. A *debit entry* is a monetary amount recorded (debited) on the left side of an account. A *credit entry* is a monetary amount recorded (credited) on the right side of an account.

Debit and Credit Rules

Each account accumulates information about both increases and decreases from various business transactions. There are two rules for recording these increases and decreases in the accounts:

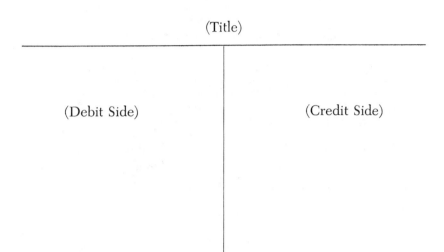

Figure 2-1. Parts of a T-account.

1. For each account, all increases are recorded on one side of the account and all decreases are recorded on the other side. This rule makes it easy to determine the total increases and decreases for a particular account. It does not indicate, however, whether the increases or decreases should be recorded on the debit (left) or credit (right) side of the account.
2. The debit and credit rule relates to the basic accounting equation:
   (a) *Asset accounts* (accounts on the left side of the accounting equation) are increased by debit entries (i.e., recorded amounts on the left side) and decreased by credit entries.
   (b) *Liabilities and owners' equity accounts* (accounts on the right side of the equation) are increased by credit entries (i.e., recorded amounts on the right side) and decreased by debit entries.

This rule and its relationship to the accounting equation are illustrated below. (Because this rule applies to the accounts of a sole proprietorship, a partnership, or a corporation, the plural "owners' equity" is used here.)

$$\text{Assets} = \text{Liabilities} + \text{Owners' Equity}$$

Asset Accounts		Liability Accounts		Owners' Equity Accounts	
(Debit)	(Credit)	(Debit)	(Credit)	(Debit)	(Credit)
Increase	Decrease	Decrease	Increase	Decrease	Increase
+	−	−	+	−	+

This rule is essential for understanding how to record business transactions whether you use a computerized or a manual accounting system. Its parts may be explained as follows:

1. Assets:
   (a) An increase in an asset is recorded on the left (debit) side of the asset account, by a debit entry.
   (b) A decrease in an asset is recorded on the right (credit) side of the asset account, by a credit entry.
2. Liabilities:
   (a) An increase in a liability is recorded on the right (credit) side of the liability account, by a credit entry.
   (b) A decrease in a liability is recorded on the left (debit) side of the liability account, by a debit entry.
3. Owners' equity:
   (a) An increase in owners' equity is recorded on the right (credit) side of the owners' equity account, by a credit entry.
   (b) A decrease in owners' equity is recorded on the left (debit) side of the owners' equity account, by a debit entry.

Balance of an Account

The *balance of an account* is the difference between the total increases and decreases recorded in the account. Usually, the balance of each account is computed when the accounting informa-

Yorky Yorkshire Terrier Farms
Trial Balance
January 31, 199X

Account Titles	Debits	Credits
Cash	$10,650	
Accounts Receivable	400	
Office Supplies	700	
Land	3,000	
Building	15,000	
Office Equipment	2,600	
Accounts Payable		$ 350
Notes Payable		2,000
C. Olafson, capital		30,000
Totals	$32,350	$32,350

Figure 2-2. Trial Balance.

tion is to be communicated in an accounting report. In a computerized system the balance is updated with each transaction.

Each asset account normally has a debit balance, because the total increases (debits) exceed the total decreases (credits) in the account. (See Figure 2-2.)

A *trial balance* is a schedule that lists the titles of all the accounts in the general ledger, the debit or credit balance of each account, and the totals of the debit and credit balances.

Each liability and owners' equity account normally has a credit balance, because the total credits (increases) exceed the total debits (decreases) in each account.

Double Entry Rule

The *double entry rule* states that when recording each transaction, the total amount of the debit entries must be equal to the total amount of the credit entries for that transaction. For each recorded transaction there must be at least one debit entry and one credit entry (although there may be more entries of each type), and the total amounts must be equal.

For example, suppose a business purchased a copier for cash at a cost of $2,500. To record this transaction, an asset account, Office Equipment, would be increased by a debit entry for $2,500 and another asset account, Cash, would be decreased by a credit entry of $2,500. Thus, the total debits equal the total credits in this transaction.

General Journal

The transactions of a business are first recorded in a *journal*, after which the information is transferred to the business's accounts. A *general journal* is a business document in which the data of the transaction is recorded, including the amounts of the debit and credit entries and an explanation of each transaction.

In a manual accounting system the general journal is a book of columnar pages. A general journal can be used to record all types of transactions. Many businesses have a number of special journals, each of which is designed for recording a particular type of business transaction. For example, one special journal is the *cash receipts journal* used to record all receipts of cash, checks, and money orders.

A *journal entry* is the recorded information for each transaction. *Journalizing* is the act of preparing the journal entry. A journal is often referred to as the *document of original entry* because each transaction is first, or originally, entered in the journal. (Before the use of computers became so widespread, a journal was called the *book of original entry*, but because a journal today may be stored on a computer disk, the term "document" is more appropriate than "book.")

There are many advantages to using a journal when initially recording a business's transactions. First, use of a journal helps to prevent errors. Because the accounts and the debit and credit amounts for each transaction are initially recorded on a single journal page rather than directly in the many accounts, this method makes it easier to prove that the debits and credits are equal. Second, all of the information about each transaction (including the explanation) is recorded in one place, thereby providing a complete "picture" of the transaction. Finally, because the transactions are recorded chronologically (day by day), the journal also provides a chronological "history" of the business's financial transactions.

Accounts and Posting

In the journalizing process each transaction is initially entered in one record, the journal, to:

1. Minimize errors;
2. Have all the debit and credit information for each transaction in one place; and
3. Have a chronological list of all of the business's financial transactions.

However, the accounting information from each transaction is not yet recorded in the accounts, the so-called *storage units* for the accounting information. Thus, we must post the accounts from the journal to the ledger accounts.

Posting is the process of transferring the debit and credit information for each journal entry to the proper accounts in the general ledger.

To fully understand the relationship between the accounting equation, the debit and credit rule, and the double entry rule, recall that the accounting equation must always be in balance. Also keep in mind that when recording a transaction, it is not always necessary to affect both sides of the equation or even two components of the equation.

It is possible to record a transaction as affecting only the left side, the right side, or both sides of the equation, provided that the equation remains in balance.

If the debit and credit rule and the double entry rule are followed, the accounting equation will always remain in balance. For example, in the preceding example of the office copier purchase, the debit entry increased the Office Equipment account while the credit entry decreased the Cash account. The total debits equalled the total credits, and thus the double entry rule was followed. Only the left side of the accounting equation (the asset component) was affected, but the equation remained in balance because there was no change in total assets. The left side of the equation, therefore, remained equal to the right side.

IMPORTANT RULES TO REMEMBER WHEN POSTING ACCOUNTS

Copy the following checklist of important rules onto an index card or in a spiral notebook for easy reference:

1. The accounting equation (assets equal liabilities plus owners' equity) must always remain in balance.
2. All increases in an account are recorded on one side of the account; all decreases are recorded on the other side of the account.
3. The debit and credit rule states that:
   (a) Asset accounts are increased by debit entries and decreased by credit entries.
   (b) Liabilities and owners' equity accounts are increased by credit entries and decreased by debit entries.
4. Asset accounts normally have debit balances. Liabilities and owners' equity accounts normally have credit balances.
5. The double entry rule states that for all recorded transactions, the total amount of the debit entries must be equal to the total amount of the credit entries.

SUMMARY

Now that you understand some of the basics of accounting, let's put what you've learned to work. In Chapter 3, we'll see how we can use what we've learned to help read and understand financial and income statements.

Chapter 3

Reading and Understanding Financial and Income Statements

FINANCIAL STATEMENTS—A MIRROR FOR SMALL BUSINESSES

Financial statements are an important management tool—not a burdensome chore imposed by bankers. When correctly prepared and properly interpreted, they contribute to an understanding of the current financial conditions, problems, and possibilities of your business. These statements, specifically, the *balance sheet*, the *income statement*, and the *statement of cash flows*, are prepared and presented with the use of technical terms and rules that are becoming increasingly complex. The interpretation of financial statements presents a formidable challenge to most owners and managers of small businesses.

No matter how technically correct they are, these statements are of no benefit unless they are actually used in making business decisions. Statements gathering dust because the businessowner does not understand what they are saying is a strong indication that an independent accountant is needed to assist. Just as it is said that an attorney who represents him or herself has a fool for a client, the same is true when you prepare your own accounting records and do the analysis yourself. An outside opinion can come as a breath of fresh air, invigorating the entire business atmosphere. But your understanding of financial statements will allow you to use them in making decisions, monitoring your business, and planning for future growth.

The Balance Sheet

The balance sheet is a "snapshot." It represents, at a moment in time, the financial position of a business. (See Figure 3-1.) It should be compared with other snapshots to provide meaningful information on changes in financial position. For that reason, the balance sheets from preceding years are usually compared with the current statement.

Yorky Yorkshire Terrier Farms
Balance Sheet
January 31, 199X

Assets			*Liabilities*		
Cash	$	10,650	Accounts Payable	$	350
Accounts Receivable		400	Notes Payable		2,000
Office Supplies		700	Total Liabilities	$	2,350
Land		3,000			
Building		15,000	Owner's Equity		
Office Equipment		2,600	C. Olafson, capital		$ 30,000
			Total Liabilities and		
Total Assets	$	32,350	Owner's Equity		$ 32,350

Figure 3-1. Sample balance sheet.

The balance sheet (or *statement of financial condition*) is so named because it represents the following equation:

$$\underset{\text{(Resources of the Business)}}{\text{Assets}} = \begin{array}{c} \text{Liabilities} \\ \text{(Amounts Owed to Outside} \\ \text{Creditors)} \\ + \\ \text{Equity (or Net Worth)} \end{array}$$

This basic equation holds, although at any given time, the amounts assigned to the individual elements of the equation may fluctuate. Assets can increase or decrease as resources are obtained, disposed of, become less valuable, or become used up (expensed) in the course of operations. Liabilities increase or decrease as obligations are incurred or liquidated. In some cases, liabilities may have to be estimated and are subject to adjustment (upward or downward) in later periods.

Equity increases or decreases primarily as a result of income or loss from operations of the business. It also increases when the owners contribute capital to the business, and decreases when capital is withdrawn or dividends are paid.

The Statement of Cash Flows

The *statement of cash flows* (which recently has superseded the *statement of changes in financial position*) reports the sources and uses of cash for the period, as analyzed into three major classifications:

Cash provided by or applied to operations
+/− Cash provided by or applied to investing activities
+/− Cash provided by or applied to financing activities
= Net increase or decrease in cash

Operations include the cash effects of essentially all items identified in the income statement (such as sales, cost of sales, operating expenses, and extraordinary items). *Investing activities* include the purchase of plant property and equipment or the proceeds from the disposition thereof, and certain investments in securities or other nonoperating assets. *Financing activities* include the borrowing and repayment of debt, as well as the contribution and redemption of equity capital and the payment of dividends thereon. (See Figure 3-2 for an example of a cash flow statement.)

(Company Name)
Consolidated Statement of Cash Flows
For the Year Ended December 31, 199X
Increase (Decrease) in Cash and Cash Equivalents

Cash flows from operating activities:		
Cash received from customers	$ 13,850	
Cash paid to suppliers and employees	(12,000)	
Dividend received from affiliate	20	
Interest received	55	
Interest paid (net of amount capitalized)	(220)	
Income taxes paid	(325)	
Insurance proceeds received	15	
Cash paid (to settle lawsuit)	(30)	
Net cash provided by operating activities		$ 1,365
Cash flows from financing activities:		
Net borrowings under line-of-credit agreement	300	
Principal payments under capital lease obligation	(125)	
Proceeds from issuance of common stock	500	
Dividends paid	(200)	
Net cash provided by financing activities		475
Net increase in cash and cash equivalents		$ 1,840
Cash and cash equivalents at beginning of year		600
Cash and cash equivalents at end of year	$ 2,440	

Figure 3-2. Sample statement of cash flows.

In addition to the basic financial statements, most financial reports that have been reported on by an independent accountant will have a section called *notes to financial statements*. If an independent accountant has been associated with the financial statements, a report will be included with the statements. The report will identify the professional service provided—an audit, a review, or a compilation—and indicate what conclusions, if any, were reached regarding the financial statements. In the case of an audit, the independent accountant will provide positive assurances that the financial statements "present fairly" the financial position and results of operations in accordance with generally accepted accounting principles, if it can be concluded that such is the case. In a review engagement, at best the accountant will express negative assurance (i.e., that based on limited procedures no reason was found to doubt that the financial statements were fairly presented). An accountant conducting a compilation merely assembles the financial statements and offers neither positive nor negative assurance.

The notes to financial statements set forth the major accounting principles used in developing the amounts reported in the statements (where a choice was made from among alternative *generally accepted accounting principles* or GAAP) and provide additional details about major accounts and transactions. Examples of the latter include details about long-term leases, long- and short-term debt (including interest rates and maturities), transactions with related parties, and contingent liabilities and commitments. Financial reports may also contain supplementary schedules that provide more detailed information about major expense captions (such as administrative expenses) or other items appearing in the basic financial statement.

Using the Financial Statement to Analyze the Performance of a Business

The information contained in basic financial statements can and should be used to provide insight into the financial strength and earnings capacity of a business. This extends beyond such single statement captions as "net income" and necessitates that relationships between accounts be examined. Although an almost unlimited number of such ratios and comparisons are possible, a relatively small group of these are traditionally the object of most attention.

The nature of the analysis depends on the perspective of the user. For example, a short-term noteholder would be primarily concerned with the business's ability to pay its current obligations. The holder of long-term debt might look to both historical and projected earnings and cash flows. The stockholders—current and future—would share a viewpoint similar to that of the long-term debtholder, with perhaps more concern for earnings than creditors might exhibit. The owner of the business is concerned with all these factors and, in addition, needs financial information that is useful on a daily basis. A selection of the financial ratios that are most often computed to analyze a business follows.

The *return on equity ratio* measures the return on the investment made by the owners.

$$\text{Return on Equity Ratio} = \frac{\text{Net Income (Income Statement)}}{\text{Average Owner's Equity (Balance Sheet)}}$$

The *return on assets ratio* measures the return on the gross investment in the business, including that financed by the owners as well as that financed by creditors. The relationship between the returns on assets and the returns on equity is indicative of the effect of the business's financial leverage—if the leverage is positive, the return on equity will be greater than the return on assets.

$$\text{Return on Assets Ratio} = \frac{\text{Net Income (Income Statement)}}{\text{Total Assets (Balance Sheet)}}$$

The *net working capital ratio* indicates the ability to meet short-term obligations, reporting the excess of current assets over current liabilities.

$$\text{Net Working Capital Ratio} = \frac{\text{Current Assets (Balance Sheet)}}{- \text{ Current Liabilities (Balance Sheet)}}$$

The *current ratio* indicates the ability to pay current liabilities as they mature, providing the ratio of current assets to current liabilities. A ratio of 1:1 or greater corresponds to positive net working capital.

$$\text{Current Ratio} = \frac{\text{Current Assets (Balance Sheet)}}{\text{Current Liabilities (Balance Sheet)}}$$

The *long-term debt ratio* indicates the balance between total equity ownership and long-term debt. The greater the percentage, the "more leveraged" is the business.

$$\text{Long-Term Debt Ratio} = \frac{\text{Long-Term Debt (Balance Sheet)}}{\substack{\text{Capitalization (Long-Term Debt Plus} \\ \text{Owners' Equity—Balance Sheet)}}}$$

The *times-interest-earned ratio* measures the ability of a business to cover the payment of interest to lenders.

$$\text{Times-Interest-Earned Ratio} = \frac{\substack{\text{Income Before Interest and Taxes} \\ \text{(Income Statement)}}}{\text{Interest Expense (Income Statement)}}$$

The *debt service* ratio is an indicator of the business's ability to pay both the interest and the current principal installments on its outstanding debts and suggests the degree of safety for creditors concerning due debt service obligations.

$$\text{Debt Service Ratio} = \frac{\substack{\text{Income Before Interest and Taxes} \\ \text{(Income Statement)}}}{\substack{\text{Interest Expense Plus Amount of Scheduled} \\ \text{Debt Repayments (Income Statement and} \\ \text{Statement of Cash Flows)}}}$$

The *collection period ratio* measures the number of days' sales that are uncollected in average accounts receivable, providing an idea of how successful the business is in collecting its customer debt.

$$\text{Collection Period Ratio} = \frac{\substack{\text{Average Accounts Receivable} \\ \text{(Balance Sheet)}}}{\text{Average Daily Sales (Income Statement)}}$$

The *receivable turnover ratio* is an alternative, but equivalent, measure of the efficiency of the business's receivable collection efforts. If the business also makes sales for cash, *total credit sales* should be substituted for *total sales*.

$$\text{Receivable Turnover Ratio} = \frac{\text{Total Sales (Income Statement)}}{\text{Average Accounts Receivable}}$$
$$\text{(Balance Sheet)}$$

The *number of days' sales in inventory ratio* is an indicator of the amount of inventory maintained relative to the business's sales (as measured by cost of goods sold).

$$\begin{array}{c}\text{Number of Days' Sales} \\ \text{in Inventory Ratio}\end{array} = \frac{\begin{array}{c}\text{Average Inventory} \\ \text{(Balance Sheet)}\end{array}}{\begin{array}{c}\text{Average Daily Cost of Sales} \\ \text{(Income Statement)}\end{array}}$$

The *inventory turnover ratio* is an alternative measure of how quickly inventory is sold.

$$\text{Inventory Turnover Ratio} = \frac{\begin{array}{c}\text{Cost of Goods Sold} \\ \text{(Income Statement)}\end{array}}{\text{Average Inventory (Balance Sheet)}}$$

Financial analysis involves many different approaches; this ratio analysis is only one of several means of gaining an understanding about a business from the financial data. Other approaches, such as the careful study of the financial statement notes, examination of the business's accounting policies, and the analysis of product-line breakdown, should also be considered.

TRACKING NET INCOME

The Accounting Period

Businesses typically operate for many years. Over the life of any business however, financial statement users need net income information on a regular basis in order to make financial decisions. An *accounting period* is the period of time for which the revenues and expenses of a business are computed.

For financial accounting, most businesses usually use a *calendar year* as their accounting period. For businesses whose operations are seasonal, a *fiscal year* is used; a fiscal year will correspond more closely to its seasonal operating activities. For example, a business whose peak sales activity usually occur during the winter and culminate at Christmas may use July 1, 19XX through June 30, 19XX as its accounting period. This enables the business to do the year-end closing activities such as taking physical inventory and verifying accounts in a normally less active and tumulteous time. This period can be called a *fiscal period* as well. Certain businesses are required to compute and report their net income on a quarterly basis. These accounting periods (and others shorter than a year) are referred to as *interim periods*. For the self-employed, a monthly income statement provides much more in benefits than the relatively small effort required to produce it as a by-product of regular accounting recordation. For almost every small enterprise the critical areas of management control will include at least the following:

Sales

Profits

Cash Flow

Job Cost Analysis (if applicable)

Receivables Status

Payables Status

Inventory Status

Financial Position Analysis

As you can see, this is a common-sense approach, which does not involve anything mysterious or highly technical and theoretical. In a small business, everything we do has to have immediate benefits, otherwise we can't afford the cost. Yet if we can make this control process effective, the self-employed owner can get into a position of power in some areas that are almost always elusive for the entrepreneur without a computerized system of accounting and recordkeeping. Although financial management can be complicated, with some work, determination, and a computer with the proper software it can be brought into focus so that an intelligent self-employed business owner without any special training can make astute judgments, based on the best information available.

Matching Principle

In the computation of net income, expenses are subtracted from revenues. Another way of expressing this principle is to say that the expired costs (i.e., efforts) are matched against the prices charged to customers (i.e., accomplishments) to determine net income. The matching principle states that to determine the net income of a business for an accounting period, the total expenses involved in obtaining the revenues of the period must be computed and matched against the revenues recorded in that period.

Accrual Accounting

In *accrual accounting*, revenue and expense transactions are recorded in the accounting period when the goods or services are provided, regardless of whether cash is received or paid by the business. To *accrue* means to accumulate. In accrual accounting, a business must be certain that all revenues have been recorded at the end of each accounting period. The business must record all revenues even if no cash inflow has been received. The business must also be certain that all expenses that should be matched against the revenue have been recorded even if no cash outflow has been made.

Accrual accounting is important because it links the revenues of a business to the accounting period in which they were earned, and it matches the expenses against the revenues in the same period. This procedure makes the resulting accounting information especially useful to users in evaluating the performance of a particular business.

Some self-employed or smaller businesses do not use accrual accounting. Instead they use *cash basis accounting*. In cash basis accounting, the net income for the accounting period is computed by subtracting the cash payments from the cash receipts from operations. This method may lead to incorrect evaluations of a business's operating results. The receipt and payment of cash may occur much earlier or later than the sale of goods or the providing of services to customers and the related costs. Accrual accounting eliminates distortions of operating results and is appropriate for businesses of all sizes. For convenience, however, cash basis accounting may be used by the self-employed and smaller businesses with a few employees in which the owner-manager finances all the operations. There are also important tax implications in regard to the choice of accrual or cash basis accounting systems. Your professional tax advisor would be the resource to use in making this important decision.

Posting Withdrawals

When an owner invests in a business, the owner contributes cash or other assets and an increase is recorded in the business's assets and in owner's equity. This investment in assets is used in the business's operations in order to earn a satisfactory net income for the owner. In many businesses, the owner is also the full-time manager. While operating the business the owner may require cash for personal expenditures or other investment opportunities. Cash may be withdrawn periodically from the business for these purposes.

Care must be taken to account properly for an owner's withdrawals of assets from a business. A withdrawal should be recorded in a manner opposite to that of recording an investment by the owner; that is, a withdrawal is recorded as a decrease in the business's assets and as a decrease in the business's owner's equity. Wihdrawals should not be confused with expenses. Withdrawals are not expenses, just as investments are not revenues.

This treatment of withdrawals is consistent with the business entity concept in which a business is considered to be an economic entity separate from its owner. The direct impact of a withdrawal is a disinvestment of assets by the owner. Because it is not considered an expense, but is instead treated as a direct reduction of assets and owner's equity, a withdrawal is not included in an income statement.

Relationship of Net Income and Withdrawals to Owner's Equity

When revenues exceed expenses, resulting in net income, an increase in net assets (assets minus liabilities) occurs. In as much as the net income of a business belongs to its owner, it is recorded as an increase in owner's equity (keeping the accounting equation in balance).

Owner's equity is increased by the initial and subsequent investments of the owner and by net income (revenues greater than expenses). Owner's equity is decreased by the withdrawals of the owner and by a net loss (expenses greater than revenues).

Recording, Retaining, and Reporting Net Income and Withdrawals Information

Because net income affects owner's equity, it would be possible to record all the transactions of a business affecting revenues and expenses directly in the owner's capital account. Remember, only the balance of an account is reported on a financial statement. Reporting the ending balance of the owner's capital account may be useful for certain purposes, but it would not be useful in reporting the business's net income. What is needed are additional accounts in the business's accounting system in which to record and retain the monetary amounts of the revenue and expense transactions so that an income statement for the accounting period can be prepared. These accounts are called *temporary* (or *nominal*) accounts because they are used only to compute the net income for the accounting period. These accounts are different from the permanent (or real) accounts that are listed on the balance sheet.

Withdrawals could also be deducted directly from the owner's capital account. It is important to report the total withdrawals for the accounting period so that the owner will know exactly how much has been taken out of the business during the period. A temporary withdrawals account is used for this purpose.

THE INCOME STATEMENT TRACKS REVENUES

The major goal of a business is to sell goods or services to customers at prices that are higher than the costs of providing the goods or services and, as a result, to earn satisfactory income (profit) for the owner. Users of financial statements need income information to evaluate a business's operating results. By recording the transactions of a business's day-to-day operations, this income information is developed.

The income of a business is commonly referred to as *net income*. Net income is the excess of revenues over expenses for a particular time period. Net income is sometimes called *net profit*, *net earnings*, or simply *earnings*. Revenues are the prices charged to a business's customers for goods or services provided during a particular time period. Expenses are the costs of providing the goods or services during that time period. Net income may be shown in an equation as follows:

$$\text{Net Income} = \text{Revenues} - \text{Expenses}$$

If expenses are greater than revenues, the resulting negative amount is called *net loss*, instead of net income. Because net income (net loss) is the difference between revenues and expenses, it is important to understand these items and their relationship.

The particular time period during which the revenues and expenses occurred is important for tax reporting considerations and in making meaningful comparisons between like periods of time.

An income statement is a financial statement summarizing the results of a business's earnings for its accounting period. It shows the revenues, expenses, and net income (or net loss) for this time period. This statement is alternatively referred to as a *statement of income, statement of earnings, profit and loss statement,* or *statement of operations.* (See Figure 3-3 for a sample income statement.)

Katherine's Boutique
Income Statement
For the Year Ended December 31, 199X

Revenues:		
Sales revenues		$ 48,200
Service revenues		89,700
Total revenues		$137,900
Expenses:		
Employees' Wages	$30,400	
Heat, light, and power	10,200	
Property Taxes	2,400	
Depreciation expense: equipment	3,875	
Depreciation expense: vehicles	7,900	
Rent expense on building	12,800	
Insurance expense	1,500	
Supplies	9,650	
Total Expenses		78,725
Net Income		$ 59,175

Figure 3-3. Sample income statement.

Listing Revenues

Revenues may be thought of as the "achievements" of a business during a particular time period. Because revenues are amounts of money charged to customers, they result in increases in assets. When goods or services are provided, the business either receives cash or an agreement for the customer to pay at a later date, and the business thus acquires an account receivable. In either case, (1) revenue has resulted and (2) assets (either cash or accounts receivable) have increased. The definition of revenue is not directly related to the inflow of cash. Cash may increase as a result of a revenue, but it is not necessary for cash to increase in order to record revenue. In addition, there are many instances when cash increases but no revenue is recorded.

For example, cash would increase as a result of borrowing money from a bank and signing a note to be repaid at a future date; or if after a sale to a customer on credit when the receivable is collected. In either case, even though there is an increase in cash, no revenue would be recorded. In the first case, the cash increased as a result of an increase in a liability. In the second case, cash increased as a result of a decrease in another asset, accounts receivable. The requirement for recording revenue is that assets must have increased (or liabilities decreased) as a result of providing goods or services to customers.

Listing Expenses

Expenses may be thought of as the "efforts" or costs expended by a business during a particular time period. Examples of expenses include the wages and salaries of employees, the cost of products sold, advertising, heat, light, power utility expenditures, property taxes, rent, and delivery costs. Because expenses are the costs of providing goods or services, expenses result in decreases in assets and increases in liabilities. When current wages are paid to employees, for example, an expense has resulted and an asset (cash) has decreased.

The outflow of cash is not a requirement to record an expense. The important point is that assets must have decreased (or liabilities increased) because of providing goods or services in the particular time period. It is also important to distinguish between the terms *cost* and *expense*. Cost refers to the amount at which a transaction is recorded. The nature of the transaction determines how a cost is recorded in an accounting system. The cost involved in a transaction can be recorded as either an asset or an expense. A cost is recorded as an asset when the business acquires a resource that is expected to provide future benefits to the business through a transaction. A cost is recorded as an expense if it results from providing goods or services to customers within a certain time period.

Debit and Credit Rules

The owner's capital account is on the right side of the accounting equation. Therefore, it is increased by credit entries and decreased by debit entries. Inasmuch as revenues increase owner's equity, all revenue accounts are increased by credit entries and decreased by debit entries. Expenses, however, decrease owner's equity. As expenses increase, owner's equity decreases. Thus the debit and credit rule for expenses is the opposite for that of owner's equity; that is, increases in expense accounts are recorded by debit entries and decreases in expense accounts are recorded by credit entries. Withdrawals similarly reduce owner's equity. An increase in the withdrawals account is recorded by a debit entry, and a decrease in the withdrawals account is recorded by a credit entry.

The entire set of debit and credit rules, as they relate to the permanent asset, liability, and owner's equity accounts and to the temporary withdrawals, revenue, and expense accounts, are summarized as follows (because the set of rules applies to the accounts of a sole proprietorship, partnership, or corporation, the plural "owners' equity" is used):

1. Asset accounts are increased by debit entries and decreased by credit entries.

2. Liability accounts are increased by credit entries and decreased by debit entries.

3. Permanent owners' equity (capital) accounts are increased by credit entries and decreased by debit entries. Temporary owners' equity accounts are governed by the following rules:

    (a) Withdrawal accounts are increased by debit entries and decreased by credit entries.

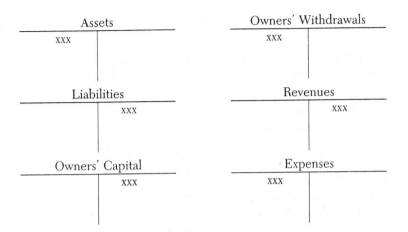

Figure 3-4. Normal account balances.

(b) Revenue accounts are increased by credit entries and decreased by debit entries.

(c) Expense accounts are increased by debit entries and decreased by credit entries.

As a result of using the debit and credit rules along with maintaining equality in the accounting equation, the accounts will have these normal balances during the accounting period. (See Figure 3-4.)

Accounts	Normal Balance
Assets	Debit
Liabilities	Credit
Owners' capital	Credit
Owners' withdrawals	Debit
Revenues	Credit
Expenses	Debit

Closing Entries

The revenue, expense, and withdrawals accounts are temporary accounts. These accounts are used to determine the changes in the owner's equity in the current accounting period as a result of net income (or net loss) and withdrawals.

To begin the next accounting period, it is important to (1) show the current balance in the owner's capital account and (2) show zero balances in the revenue, expense, and withdrawals accounts. The owner's capital account should be up to date to show the owner's current investment in the assets of the company. The revenue, expense, and withdrawals accounts will be used in the next accounting period to accumulate the net income and withdrawals information for that period. It is important to start with a zero balance in each of these accounts at the beginning of the period so that at the end of the period, the balances in the accounts will show the revenues, expenses, and withdrawals for only one period.

Closing entries are journal entries made at the end of an accounting period to create zero balances in each revenue, expense, and withdrawals account and to transfer these account balances to the owner's permanent capital account. Closing entries are made like any journal entry. They are recorded first in the general journal and then posted to the respective accounts. The term "closed or closing" signifies the transfer of the balance from one account to another account. The revenue and expense account balances are not closed directly to the owner's capital account. These account balances are first transferred to an account entitled *income summary*. The income summary account is a temporary account used in the closing process to accumulate the amount of net income (or net loss) before transferring this amount to the owner's capital account.

Closing the Income Summary Account

After the revenue and expense accounts have been closed to the income summary account, the balance in this account is the net income (or net loss). A *credit balance* indicates that the business has earned a net income for the accounting period, because revenues exceeded expenses. A *debit balance* indicates a net loss, because expenses exceed revenues.

The net income (or net loss) amount is now transferred to the owner's permanent capital account. For net income, the journal entry is a debit to the income summary account for its balance, and a credit to the owner's capital account for the same amount. The debit to income summary reduces the account balance to zero, making it ready for the closing entries of the next accounting period. The credit to the owner's capital account increases the account for the net income. A net loss would be handled in the opposite manner; a debit to the owner's capital account for the amount of the net loss and a credit to the income summary account to reduce it to zero.

Closing the Withdrawals Account

The debit balance of the withdrawals account is transferred directly to the owner's permanent capital account, inasmuch as the withdrawals are disinvestments by the owner. The closing entry is a debit to the owner's permanent capital account and a credit to the withdrawals account for the total withdrawals of the period. The debit entry brings the owner's capital account up to date at the end of the period. The credit to the withdrawals account reduces the account balance to zero so that it can accumulate the withdrawals of the next period. The withdrawals account is never closed to the income summary account, because withdrawals are not part of net income.

Summary of Closing Process

The steps in the closing process at the end of each period are as follows:

1. Close all the revenue accounts to a zero balance by debiting each revenue account for its balance and crediting the income summary account for the total revenues.

2. Close all the expense accounts to a zero balance by crediting each expense account for its balance and debiting the income summary account for the total expenses.

3. Compute the balance in the income summary account after completing steps 1 and 2. Close a credit balance (net income) in the account by debiting the income summary and crediting the owner's capital account for the amount of the net income. Close a debit balance (net loss) in the account by crediting the income summary and debiting the owner's capital account.

4. Close the owner's withdrawals account by crediting the account and debiting the owner's capital account for the balance of the withdrawals account.

5. Prepare a postclosing trial balance to prove the equality of the debit and credit balances in the asset, liability, and owner's capital account balances.

The term debit, from the Latin noun debitum (debt), and the other side, credit, from the Latin noun creditum (trust, loan) form the sides of the accounting equation (debits equal credits).

Chapter 4

How the Self-Employed Can Win the Tax War

When starting your business, you should set up a system of record-keeping suitable for both your business and your personality. Keep in mind the taxes you will have to pay and when you will have to pay them. Choose an accounting method and a tax year, and set up your books using an accounting method that clearly shows your income for the accounting period that is your tax year.

Every taxpayer (business or individual) must figure taxable income and file a tax return on the basis of an annual accounting period. The term *tax year* is the annual accounting period you use for keeping your records and reporting your income and expenses. The accounting periods the IRS permits you to use are:

1. A calendar year; or
2. A fiscal year.

You adopt a tax year when you file your first income tax return. You must establish your first tax year by the due date (not including extensions) for filing a return for that year.

The due date for individuals and partnerships is the fifteenth day of the fourth month after the end of the tax year. *Individuals* include sole proprietors, partners, and S corporation shareholders. The due date for filing returns for corporations and S corporations is the fifteenth day of the third month after the end of the tax year. If the fifteenth day of the month falls on a Saturday, Sunday, or legal holiday, the due date is the next day that is not a Saturday, Sunday, or legal holiday.

Employment taxes are figured on a calendar year basis. You must use the calendar quarter for withholding income tax and Social Security and Medicare taxes. You must use the calendar year for federal unemployment tax.

SETTING UP TAX YEARS

Your regular accounting period is either a calendar tax year or a fiscal tax year.

Calendar Tax Year

If you adopt the calendar year for your annual accounting period, you must maintain your books and records and report your income and expenses for the period from January 1 through December 31 of each year.

If you filed your first return using the calendar tax year, and you later begin business as a sole proprietor, become a partner in a partnership, or become a shareholder in an S corporation, you must continue to use the calendar tax year unless you get permission from the IRS to change. You must report your income from all sources, including your sole proprietorship, salaries, partnership income, and dividends, using the same tax year.

You must adopt the calendar tax year if:

1. You do not keep adequate records (according to the IRS);

2. You have no annual accounting period;

3. Your present tax year does not qualify as a fiscal year.

Fiscal Tax Year

A regular fiscal tax year is 12 consecutive months ending on the last day of any month except December. A 52- to 53-week year is a fiscal tax year that varies from 52 to 53 weeks. If you adopt a fiscal tax year, you must maintain your books and records and report your income and expenses using the same tax year.

52- to 53-Week Tax Year

You can elect to use a 52 to 53-week tax year if you keep your books and records and report your income on that basis. If you make this election, your tax year will always be either 52 or 53 weeks long, and will always end on the same day of the week. You may choose to have your year always end on either:

1. The date a specified day of the week last occurs in a particular month; or
2. The date that day of the week occurs nearest to the last day of a particular month.

For example, if you elect a tax year that always ends on the last Monday in March, then for the tax year ending in 1994, your tax year would end on March 28, 1994. If you elected a tax year ending on the Monday nearest to the end of January, then for the tax year ending in 1994, your tax year would end on January 31, 1994. You make the election by filing your tax return for the 52 to 53-week year and attaching a statement showing:

1. The day of the week on which the tax year will always end;
2. Whether it will end on the last such day of the week in the calendar month or on the date such day of the week occurs nearest the end of the month; and
3. The month in which, or with reference to which, the tax year will end.

MAKING A CHANGE IN YOUR ACCOUNTING PERIOD

If you change your accounting period, you figure your tax for the short tax year by putting your taxable income for the short period on an annual basis.

You Must Get IRS Approval

You must, with certain exceptions, get approval from the IRS to change your tax year. To get this approval, you must file a current Form 1128 and enclose the user fee of $200. This form must be filed by the fifteenth day of the second calendar month after the close of the short tax year. The *short tax year* begins on the first day after the end of your present tax year and ends on the day before the first day of your new tax year.

THE IRS AND YOUR CHOICE OF A BOOKKEEPING SYSTEM

You must decide whether to use a single- or a double-entry bookkeeping system. The single-entry system is easy to maintain, but it may not be suitable for everyone. You may find the double-entry system better because it has built-in checks and balances to assure accuracy and control.

Single Entry

The single-entry bookkeeping system is based on the income statement (profit or loss statement) and includes only your business income and expenses. It can be a simple and very practical system if you are just starting a small business. For tax purposes, this system records the flow of income and expenses through the use of a daily summary of cash receipts and a monthly summary of cash receipts and disbursements.

Double Entry

The double-entry bookkeeping system uses journals and ledgers and is based on both the income statement and the balance sheet. Transactions are first entered in a journal, and then summary totals (usually monthly) of the journal entry transactions are entered in ledger accounts. Ledger accounts include income, expense, asset, liability, and net worth. Income and expense accounts are closed at the end of the annual accounting period. Asset, liability, and net worth accounts are kept on a permanent basis.

The double-entry system is self-balancing. Every journal entry is made up of both debts and credits, and the sum of the debits must equal the sum of the credits in each journal entry. After the journal entries are entered in the ledger accounts, the total debits equal the total credits and the accounts are in balance.

At the end of each accounting period, financial statements may be prepared. These statements are generally the income statement and the balance sheet. The income statement reflects the current operations for the year. The balance sheet shows the financial position of the business in terms of assets, liabilities, and net worth on a given date.

The IRS does not dictate which bookkeeping system you must use. Later in this book will be thorough descriptions, in-depth analysis, level of accounting skill necessary, and costs for the leading accounting system software available. Although manual systems are available, they will never equal a computerized system in ease and level of control in operating your business and managing its finances. If you are not computer literate and are unwilling to learn how to use this miracle of business management, then perhaps you should think of limiting your business enterprise to an elementary level.

A detailed examination of journals and ledgers can be found in chapter two. For more information on financial statements including the income statement and balance sheet please see chapter three.

THE IRS AND RECORDKEEPING

You should deposit all business receipts in a separate bank account. If possible, you should also make all disbursements by check. In regard to all business entities, with the exception of corporations, a disbursement from the business account is not necessary to qualify the expenditure as a business expense. A check written on a personal account for business purposes will qualify if that expense is otherwise allowable. It is important to document both business income and business expenses.

Write checks payable to yourself only when making withdrawals of income from your business for your own use. Avoid writing business checks payable to cash as it is important to identify which disbursements are business and which are personal. In the event of an IRS audit, this is an area that will get close scrutiny. The IRS auditor will not only look at each check to see to whom it was paid, but will also look at the reverse of the check to see by whom and how the check was endorsed. If you must write a check for cash to pay a business expense, include the receipt for the cash payment in your records. If you cannot get a receipt or a cash payment, put a statement in your records at the time of the transaction to explain the payment.

Get receipts for all business expenditures! For all business trips, make sure always to get receipts from hotels and motels. Toll receipts can also help to substantiate travel expenses. Obtain receipts from the post office when you purchase stamps and mail larger envelopes and packages. You should establish a petty cash fund for small expenses. All business expenses paid by cash should be clearly substantiated by documents showing their business purpose.

Support your entries with sales slips, invoices, canceled checks, paid bills, duplicate deposit slips, and any other documents that explain and support entries made in your books. File these materials in a safe place. Memorandums or sketchy records that approximate income, deductions, or other items affecting your tax liability will not be considered adequate by the IRS. Remember, where the IRS is concerned, the burden of proof is on the taxpayer. You will not be given the benefit of the doubt.

CLASSIFY YOUR BOOKS OF ACCOUNTS

Classify your accounts by separating them into five groups:

1. Income;
2. Expenses;
3. Assets;
4. Liabilities; and
5. Equity (net worth).

For your assets, record the date of acquisition, cost or other basis, depreciation, depletion, and anything else affecting their basis. Basis is the amount of your investment in a property for tax purposes.

KEEPING YOUR RECORDS

You must keep the books and records of your business available at all times for inspection by the IRS. Records must be kept as long as they may be needed in the administration of any Internal Revenue law.

Keep records supporting items reported on a tax return until the period of limitations for that tax year has expired. Usually, this is the later of:

1. Three years after the date your return is due or filed; or
2. Two years after the date the tax was paid.

However, you should keep some records indefinitely. For example, if you adopt the *last-in-first-out* (LIFO) method of valuing your inventory or change your accounting method, records supporting these decisions and approvals from the IRS may be needed for an indefinite time.

Keep records that support your basis in property for as long as they are needed to figure the correct basis of your original or replacement property (including capital improvements).

Keep copies of your tax returns. They will help you in preparing future tax returns and in making computations if you later file an amended return or a claim for a refund.

Microfilm

Microfilm and microfiche reproductions of general books of accounts (such as cash books, journals, voucher registers, and ledgers) are accepted by the IRS for recordkeeping purposes if they comply with Revenue Procedure 81-46, in Cumulative Bulletin 1981-2 on page 621. If your micrographic system does not meet the requirements of Revenue Procedure 81-46, you may be subject to penalties.

Computerized Systems

If you maintain your records with an automated data processing system, as this book strongly advocates, you must be able to produce legible records from the system to provide the information needed to determine your correct tax liability.

You must keep a complete description of the computerized portion of your accounting system. This documentation must be sufficiently detailed to show the applications being performed; the procedures used in each application; or the controls used to ensure accurate and reliable processing; and controls used to prevent the unauthorized addition, alteration, or deletion of retained records. These records must be retained for as long as they may be material in the administration of any Internal Revenue law.

See IRS Revenue Procedure 91-59, in Cumulative Bulletin 1991-2 on page 841, for more information.

ORGANIZING EFFECTIVE TAX RECORDS

Identify the Source of Income

The money or the property you receive can come from many sources. Your records should identify the source of any income so that you can show whether an income item is taxable or nontaxable. A good practice is to photocopy all checks that are received and file the copies with the corresponding bank deposit duplicates.

Maintain a Record of Deductible Expenses

You may forget expenses when you prepare your tax return unless you record them when they occur. You should also retain the invoice, paid receipt, or canceled check that supports an item of expense in a safe, well-organized file. Figures 4-1 through 4-3 will give you a good idea of what you can deduct.

Type of acquisition:	*When your holding period starts:*
Stocks and bonds bought on a securities market	Day after trading date you bought security. Ends on trading date after you sold security.
U.S. Treasury notes and bonds	If bought at auction, day after notification of bid acceptance. If bought through subscription, day after subscription was submitted.
Nontaxable exchanges	Day after date you acquired old property.
Gift	If your basis is giver's adjusted basis, same day as giver's holding period began. If your basis is fair market value, day after date of gift.
Real property bought	Generally, day after date you received title to the property
Real property repossessed	Day you originally acquired the property but does not include time between the original sale and date of repossession.

Figure 4-1. Holding period for different types of acquisition.

Element to be proved (1)	Expense			
	Travel (2)	Entertainment (3)	Gift (4)	Transportation (Car) (5)
Amount	Amount of each separate expense for travel, lodging, and meals. Incidental expenses may be totaled in reasonable categories, such as taxis, daily meals for traveler, etc.	Amount of each separate expense. Incidental expenses such as taxis, telephones, etc., may be totaled on a daily basis.	Cost of gift.	1) Amount of each separate expense including cost of the car, 2) Mileage for each business use of the car, and 3) Total miles for the tax year.
Time	Date you left and returned for each trip, and number of days for business.	Date of entertainment or use of a facility for entertainment. For meals or entertainment directly before or after a business discussion, the date and duration of the business discussion.	Date of gift.	Date of the expense or use.
Place	Name of city or other designation.	Name and address of location of place of entertainment, or place of use of a facility for entertainment. Type of entertainment if not otherwise apparent. Place where business discussion was held if entertainment is directly before or after a business discussion.	Not applicable.	Name of city or other designation if applicable.
Description	Not applicable.	Not applicable.	Description of gift.	Not applicable.
Business Purpose	Business reason for travel or the business benefit gained or expected to be gained.	Business reason or the business benefit gained or expected to be gained. Nature of business discussion or activity.	Business reason for giving the gift or the business benefit gained or expected to be gained.	Business reason for the expense or use of the car.
Business Relationship	Not applicable.	Occupations or other information—such as names or other designations—about persons entertained that shows their business relationship to you. If all people entertained did not take part in business discussion, identify those who did. You must also prove that you or your employee was present if entertainment was a business meal.	Occupation or other information— such as name or other designation— about recipient that shows his or her business relationship to you.	Not applicable.

Figure 4-2. Elements to prove certain business expenses.

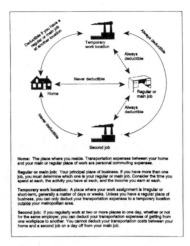

Home: The place where you reside. Transportation expenses between your home and your main or regular place of work are personal commuting expenses.

Regular or main job: Your principal place of business. If you have more than one job, you must determine which one is your regular or main job. Consider the time you spend at each, the activity you have at each, and the income you earn at each.

Temporary work location: A place where your work assignment is irregular or short-term, generally a matter of days or weeks. Unless you have a regular place of business, you can only deduct your transportation expenses to a temporary location outside your metropolitan area.

Second job: If you regularly work at two or more places in one day, whether or not for the same employer, you can deduct your transportation expenses of getting from one workplace to another. You cannot deduct your transportation costs between your home and a second job on a day off from your main job.

Figure 4-3. When are local transportation expenses deductible?

Figure Depreciation Deduction

You should note on a permanent record all business assets you can depreciate. Depreciation allows you to recover the cost of business property by deducting part of it each year on your tax return. You must keep a record of the cost and other information regarding your assets to figure your depreciation deduction and any gain or loss upon disposition of the asset. If assets are sold or capital improvements have been made to them, only a permanent record will show how much of their cost you have recovered. This information is also needed to correctly report a disposition of an asset on your tax return.

Figure Earnings for Self-Employment Tax Purposes

The self-employment tax is part of the system for providing Social Security coverage for people who work for themselves. The Social Security benefits you receive when you retire or become disabled, or that will be paid to your family in the event of your death, depend on the amount you contributed to your Social Security account based on your net earnings. Your records should show how much of your earnings are subject to self-employment tax and how much self-employment tax you paid on those earnings.

Support Items Reported on Tax Returns

If any of your tax returns are examined by the IRS, you may (will) be asked to explain and support the items reported on them. A complete set of records will speed up the examination and generally impress the examiner favorably. Adequate and complete records are always supported by sales slips, invoices, receipts, bank deposit slips, canceled checks, and other documents.

Keep Financial Account Statements as Proof of Payment

If you cannot provide a canceled check to prove payment of an expense item, you may be able to prove it with certain financial account statements. These include account statements prepared by a third party who is under contract to prepare statements for the financial institution. To be acceptable, it must meet certain requirements:

1. An account statement showing a check clearing is accepted as proof if it shows the check number, amount, payee name, and the date the check amount was posted to the account by the financial institution.
2. An account statement prepared by a financial institution showing an electronic funds transfer is accepted as proof if it shows the amount transferred, payee name, and the date the transfer was posted to the account by the financial institution.
3. An account statement prepared by a financial institution showing a credit card charge (an increase in the cardholder's loan balance) is accepted as proof if it shows the amount charged, payee name, and the date charged (transaction date).

These account statements must have a high degree of legibility and readability. For this purpose, legibility is the quality of a letter or number enabling it to be identified positively, excluding all other letters and numbers. Readability is the quality of a group of letters or numbers enabling it to be recognized as words or complete numbers. However, this does not mean the information must be typed or printed. The information can be handwritten, photocopied, or faxed (although this last type is not a good idea unless the original fax is copied onto plain paper since the fax paper will darken over time and be completely illegible after some interval). While there is no specific prohibition against pencil there is the doubt raised as to the credibility of the records since pencil can be erased and altered too easily.

The IRS also cautions that proof of payment of an amount alone does not establish that you are entitled to a tax deduction. You should also keep the other supporting documents previously discussed.

KNOW THE RECORDS REQUIRED OF EMPLOYERS

As an employer, you must keep all your records on employment taxes (income tax withholding, Social Security, Medicare, and federal unemployment tax) for at least four years after the due date of the return or after the date the tax is paid, which is later. In addition to the following items required for each specific kind of employment tax, your records should contain your employer identification number, copies of the returns you have filed, and the dates and amounts of the deposits you made.

Income Tax Withholding

The specific records you must keep for income tax withholding are:

1. Each employee's name, address, and Social Security number;
2. The total amount and date of each wage payment and the period of time the payment covers;

3. For each wage payment, the amount subject to withholding;

4. The amount of withholding tax collected on each payment and the date it was collected;

5. If the taxable amount is less than the total payment, the reason that it is less;

6. Copies of any statements furnished by employees relating to nonresident alien status, residence in Puerto Rico or the Virgin Islands, or residence or physical presence in a foreign country;

7. The fair market value and date of each payment of noncash compensation made to a retail commission salesperson, if no income tax was withheld;

8. For accident or health plans, information about the amount of each payment;

9. The withholding allowance certificates (Form W-4) filed by each employee;

10. Any agreement between you and the employee for the voluntary withholding of additional amounts of tax;

11. The dates in each calendar quarter on which any employee worked for you, but not in the course of your trade or business, and the amount paid for that work;

12. Copies of statements given to you by employees reporting tips received in their work, unless the information shown on the statements appears in another item on this list;

13. Requests by employees to have their withheld tax figured on the basis of their individual cumulative wages; and

14. The Forms W-5 of your employees who are eligible for the earned income credit and wish to receive part of their credit in advance, rather than when they file their income tax returns.

An employees' earnings ledger, which is available at most office supply stores, normally has space for the information required in items 1 to 4. Payroll software also contains all the information you are required to report and retain for the IRS.

Social Security and Medicare Taxes

You must also maintain the following information in your records on the Social Security and Medicare (FICA) taxes of your employees:

1. The amount of each wage payment subject to Social Security tax;
2. The amount of each wage payment subject to Medicare tax;
3. The amount of Social Security and Medicare tax collected for each payment and the date collected; and
4. If the total wage payment and the taxable amount differ, the reason for the variance.

Federal Unemployment Tax

The Federal Unemployment Tax Act (FUTA) requires you to maintain records containing the following information:

1. The total amount paid to each of your employees during the calendar year;
2. The amount of compensation subject to the unemployment tax;
3. The amount you paid into the state unemployment fund; and
4. Any other information required to be shown on Form 940 (or Form 940-EZ).

S CORPORATION REQUIREMENTS

A qualifying corporation may choose to be generally exempt from federal income tax. Its shareholders will then include in their income their share of the corporation's separately stated items of income, deduction, loss, and credit and their share of nonseparately stated income or loss. A corporation that makes this choice is an S *corporation*.

Although it generally will not be liable for federal income tax, an S corporation may have to pay a tax on excess net passive investment income, a tax on capital gains, a tax on built-in gains, or the tax from recomputing a prior year's investment credit. An S corporation files its return on Form 1120S.

To make the election to become an S corporation, a corporation, in addition to other requirements, must not have more than 35 shareholders. Moreover, each shareholder must consent to the election.

OBTAINING A TAXPAYER IDENTIFICATION NUMBER

Generally, you can use your Social Security number as your *taxpayer identification number*. You must put this number on each of your individual income tax forms, such as Form 1040 and its schedules.

However, every partnership and corporation (including S corporations) and certain sole proprietors must have an *employer identification number* (EIN) to use as a taxpayer identification number. Sole proprietors must have EINs if they:

1. Pay wages to one or more employees; or
2. Must file any pension or excise tax returns, including those for alcohol, tobacco, or firearms.

If you are required to have an EIN, include it along with your Social Security number on your Schedule C (Form 1040). If you are not required to have an EIN, use your Social Security number as your business taxpayer identification number.

Application for Identification Number

To apply for a Social Security number, you should use Form SS-5. If you are under 18 years of age, you must furnish evidence of age, identity, and U.S. citizenship along with this form. If you are 18 or older, you must appear in person with this evidence at a Social Security office. If you are an alien, you must appear in person and bring your birth certificate and either your alien registration card or your U.S. immigration form. This form is available from Social Security Administration offices or from the Internal Revenue Service by calling 1-800-829-3676.

To apply for an EIN, use Form SS-4. This form is available from IRS and Social Security Administration offices.

MAKING PAYMENTS TO OTHERS

If you make payments that require an information return (Form 1099), you must include the payee's taxpayer identification number on the information return.

To get the payee's number, use Form W-9. This form is available from the IRS. A payee who does not provide you with an identification number may be subject to backup withholding of 20 percent on the payments you make.

FILING SCHEDULE C

If you are a sole proprietor, you report your income and expenses from your business or profession in Schedule C or Schedule C-EZ (Form 1040). File Schedule C with your Form 1040. Report the amount of net profit (or loss) from Schedule C on the appropriate line of Form 1040. If you operate more than one business as a sole proprietor, you must prepare a separate Schedule C for each business and attach all of these schedules to your tax return. If you do not prepare a separate Schedule C for each business, you may have to pay a penalty because you did not properly report your income and deductions.

It is important to use the correct business code, similar to the SIC (*Standard Industrial Classification*) code, found on page two of Schedule C. This information will identify market segments of the public for IRS Taxpayer Education programs and is also used by the U.S. Census Bureau for its economic census. In addition, the information is a component in the *Taxpayer Compliance Program* (TCP), which the IRS uses in secret computer programs to determine which returns to select for an audit. By comparing the income and deductions of your business with a composite of other businesses within that category, the computer can discover inconsistencies and score points (through DIF), which will target the return for examination by an agent-analyst when a certain point threshold is reached or exceeded. (See DIF, in the section "The IRS Examination and Appeals Process," later in this chapter.) The agent-analyst will determine whether the return is to be sent to your local IRS field office for an in-office examination (audit) or to a revenue officer for an on-site audit.

Figures 4-4 through 4-19 are samples of some of the IRS forms you may need when filing your return. Most tax software packages will include such forms, but they are presented here for illustrative purposes.

THE IRS EXAMINATION AND APPEALS PROCESS

The IRS examines returns for correctness of income, exemptions, credits, and deductions. Most taxpayers' returns are accepted as filed. But if your return is selected for examination, it does not suggest that you are dishonest. The examination may or may not result in your having to pay more tax; your case may be closed without change; or you may receive a refund.

You are entitled to courteous and considerate treatment by IRS employees at all times. If you ever feel that you are not being treated with fairness, courtesy, and consideration by an IRS employee, you should tell the employee's supervisor. IRS Publication 1, *Your Rights as a Taxpayer* explains taxpayers' rights. You can get free publications by calling the IRS at 1-800-829-3676. The best times to call are 8:00 to 9:30 A.M. and 3:00 to 4:30 P.M.

You need pay only the required tax. You have the right to plan your business and personal finances so that you will pay the least tax that

a Control number		Void ☐
b Employer's identification number		1 Wages, tips, other compensation	2 Federal income tax withheld
c Employer's name, address, and ZIP code		3 Social security wages	4 Social security tax withheld
		5 Medicare wages and tips	6 Medicare tax withheld
		7 Social security tips	8 Allocated tips
d Employee's social security number		9 Advance EIC payment	10 Dependent care benefits
e Employee's name, address, and ZIP code		11 Nonqualified plans	12 Benefits included in Box 1
		13 See Instrs. for Box 13	14 Other
		15 Statutory employee ☐ Deceased ☐ Pension plan ☐ Legal rep. ☐ 942 emp ☐ Subtotal ☐ Deferred compensation ☐	
16 State	Employer's state I.D. No.	17 State wages tips etc	18 State income tax	19 Locality name	20 Local wages tips etc	21 Local income tax

Form **W-2** Wage and Tax **1993**
Statement

Copy B To Be Filed With Employee's FEDERAL Tax Return

Department of the Treasury—Internal Revenue Service

This information is being furnished to the Internal Revenue Service

OMB No. 1545-0008

Figure 4-4. Sample W-2 form.

□ CORRECTED (if checked)			
PAYER'S name, street address, city, state, and ZIP code	1 Rents $	OMB No. 1545-0115	**Miscellaneous**
	2 Royalties $	19**93**	**Income**
	3 Prizes, awards, etc. $		
PAYER'S Federal identification number	RECIPIENT'S identification number	4 **Federal income tax withheld** $	5 Fishing boat proceeds $	**Copy B** **For Recipient**
RECIPIENT'S name		6 Medical and health care payments $	7 Nonemployee compensation $	This is important tax information and is being furnished to the Internal Revenue Service. If you are required to file a return, a negligence penalty or other sanction may be imposed on you if this income is taxable and the IRS determines that it has not been reported.
Street address (including apt. no.)		8 Substitute payments in lieu of dividends or interest $	9 Payer made direct sales of $5,000 or more of consumer products to a buyer (recipient) for resale ► □	
City, state, and ZIP code		10 Crop insurance proceeds $	11 State income tax withheld $	
Account number (optional)		12 State/Payer's state number		

Form **1099-MISC**   (Keep for your records.)   Department of the Treasury - Internal Revenue Service

Figure 4-5. Sample 1099 form.

DO NOT STAPLE

a Control number	33333	**For Official Use Only ►** OMB No. 1545-0008				
b **Kind of Payer**	941/941E ☐ CT-1 ☐	Military ☐ 942 ☐	943 ☐ Medicare govt. emp. ☐	**1** Wages, tips, other compensation	**2** Federal income tax withheld	
				3 Social security wages	**4** Social security tax withheld	
c Total number of statements	**d** Establishment number			**5** Medicare wages and tips	**6** Medicare tax withheld	
	e Employer's identification number			**7** Social security tips	**8** Allocated tips	
f Employer's name				**9** Advance EIC payments	**10** Dependent care benefits	
				11 Nonqualified plans	**12** Deferred compensation	
				13 Adjusted total social security wages and tips		
				14 Adjusted total Medicare wages and tips		
g Employer's address and ZIP code						
h Other EIN used this year				**15** Income tax withheld by third-party payer		
i Employer's state I.D. No.						

Under penalties of perjury, I declare that I have examined this return and accompanying documents, and, to the best of my knowledge and belief, they are true, correct, and complete.

Signature ► _____ Title ► _____ Date ► _____

Telephone number ( )

Form **W-3 Transmittal of Wage and Tax Statements 1993**   Department of the Treasury Internal Revenue Service

Please return this entire page with Copy A of Forms W-2 to the Social Security Administration address for your state as listed below. **Household employers filing Forms W-2 for household employees should send the forms to the Albuquerque Data Operations Center.** You may order forms by calling 1-800-TAX-FORM (1-800-829-3676).

Where To File

If your legal residence, principal place of business, or office, or agency is located in ▼	Use this address ▼
Alaska, Arizona, California, Colorado, Hawaii, Idaho, Iowa, Minnesota, Missouri, Montana, Nebraska, Nevada, North Dakota, Oregon, South Dakota, Utah, Washington, Wisconsin, Wyoming	Social Security Administration Data Operations Center Salinas, CA 93911
Alabama, Arkansas, Florida, Georgia, Illinois, Kansas, Louisiana, Mississippi, New Mexico, Oklahoma, South Carolina, Tennessee, Texas	Social Security Administration Data Operations Center Albuquerque, NM 87180
Connecticut, Delaware, District of Columbia, Indiana, Kentucky, Maine, Maryland, Massachusetts, Michigan, New Hampshire, New Jersey, New York, North Carolina, Ohio, Pennsylvania, Rhode Island, Vermont, Virginia, West Virginia	Social Security Administration Data Operations Center Wilkes-Barre, PA 18769
If you have no legal residence or principal place of business in any state	Social Security Administration Data Operations Center Wilkes-Barre, PA 18769

Note: Extra postage may be necessary if the report you send contains more than a few pages or if the envelope is larger than letter size.

Paperwork Reduction Act Notice.—We ask for the information on this form to carry out the Internal Revenue laws of the United States. You are required to give us the information. We need it to ensure that you are complying with these laws and to allow us to figure and collect the right amount of tax.

The time needed to complete and file this form will vary depending on individual circumstances. The estimated average time is 27 minutes. If you have comments concerning the accuracy of this time estimate or suggestions for making this form more simple, we would be happy to hear from you. You can write to both the **Internal Revenue Service**, Washington, DC 20224, Attention: IRS Reports Clearance Officer T:FP; and the **Office of Management and Budget**, Paperwork Reduction Project (1545-0008), Washington, DC 20503. Do NOT send the form to either of these offices. Instead, see **Where To File.**

Items To Note

Format Change.—Major changes have been made to the format of Form W-3. Entity information is reported on the left and amounts are reported on the right. Boxes 1 through 10 are the same boxes as shown on Form W-2. A reference chart is included on page 7 of the Instructions for Form W-2.

Top Margin.—The top margin of Form W-3 has changed from ¼ to ⅜ inch.

Sick Pay Reporting.—Most instructions on sick pay reporting have been removed because of new **Pub. 952**, Sick Pay Reporting.

Reconciliation.—Instructions were added on reconciling and reducing discrepancies.

General Instructions

This form is a transmittal for Copy A of Forms W-2.

Note: Amounts reported on related employment tax Forms (W-2, 941, 942, or 943) should agree with the amounts reported on Form W-3. If there are differences, you may be contacted by the IRS. You should retain your reconciliation for future reference. See **Reconciling Forms W-2, W-3, and 941** on page 3.

Cat. No. 10159Y

Figure 4-6. Sample W-3 form.

Form **940** Department of the Treasury Internal Revenue Service	**Employer's Annual Federal Unemployment (FUTA) Tax Return** ▶ **For Paperwork Reduction Act Notice, see separate instructions.**	OMB No. 1545-0028 **1993**

If incorrect, make any necessary change. ▶	⌐ Name (as distinguished from trade name)	Calendar year ⌐	T
			FF
	Trade name, if any		FD
			FP
	Address and ZIP code	Employer identification number	I
	L		T

A Are you required to pay unemployment contributions to only one state? (If no, skip questions B through D.) . ☐ **Yes** ☐ **No**

B Did you pay all state unemployment contributions by January 31, 1994? (If a 0% experience rate is granted, check "Yes.") (If no, skip questions C and D.) . . . . ☐ **Yes** ☐ **No**

C Were all wages that were taxable for FUTA tax also taxable for your state's unemployment tax? (If no, skip D.) ☐ **Yes** ☐ **No**

D Did you pay all wages in states or territories other than the U.S. Virgin Islands? . . . . ☐ **Yes** ☐ **No**

If you answered "No" to any of these questions, you must file Form 940. If you answered "Yes" to all the questions, you may file Form 940-EZ, which is a simplified version of Form 940. You can get Form 940-EZ by calling 1-800-TAX-FORM (1-800-829-3676).

E If you will not have to file returns in the future, check here, complete, and sign the return . . . . ▶ ☐

F If this is an Amended Return, check here . . . . ▶ ☐

Part I   **Computation of Taxable Wages**

1	Total payments (including exempt payments) during the calendar year for services of employees .	**1**	
2	Exempt payments. (Explain each exemption shown, attach additional sheets if necessary.) ▶	Amount paid	
		2	
3	Payments of more than $7,000 for services. Enter only amounts over the first $7,000 paid to each employee. Do not include payments from line 2. The $7,000 amount is the Federal wage base. Your state wage base may be different. **Do not use the state wage limitation**	**3**	
4	Total exempt payments (add lines 2 and 3)	**4**	
5	**Total taxable wages** (subtract line 4 from line 1, enter result, and go to part II) . . . . . ▶	**5**	

Be sure to complete both sides of this return and sign in the space provided on the back.   Cat. No. 11234O   Form **940** (1993)

Figure 4-7. Sample FUTA form—Form 940.

Form 940 (1993)   Page **2**

Part II Tax Due or Refund

1	Gross FUTA tax. Multiply the wages in Part I, line 5, by .062	**1**
2	Maximum credit. Multiply the wages in Part I, line 5, by .054 . . . . **2**	
3	**Computation of tentative credit (Note:** *All taxpayers must complete the applicable columns.*)	

Note: *The additional credit shown in column (h) is limited to 3% of the taxable payroll for the U.S. Virgin Islands. Use 3% (.03) in column (f). See Part II, line 3, columns (f) and (h), on page 4 of the separate instructions.*

(a) Name of state	(b) State reporting number(s) as shown on employer's state contribution returns	(c) Taxable payroll (as defined in state act)	(d) State experience rate period		(e) State experience rate	(f) Contributions if rate had been 5.4% (col. (c) x .054)	(g) Contributions payable at experience rate (col. (c) x col. (e))	(h) Additional credit (col. (f) minus col.(g)). If 0 or less, enter 0.	(i) Contributions actually paid to state
			From	To					

3a	Totals . . . ▶	
3b	Total tentative credit (add line 3a, columns (h) and (i) only—see instructions for limitations on late payments) ▶	
4		
5		
6	**Credit:** Enter the smaller of the amount in Part II, line 2, or line 3b.	**6**
7	**Total FUTA tax** (subtract line 6 from line 1)	**7**
8	Total FUTA tax deposited for the year, including any overpayment applied from a prior year . .	**8**
9	**Balance due** (subtract line 8 from line 7). This should be $100 or less. Pay to the Internal Revenue Service. See page 2 of the separate instructions for details . . . . ▶	**9**
10	**Overpayment** (subtract line 7 from line 8). Check if it is to be: ☐ **Applied to next return,** or ☐ **Refunded** . . . . ▶	**10**

Part III Record of Quarterly Federal Unemployment Tax Liability *(Do not include state liability)*

Quarter	First	Second	Third	Fourth	Total for year
Liability for quarter					

Under penalties of perjury, I declare that I have examined this return, including accompanying schedules and statements, and to the best of my knowledge and belief, it is true, correct, and complete, and that no part of any payment made to a state unemployment fund claimed as a credit was or is to be deducted from the payments to employees.

Signature ▶ _____   Title (Owner, etc.) ▶ _____   Date ▶ _____

Figure 4-7. Sample FUTA form—Form 940. (Continued)

Form **940-EZ**	Employer's Annual Federal	OMB No. 1545-1110
Department of the Treasury Internal Revenue Service	Unemployment (FUTA) Tax Return	19**93**

				T	
	Name (as distinguished from trade name)	Calendar year		FF	
If incorrect, make any necessary changes. ▶				FD	
	Trade name, if any			FP	
				I	
	Address and ZIP code	Employer identification number		T	

Follow the chart under **Who May Use Form 940-EZ** on page 2. If you cannot use Form 940-EZ, you must use Form 940 instead.

A Enter the amount of contributions paid to your state unemployment fund. (See instructions for line A on page 4.) ▶ $ ....

B (1) Enter the name of the state where you have to pay contributions . . . . ▶ ....

(2) Enter your state reporting number as shown on state unemployment tax return. ▶

If you will not have to file returns in the future, check here (see Who Must File, on page 2) complete, and sign the return . . . . . ▶ ☐

If this is an **Amended Return** check here . . . . ▶ ☐

Part I   Taxable Wages and FUTA Tax

1	Total payments (including payments shown on lines 2 and 3) during the calendar year for services of employees		**1**		
		Amount paid			
2	Exempt payments. (Explain all exempt payments, attaching additional sheets if necessary.) ▶	**2**			
3	Payments for services of more than $7,000. Enter only amounts over the first $7,000 paid to each employee. Do not include any exempt payments from line 2. Do not use your state wage limitation. The $7,000 amount is the Federal wage base. Your state wage base may be different	**3**			
4	Total exempt payments (add lines 2 and 3)		**4**		
5	**Total taxable wages** (subtract line 4 from line 1) . . . . ▶		**5**		
6	**FUTA tax.** Multiply the wages on line 5 by .008 and enter here. (If the result is over $100, also complete Part II.) .		**6**		
7	Total FUTA tax deposited for the year, including any overpayment applied from a prior year (from your records)		**7**		
8	**Amount you owe** (subtract line 7 from line 6). This should be $100 or less. Pay to "Internal Revenue Service" . ▶		**8**		
9	**Overpayment** (subtract line 6 from line 7). Check if it is to be: ☐ **Applied to next return, or** ☐ Refunded ▶		**9**		

Part II   Record of Quarterly Federal Unemployment Tax Liability (Do not include state liability.) Complete only if line 6 is over $100.

Quarter	First (Jan. 1 – Mar. 31)	Second (Apr. 1 – June 30)	Third (July 1 – Sept. 30)	Fourth (Oct. 1 – Dec. 31)	Total for year
Liability for quarter					

Under penalties of perjury, I declare that I have examined this return, including accompanying schedules and statements, and, to the best of my knowledge and belief, it is true, correct, and complete, and that no part of any payment made to a state unemployment fund claimed as a credit was, or is to be, deducted from the payments to employees.

Signature ▶   Title (Owner, etc.) ▶   Date ▶

Cat. No. 10983G   Form **940-EZ** (1993)

Figure 4-8. Sample FUTA form—Form 940-EZ.

THE IRS EXAMINATION AND APPEALS PROCESS

Paperwork Reduction Act Notice.—We ask for the information on this form to carry out the Internal Revenue laws of the United States. You are required to give us the information. We need it to ensure that you are complying with these laws and to allow us to figure and collect the correct tax.

The time needed to complete and file this form will vary depending on individual circumstances. The estimated average time is:

Recordkeeping	5 hr., 55 min.
Learning about the law or the form	7 min.
Preparing and sending the form to the IRS	28 min.

If you have comments concerning the accuracy of these time estimates or suggestions for making this form more simple, we would be happy to hear from you. You can write to both the **Internal Revenue Service,** Attention: Reports Clearance Officer, T:FP, Washington, DC 20224; and the **Office of Management and Budget,** Paperwork Reduction Project (1545-1110), Washington, DC 20503. **DO NOT** send the form to either of these offices. Instead, see **Where To File** on page 4.

Who May Use Form 940-EZ.—You may use Form 940-EZ if:

1. You paid unemployment taxes ("contributions") to only one state;

2. You paid these taxes by the January 31 due date of Form 940-EZ;

3. All wages that were taxable for FUTA tax were also taxable for your state's unemployment tax. Otherwise, use Form 940. For example, if you paid wages to corporate officers (these wages are taxable for FUTA tax) in a state that exempts these wages from its unemployment taxes, you cannot use Form 940-EZ; and

4. You pay wages in a state that is not a credit reduction state. A state that has not repaid money it borrowed from the Federal government to pay unemployment benefits is a credit reduction state. The Department of Labor determines these states.

Note: *Do not file Form 940-EZ if you have already filed Form 940 for 1993.*

The following chart will lead you to the right form to use.

```
┌────────────────────────┐
│ Did you pay            │
│ unemployment           │
│ contributions to only one │──── No ──►
│ state?                 │
└────────────────────────┘
          │
         Yes
          ▼
┌────────────────────────┐
│ Did you pay all state  │
│ unemployment           │──── No ──►
│ contributions by       │
│ January 31?            │
└────────────────────────┘
          │
         Yes
          ▼
┌────────────────────────┐
│ Were all wages that were │
│ taxable for FUTA tax also │──── No ──►
│ taxable for your state's │
│ unemployment tax?      │
└────────────────────────┘
          │
         Yes
          ▼
┌────────────────────────┐
│ Were all wages paid in a │
│ state that is not a credit │──── No ──►
│ reduction state?       │
└────────────────────────┘
          │
         Yes
          ▼
┌──────────────────┐   ┌──────────────────────┐
│ You may use Form │   │ You cannot use Form  │
│ 940-EZ           │   │ 940-EZ; use Form 940 │
│                  │   │ instead.             │
└──────────────────┘   └──────────────────────┘
```

General Instructions

Purpose of Form.—The Federal Unemployment Tax Act (FUTA), together with state unemployment systems, provides for payments of unemployment compensation to workers who have lost their jobs. Most employers pay both Federal and state unemployment taxes. Use this form for your annual FUTA tax report. **Only the employer pays this tax.** The $7,000 amount is the Federal wage base. Your state wage base may be different.

Who Must File

General Rule (household and agricultural employers see next column).—File if either of the following applies:

1. You paid wages of $1,500 or more in any calendar quarter in 1992 or 1993; or

2. You had at least one employee for some part of a day in any 20 different weeks in 1992 or 1993.

Count all regular, temporary, and part-time employees. A partnership should not count its partners. If a business changes hands during the year, each employer meeting test 1 or 2 must file. Do not report wages paid by the other.

Household Employers.—File a FUTA tax return **ONLY** if you paid cash wages of $1,000 or more in any calendar quarter in 1992 or 1993 for household work in a private home, local college club, or a local chapter of a college fraternity or sorority. **Note:** *See Pub. 926, Employment Taxes for Household Employers, for more information including filled-in examples of Form 940-EZ.*

Agricultural Employers.—File a FUTA tax return if either of the following applies:

1. You paid cash wages of $20,000 or more to farmworkers during any calendar quarter in 1992 or 1993; or

2. You employed 10 or more farmworkers during some part of a day (whether or not at the same time) for at least 1 day during any 20 different weeks in 1992 or 1993.

Count aliens admitted on a temporary basis to the United States to perform farmwork, also known as workers with "H-2(a)" visas, to see if you meet either of the tests. Wages paid to these aliens are not subject to FUTA tax before 1995.

Nonprofit Organizations.—Religious, educational, charitable, etc., organizations described in section 501(c)(3) of the Internal Revenue Code and exempt from tax under section 501(a) are not subject to FUTA tax and are not required to file.

Completing Form 940-EZ.—If your FUTA tax for 1993 (line 6) is $100 or less, complete only Part I of the form. If your FUTA tax is over $100, complete Parts I and II. See the instructions for Part II for information on FUTA tax deposits.

If You Are Not Liable for FUTA Tax.—If you receive Form 940-EZ and are not liable for FUTA tax for 1993, write "Not Liable" across the front of the form, sign the return, and return it to the IRS. **Note:** *If you will not have to file returns in the future,*

(Instructions continued on next page.)

Figure 4-8. Sample FUTA form—Form 940-EZ. (Continued)

Form **941**
(Rev. January 1993)
Department of the Treasury
Internal Revenue Service

41,41,

Employer's Quarterly Federal Tax Return
► See separate instructions for information on completing this form.
Please type or print.

OMB No. 1545-0029
Expires 1-31-96

Enter state code for state in which deposits made ► (see page 2 of instructions).

Name (as distinguished from trade name)	Date quarter ended
Trade name, if any	Employer identification number
Address (number and street)	City, state, and ZIP code

T
FF
FD
FP
I
T

If address is different from prior return, check here ►

IRS Use

If you do not have to file returns in the future, check here . ► ☐ Date final wages paid .
If you are a seasonal employer, see **Seasonal employers** on page 1 and check here . ☐

1   Number of employees (except household) employed in the pay period that includes March 12th ►

2   Total wages and tips subject to withholding, plus other compensation **2**

3   Total income tax withheld from wages, tips, pensions, annuities, sick pay, gambling, etc. . **3**

4   Adjustment of withheld income tax for preceding quarters of calendar year (see instructions) . . **4**

5   Adjusted total of income tax withheld (line 3 as adjusted by line 4—see instructions) . . . **5**

6a Taxable social security wages . . . . . $_____ . 12.4% (.124) = **6a**

b   Taxable social security tips . . . . . . $_____ . 12.4% (.124) = **6b**

7   Taxable Medicare wages and tips . . . $_____ . 2.9% (.029) = **7**

8   Total social security and Medicare taxes (add lines 6a, 6b, and 7) **8**

9   Adjustment of social security and Medicare taxes (see instructions for required explanation) . **9**

10 Adjusted total of social security and Medicare taxes (line 8 as adjusted by line 9—see instructions) **10**

11 Backup withholding (see instructions) **11**

12 Adjustment of backup withholding tax for preceding quarters of calendar year **12**

13 Adjusted total of backup withholding (line 11 as adjusted by line 12) **13**

14 **Total taxes** (add lines 5, 10, and 13) **14**

15 Advance earned income credit (EIC) payments made to employees, if any **15**

16 Net taxes (subtract line 15 from line 14). **This should equal line 20, col. (d), below or line D of Schedule B** (plus line D of Schedule A if you treated backup withholding as a separate liability) **16**

17 **Total deposits for quarter,** including overpayment applied from a prior quarter, from your records **17**

18 **Balance due** (subtract line 17 from line 16). This should be less than $500. Pay to the Internal Revenue Service **18**

19 **Overpayment,** if line 17 is more than line 16, enter excess here $_____ and check if to be:
☐ Applied to next return   **OR**   ☐ Refunded.

20 **Monthly Summary of Federal Tax Liability. If line 16 is less than $500, you need not complete line 20.** If you are a monthly depositor, summarize your monthly tax liability below. If you are a semiweekly depositor or have accumulated a tax liability of $100,000 or more on any day, attach Schedule B (Form 941) and check here (see instructions) . . . . ☐

	(a) First month	**(b)** Second month	**(c)** Third month	**(d)** Total for quarter
Liability for month				

Sign Here

Under penalties of perjury, I declare that I have examined this return, including accompanying schedules and statements, and to the best of my knowledge and belief, it is true, correct, and complete.

Signature ►   Print Your Name and Title ►   Date ►

For Paperwork Reduction Act Notice, see page 1 of separate instructions.   Cat. No. 17001Z   Form **941** (Rev. 1-93)

☆ U.S. GOVERNMENT PRINTING OFFICE: 1993 361-279

Figure 4-9. Employer's quarterly federal tax return.

86

Form **1120S**	**U.S. Income Tax Return for an S Corporation**	OMB No. 1545-0130
Department of the Treasury Internal Revenue Service	▶ Do not file this form unless the corporation has timely filed Form 2553 to elect to be an S corporation. ▶ See separate instructions.	19**93**

For calendar year 1993, or tax year beginning .... , 1993, and ending .... , 19 .....

A Date of election as an S corporation	Use IRS label. Other-wise, please print or type.	Name	C Employer identification number
B Business code no. (see Specific Instructions)		Number, street, and room or suite no. (If a P.O. box, see page 9 of the instructions.)	D Date incorporated
		City or town, state, and ZIP code	E Total assets (see Specific Instructions) $

F Check applicable boxes: (1) ☐ Initial return   (2) ☐ Final return   (3) ☐ Change in address   (4) ☐ Amended return
G Check this box if this S corporation is subject to the consolidated audit procedures of sections 6241 through 6245 (see instructions before checking this box) . ▶ ☐
H Enter number of shareholders in the corporation at end of the tax year . . . . ▶

Caution: *Include **only** trade or business income and expenses on lines 1a through 21. See the instructions for more information.*

Income

1a	Gross receipts or sales |_____ **b** Less returns and allowances|_____ **c** Bal ▶	**1c**
2	Cost of goods sold (Schedule A, line 8)		**2**
3	Gross profit. Subtract line 2 from line 1c		**3**
4	Net gain (loss) from Form 4797, Part II, line 20 *(attach Form 4797)* . . .		**4**
5	Other income (loss) (see instructions) *(attach schedule)*		**5**
6	**Total income (loss).** Combine lines 3 through 5 . . . . ▶		**6**

Deductions (See instructions for limitations.)

7	Compensation of officers		**7**
8a	Salaries and wages |_____ **b** Less employment credits |_____ **c** Bal ▶	**8c**
9	Repairs and maintenance		**9**
10	Bad debts		**10**
11	Rents		**11**
12	Taxes and licenses		**12**
13	Interest		**13**
14a	Depreciation (see instructions)	**14a**	
b	Depreciation claimed on Schedule A and elsewhere on return .	**14b**	
c	Subtract line 14b from line 14a		**14c**
15	Depletion **(Do not deduct oil and gas depletion.)**		**15**
16	Advertising		**16**
17	Pension, profit-sharing, etc., plans		**17**
18	Employee benefit programs		**18**
19	Other deductions (see instructions) *(attach schedule)*		**19**
20	**Total deductions.** Add lines 7 through 19 . . . . ▶		**20**
21	Ordinary income (loss) from trade or business activities. Subtract line 20 from line 6		**21**

Tax and Payments

22	**Tax: a** Excess net passive income tax *(attach schedule)*. . .	**22a**	
b	Tax from Schedule D (Form 1120S)	**22b**	
c	Add lines 22a and 22b (see instructions for additional taxes) . . .		**22c**
23	**Payments: a** 1993 estimated tax payments	**23a**	
b	Tax deposited with Form 7004	**23b**	
c	Credit for Federal tax paid on fuels *(attach Form 4136)* . . .	**23c**	
d	Add lines 23a through 23c		**23d**
24	Estimated tax penalty (see instructions). Check if Form 2220 is attached. . . . . ▶ ☐		**24**
25	**Tax due.** If the total of lines 22c and 24 is larger than line 23d, enter amount owed. See instructions for depositary method of payment		**25**
26	**Overpayment.** If line 23d is larger than the total of lines 22c and 24, enter amount overpaid ▶		**26**
27	Enter amount of line 26 you want: **Credited to 1994 estimated tax ▶**	Refunded ▶	**27**

Please Sign Here

Under penalties of perjury, I declare that I have examined this return, including accompanying schedules and statements, and to the best of my knowledge and belief, it is true, correct, and complete. Declaration of preparer (other than taxpayer) is based on all information of which preparer has any knowledge.

▶ _____ Signature of officer   Date   ▶ _____ Title

Paid Preparer's Use Only	Preparer's signature ▶		Date		Check if self-employed ☐	Preparer's social security number
	Firm's name (or yours if self-employed) and address	▶			E.I. No. ▶	
					ZIP code ▶	

For Paperwork Reduction Act Notice, see page 1 of separate instructions.   Cat. No. 11510H   Form **1120S** (1993)

Figure 4-10. Sample S corporation tax return.

HOW THE SELF-EMPLOYED CAN WIN THE TAX WAR

Schedule A	**Cost of Goods Sold** (See instructions.)	

1	Inventory at beginning of year	1
2	Purchases	2
3	Cost of labor	3
4	Additional section 263A costs (see instructions) *(attach schedule)*	4
5	Other costs *(attach schedule)*	5
6	**Total.** Add lines 1 through 5	6
7	Inventory at end of year	7
8	**Cost of goods sold.** Subtract line 7 from line 6. Enter here and on page 1, line 2	8

9a Check all methods used for valuing closing inventory:

    (i) ☐ Cost

    (ii) ☐ Lower of cost or market as described in Regulations section 1.471-4

    (iii) ☐ Writedown of "subnormal" goods as described in Regulations section 1.471-2(c)

    (iv) ☐ Other (specify method used and attach explanation) ▶ ....

  b Check if the LIFO inventory method was adopted this tax year for any goods *(if checked, attach Form 970)* ▶ ☐

  c If the LIFO inventory method was used for this tax year, enter percentage (or amounts) of closing inventory computed under LIFO | 9c |

  d Do the rules of section 263A (for property produced or acquired for resale) apply to the corporation? ☐ Yes ☐ No

  e Was there any change in determining quantities, cost, or valuations between opening and closing inventory? ☐ Yes ☐ No
If "Yes," attach explanation.

Schedule B	**Other Information**	

		Yes	No
1	Check method of accounting: **(a)** ☐ Cash **(b)** ☐ Accrual **(c)** ☐ Other (specify) ▶		
2	Refer to the list in the instructions and state the corporation's principal: **(a)** Business activity ▶ .... **(b)** Product or service ▶		
3	Did the corporation at the end of the tax year own, directly or indirectly, 50% or more of the voting stock of a domestic corporation? (For rules of attribution, see section 267(c).) If "Yes," attach a schedule showing: **(a)** name, address, and employer identification number and **(b)** percentage owned.		
4	Was the corporation a member of a controlled group subject to the provisions of section 1561?		
5	At any time during calendar year 1993, did the corporation have an interest in or a signature or other authority over a financial account in a foreign country (such as a bank account, securities account, or other financial account)? (See instructions for exceptions and filing requirements for Form TD F 90-22.1.) If "Yes," enter the name of the foreign country ▶		
6	Was the corporation the grantor of, or transferor to, a foreign trust that existed during the current tax year, whether or not the corporation has any beneficial interest in it? If "Yes," the corporation may have to file Forms 3520, 3520-A, or 926.		
7	Check this box if the corporation has filed or is required to file **Form 8264,** Application for Registration of a Tax Shelter. ▶ ☐		
8	Check this box if the corporation issued publicly offered debt instruments with original issue discount ▶ ☐ If so, the corporation may have to file **Form 8281,** Information Return for Publicly Offered Original Issue Discount Instruments.		
9	If the corporation: **(a)** filed its election to be an S corporation after 1986, **(b)** was a C corporation before it elected to be an S corporation **or** the corporation acquired an asset with a basis determined by reference to its basis (or the basis of any other property) in the hands of a C corporation, and **(c)** has net unrealized built-in gain (defined in section 1374(d)(1)) in excess of the net recognized built-in gain from prior years, enter the net unrealized built-in gain reduced by net recognized built-in gain from prior years (see instructions) ▶ $		
10	Check this box if the corporation had subchapter C earnings and profits at the close of the tax year (see instructions) ▶ ☐		

Designation of Tax Matters Person (See instructions.)

Enter below the shareholder designated as the tax matters person (TMP) for the tax year of this return:

Name of designated TMP ▶	Identifying number of TMP ▶

Address of designated TMP ▶

Figure 4-10. Sample S corporation tax return. (Continued)

Form 1120S (1993)   Page **3**

Schedule K   **Shareholders' Shares of Income, Credits, Deductions, etc.**

	(a) Pro rata share items		(b) Total amount
Income (Loss)	**1** Ordinary income (loss) from trade or business activities (page 1, line 21)	**1**	
	2 Net income (loss) from rental real estate activities *(attach Form 8825)*	**2**	
	3a Gross income from other rental activities . . . . . . `3a`		
	b Expenses from other rental activities *(attach schedule)*. . `3b`		
	c Net income (loss) from other rental activities. Subtract line 3b from line 3a	**3c**	
	4 Portfolio income (loss):		
	a Interest income	**4a**	
	b Dividend income	**4b**	
	c Royalty income	**4c**	
	d Net short-term capital gain (loss) *(attach Schedule D (Form 1120S))*	**4d**	
	e Net long-term capital gain (loss) *(attach Schedule D (Form 1120S))*.	**4e**	
	f Other portfolio income (loss) *(attach schedule)*	**4f**	
	5 Net gain (loss) under section 1231 (other than due to casualty or theft) *(attach Form 4797)*	**5**	
	6 Other income (loss) *(attach schedule)*	**6**	
Deductions	**7** Charitable contributions (see instructions) *(attach schedule)*	**7**	
	8 Section 179 expense deduction *(attach Form 4562)*.	**8**	
	9 Deductions related to portfolio income (loss) (see instructions) (itemize)	**9**	
	10 Other deductions *(attach schedule)*	**10**	
Investment Interest	**11a** Interest expense on investment debts	**11a**	
	b (1) Investment income included on lines 4a, 4b, 4c, and 4f above	**11b(1)**	
	(2) Investment expenses included on line 9 above	**11b(2)**	
Credits	**12a** Credit for alcohol used as a fuel *(attach Form 6478)*	**12a**	
	b Low-income housing credit (see instructions):		
	(1) From partnerships to which section 42(j)(5) applies for property placed in service before 1990	**12b(1)**	
	(2) Other than on line 12b(1) for property placed in service before 1990.	**12b(2)**	
	(3) From partnerships to which section 42(j)(5) applies for property placed in service after 1989	**12b(3)**	
	(4) Other than on line 12b(3) for property placed in service after 1989	**12b(4)**	
	c Qualified rehabilitation expenditures related to rental real estate activities *(attach Form 3468)* .	**12c**	
	d Credits (other than credits shown on lines 12b and 12c) related to rental real estate activities (see instructions).	**12d**	
	e Credits related to other rental activities (see instructions)	**12e**	
	13 Other credits (see instructions)	**13**	
Adjustments and Tax Preference Items	**14a** Depreciation adjustment on property placed in service after 1986	**14a**	
	b Adjusted gain or loss	**14b**	
	c Depletion (other than oil and gas)	**14c**	
	d (1) Gross income from oil, gas, or geothermal properties	**14d(1)**	
	(2) Deductions allocable to oil, gas, or geothermal properties	**14d(2)**	
	e Other adjustments and tax preference items *(attach schedule)*	**14e**	
Foreign Taxes	**15a** Type of income ▶		
	b Name of foreign country or U.S. possession ▶		
	c Total gross income from sources outside the United States *(attach schedule)*	**15c**	
	d Total applicable deductions and losses *(attach schedule)*	**15d**	
	e Total foreign taxes (check one): ▶ ☐ Paid ☐ Accrued	**15e**	
	f Reduction in taxes available for credit *(attach schedule)*	**15f**	
	g Other foreign tax information *(attach schedule)*	**15g**	
Other	**16a** Total expenditures to which a section 59(e) election may apply	**16a**	
	b Type of expenditures ▶		
	17 Tax-exempt interest income	**17**	
	18 Other tax-exempt income	**18**	
	19 Nondeductible expenses	**19**	
	20 Total property distributions (including cash) other than dividends reported on line 22 below	**20**	
	21 Other items and amounts required to be reported separately to shareholders (see instructions) *(attach schedule)*		
	22 Total dividend distributions paid from accumulated earnings and profits	**22**	
	23 **Income (loss).** (Required only if Schedule M-1 must be completed.) Combine lines 1 through 6 in column (b). From the result, subtract the sum of lines 7 through 11a, 15e, and 16a.	**23**	

Figure 4-10. Sample S corporation tax return. (Continued)

Form 1120S (1993)   Page **4**

Schedule L — Balance Sheets

Assets	Beginning of tax year (a)	(b)	End of tax year (c)	(d)
1 Cash				
2a Trade notes and accounts receivable				
b Less allowance for bad debts				
3 Inventories				
4 U.S. Government obligations				
5 Tax-exempt securities				
6 Other current assets (attach schedule)				
7 Loans to shareholders				
8 Mortgage and real estate loans				
9 Other investments (attach schedule)				
10a Buildings and other depreciable assets				
b Less accumulated depreciation				
11a Depletable assets				
b Less accumulated depletion				
12 Land (net of any amortization)				
13a Intangible assets (amortizable only)				
b Less accumulated amortization				
14 Other assets (attach schedule)				
15 Total assets				
Liabilities and Shareholders' Equity				
16 Accounts payable				
17 Mortgages, notes, bonds payable in less than 1 year				
18 Other current liabilities (attach schedule)				
19 Loans from shareholders				
20 Mortgages, notes, bonds payable in 1 year or more				
21 Other liabilities (attach schedule)				
22 Capital stock				
23 Paid-in or capital surplus				
24 Retained earnings				
25 Less cost of treasury stock	(	)	(	)
26 Total liabilities and shareholders' equity				

Schedule M-1 — Reconciliation of Income (Loss) per Books With Income (Loss) per Return (You are not required to complete this schedule if the total assets on line 15, column (d), of Schedule L are less than $25,000.)

1 Net income (loss) per books

2 Income included on Schedule K, lines 1 through 6, not recorded on books this year (itemize): ....

3 Expenses recorded on books this year not included on Schedule K, lines 1 through 11a, 15e, and 16a (itemize):
a Depreciation $ ....
b Travel and entertainment $ ....

4 Add lines 1 through 3

5 Income recorded on books this year not included on Schedule K, lines 1 through 6 (itemize):
a Tax-exempt interest $ ....

6 Deductions included on Schedule K, lines 1 through 11a, 15e, and 16a, not charged against book income this year (itemize):
a Depreciation $ ....

7 Add lines 5 and 6

8 Income (loss) (Schedule K, line 23). Line 4 less line 7

Schedule M-2 — Analysis of Accumulated Adjustments Account, Other Adjustments Account, and Shareholders' Undistributed Taxable Income Previously Taxed (See instructions.)

	(a) Accumulated adjustments account	(b) Other adjustments account	(c) Shareholders' undistributed taxable income previously taxed
1 Balance at beginning of tax year			
2 Ordinary income from page 1, line 21			
3 Other additions			
4 Loss from page 1, line 21	( )		
5 Other reductions	( )	( )	
6 Combine lines 1 through 5			
7 Distributions other than dividend distributions			
8 Balance at end of tax year. Subtract line 7 from line 6			

Figure 4-10. Sample S corporation tax return. (Continued)

| Form **SS-4**
(Rev. April 1991)
Department of the Treasury
Internal Revenue Service | **Application for Employer Identification Number**
(For use by employers and others. Please read the attached instructions before completing this form.) | **EIN**
OMB No. 1545-0003
Expires 4-30-94 |

Please type or print clearly.

1 Name of applicant (True legal name) (See instructions.)

| **2** Trade name of business, if different from name in line 1 | **3** Executor, trustee, "care of" name |

| **4a** Mailing address (street address) (room, apt., or suite no.) | **5a** Address of business (See instructions.) |
| **4b** City, state, and ZIP code | **5b** City, state, and ZIP code |

6 County and state where principal business is located

7 Name of principal officer, grantor, or general partner (See instructions.) ▶

8a Type of entity (Check only one box.) (See instructions.)
☐ Individual SSN _____
☐ REMIC ☐ Personal service corp.
☐ State/local government ☐ National guard
☐ Other nonprofit organization (specify) _____
☐ Other (specify) ▶ _____

☐ Estate ☐ Trust
☐ Plan administrator SSN _____ ☐ Partnership
☐ Other corporation (specify) _____ ☐ Farmers' cooperative
☐ Federal government/military ☐ Church or church controlled organization
If nonprofit organization enter GEN (if applicable) _____

8b If a corporation, give name of foreign country (if applicable) or state in the U.S. where incorporated ▶

| Foreign country | State |

9 Reason for applying (Check only one box.)
☐ Started new business
☐ Hired employees
☐ Created a pension plan (specify type) ▶ _____
☐ Banking purpose (specify) ▶

☐ Changed type of organization (specify) ▶ _____
☐ Purchased going business
☐ Created a trust (specify) ▶ _____
☐ Other (specify) ▶

10 Date business started or acquired (Mo., day, year) (See instructions.)

11 Enter closing month of accounting year. (See instructions.)

12 First date wages or annuities were paid or will be paid (Mo., day, year). **Note:** *If applicant is a withholding agent, enter date income will first be paid to nonresident alien. (Mo., day, year)* . . . . ▶

13 Enter highest number of employees expected in the next 12 months. **Note:** *If the applicant does not expect to have any employees during the period, enter "0."* . . . . ▶

| Nonagricultural | Agricultural | Household |

14 Principal activity (See instructions.) ▶

15 Is the principal business activity manufacturing? . . . . ☐ Yes ☐ No
If "Yes," principal product and raw material used ▶

16 To whom are most of the products or services sold? Please check the appropriate box. ☐ Business (wholesale)
☐ Public (retail) ☐ Other (specify) ▶ ☐ N/A

17a Has the applicant ever applied for an identification number for this or any other business? . . . . ☐ Yes ☐ No
Note: *If "Yes," please complete lines 17b and 17c.*

17b If you checked the "Yes" box in line 17a, give applicant's true name and trade name, if different than name shown on prior application.

True name ▶   Trade name ▶

17c Enter approximate date, city, and state where the application was filed and the previous employer identification number if known.

| Approximate date when filed (Mo., day, year) | City and state where filed | Previous EIN |

Under penalties of perjury, I declare that I have examined this application, and to the best of my knowledge and belief, it is true, correct, and complete | Telephone number (include area code)

Name and title (Please type or print clearly.) ▶

Signature ▶   Date ▶

Note: *Do not write below this line. For official use only.*

| Please leave blank ▶ | Geo. | Ind. | Class | Size | Reason for applying |

For Paperwork Reduction Act Notice, see attached instructions.   Cat. No. 16055N   Form **SS-4** (Rev. 4-91)

Figure 4-11. Sample EIN application.

Form SS-4 (Rev. 4-91)   Page **2**

General Instructions

(Section references are to the Internal Revenue Code unless otherwise noted.)

Paperwork Reduction Act Notice.—We ask for the information on this form to carry out the Internal Revenue laws of the United States. You are required to give us this information. We need it to ensure that you are complying with these laws and to allow us to figure and collect the right amount of tax.

The time needed to complete and file this form will vary depending on individual circumstances. The estimated average time is:

Recordkeeping	7 min.
Learning about the law or the form	21 min.
Preparing the form	42 min.
Copying, assembling, and sending the form to IRS	20 min.

If you have comments concerning the accuracy of these time estimates or suggestions for making this form more simple, we would be happy to hear from you. You can write to both the **Internal Revenue Service,** Washington, DC 20224, Attention: IRS Reports Clearance Officer, T:FP; and the **Office of Management and Budget,** Paperwork Reduction Project (1545-0003), Washington, DC 20503. **DO NOT** send the tax form to either of these offices. Instead, see **Where To Apply.**

Purpose.—Use Form SS-4 to apply for an employer identification number (EIN). The information you provide on this form will establish your filing requirements.

Who Must File.—You must file this form if you have not obtained an EIN before and

● You pay wages to one or more employees.

● You are required to have an EIN to use on any return, statement, or other document, even if you are not an employer.

● You are required to withhold taxes on income, other than wages, paid to a nonresident alien (individual, corporation, partnership, etc.). For example, individuals who file **Form 1042,** Annual Withholding Tax Return for U.S. Source Income of Foreign Persons, to report alimony paid to nonresident aliens must have EINs.

Individuals who file **Schedule C,** Profit or Loss From Business, or **Schedule F,** Profit or Loss From Farming, of **Form 1040,** U.S. Individual Income Tax Return, must use EINs if they have a Keogh plan or are required to file excise, employment, or alcohol, tobacco, or firearms returns.

The following must use EINs even if they do not have any employees:

● Trusts, except an IRA trust, unless the IRA trust is required to file **Form 990-T,** Exempt Organization Business Income Tax Return, to report unrelated business taxable income or is filing Form 990-T to obtain a refund of the credit from a regulated investment company.

● Estates

● Partnerships

● REMICS (real estate mortgage investment conduits)

● Corporations

● Nonprofit organizations (churches, clubs, etc.)

● Farmers' cooperatives

● Plan administrators

New Business.—If you become the new owner of an existing business, **DO NOT** use the EIN of the former owner. If you already have an EIN, use that number. If you do not have an EIN, apply for one on this form. If

you become the "owner" of a corporation by acquiring its stock, use the corporation's EIN.

If you already have an EIN, you may need to get a new one if either the organization or ownership of your business changes. If you incorporate a sole proprietorship or form a partnership, you must get a new EIN. However, **DO NOT** apply for a new EIN if you change only the name of your business.

File Only One Form SS-4.—File only one Form SS-4, regardless of the number of businesses operated or trade names under which a business operates. However, each corporation in an affiliated group must file a separate application.

If you do not have an EIN by the time a return is due, write "Applied for" and the date you applied in the space shown for the number. **DO NOT** show your social security number as an EIN on returns.

If you do not have an EIN by the time a tax deposit is due, send your payment to the Internal Revenue service center for your filing area. (See **Where To Apply** below.) Make your check or money order payable to Internal Revenue Service and show your name (as shown on Form SS-4), address, kind of tax, period covered, and date you applied for an EIN.

For more information about EINs, see **Pub. 583,** Taxpayers Starting a Business.

How To Apply.—You can apply for an EIN either by mail or by telephone. You can get an EIN immediately by calling the Tele-TIN phone number for the service center for your state, or you can send the completed Form SS-4 directly to the service center to receive your EIN in the mail.

Application by Tele-TIN.—The Tele-TIN program is designed to assign EINs by telephone. Under this program, you can receive your EIN over the telephone and use it immediately to file a return or make a payment.

To receive an EIN by phone, complete Form SS-4, then call the Tele-TIN phone number listed for your state under **Where To Apply.** The person making the call must be authorized to sign the form (see **Signature block** on page 3).

An IRS representative will use the information from the Form SS-4 to establish your account and assign you an EIN. Write the number you are given on the upper right-hand corner of the form, sign and date it, and promptly mail it to the Tele-TIN Unit at the service center address for your state.

Application by mail.—Complete Form SS-4 at least 4 to 5 weeks before you will need an EIN. Sign and date the application and mail it to the service center address for your state. You will receive your EIN in the mail in approximately 4 weeks.

Note: *The Tele-TIN phone numbers listed below will involve a long-distance charge to callers outside of the local calling area, and should only be used to apply for an EIN. Use 1-800-829-1040 to ask about an application by mail.*

Where To Apply.—

If your principal business, office or agency, or legal residence in the case of an individual, is located in:	Call the Tele-TIN phone number shown or file with the Internal Revenue service center at:
Florida, Georgia, South Carolina	Atlanta, GA 39901 (404) 455-2360
New Jersey, New York City and counties of Nassau, Rockland, Suffolk, and Westchester	Holtsville, NY 00501 (516) 447-4955
New York (all other counties), Connecticut, Maine, Massachusetts, New Hampshire, Rhode Island, Vermont	Andover, MA 05501 (508) 474-9717
Illinois, Iowa, Minnesota, Missouri, Wisconsin	Kansas City, MO 64999 (816) 926-5999
Delaware, District of Columbia, Maryland, Pennsylvania, Virginia	Philadelphia, PA 19255 (215) 961-3980
Indiana, Kentucky, Michigan, Ohio, West Virginia	Cincinnati, OH 45999 (606) 292-5467
Kansas, New Mexico, Oklahoma, Texas	Austin, TX 73301 (512) 462-7845
Alaska, Arizona, California (counties of Alpine, Amador, Butte, Calaveras, Colusa, Contra Costa, Del Norte, El Dorado, Glenn, Humboldt, Lake, Lassen, Marin, Mendocino, Modoc, Napa, Nevada, Placer, Plumas, Sacramento, San Joaquin, Shasta, Sierra, Siskiyou, Solano, Sonoma, Sutter, Tehama, Trinity, Yolo, and Yuba), Colorado, Idaho, Montana, Nebraska, Nevada, North Dakota, Oregon, South Dakota, Utah, Washington, Wyoming	Ogden, UT 84201 (801) 625-7645
California (all other counties), Hawaii	Fresno, CA 93888 (209) 456-5900
Alabama, Arkansas, Louisiana, Mississippi, North Carolina, Tennessee	Memphis, TN 37501 (901) 365-5970

If you have no legal residence, principal place of business, or principal office or agency in any Internal Revenue District, file your form with the Internal Revenue Service Center, Philadelphia, PA 19255 or call (215) 961-3980.

Specific Instructions

The instructions that follow are for those items that are not self-explanatory. Enter N/A (nonapplicable) on the lines that do not apply.

Line 1.—Enter the legal name of the entity applying for the EIN.

Individuals.—Enter the first name, middle initial, and last name.

Trusts.—Enter the name of the trust.

Estate of a decedent.—Enter the name of the estate.

Partnerships.—Enter the legal name of the partnership as it appears in the partnership agreement.

Corporations.—Enter the corporate name as set forth in the corporation charter or other legal document creating it.

Plan administrators.—Enter the name of the plan administrator. A plan administrator who already has an EIN should use that number.

Line 2.—Enter the trade name of the business if different from the legal name.

Note: *Use the full legal name entered on line 1 on all tax returns to be filed for the entity. However, if a trade name is entered on line 2, use only the name on line 1 or the name on line 2 consistently when filing tax returns.*

Line 3.—Trusts enter the name of the trustee. Estates enter the name of the executor, administrator, or other fiduciary. If the entity applying has a designated person to receive tax information, enter that person's name as the "care of" person. Print or type the first name, middle initial, and last name.

Lines 5a and 5b.—If the physical location of the business is different from the mailing address (lines 4a and 4b), enter the address of the physical location on lines 5a and 5b.

Figure 4-11. Sample EIN application. (Continued)

Line 7.—Enter the first name, middle initial, and last name of a principal officer if the business is a corporation; of a general partner if a partnership; and of a grantor if a trust.

Line 8a.—Check the box that best describes the type of entity that is applying for the EIN. If not specifically mentioned, check the "other" box and enter the type of entity. Do not enter N/A.

Individual.—Check this box if the individual files Schedule C or F (Form 1040) and has a Keogh plan or is required to file excise, employment, or alcohol, tobacco, or firearms returns. If this box is checked, enter the individual's SSN (social security number) in the space provided.

Plan administrator.—The term plan administrator means the person or group of persons specified as the administrator by the instrument under which the plan is operated. If the plan administrator is an individual, enter the plan administrator's SSN in the space provided.

New withholding agent.—If you are a new withholding agent required to file Form 1042, check the "other" box and enter in the space provided "new withholding agent."

REMICs.—Check this box if the entity is a real estate mortgage investment conduit (REMIC). A REMIC is any entity

1. To which an election to be treated as a REMIC applies for the tax year and all prior tax years,

2. In which all of the interests are regular interests or residual interests,

3. Which has one class of residual interests (and all distributions, if any, with respect to such interests are pro rata),

4. In which as of the close of the 3rd month beginning after the startup date and at all times thereafter, substantially all of its assets consist of qualified mortgages and permitted investments,

5. Which has a tax year that is a calendar year, and

6. With respect to which there are reasonable arrangements designed to ensure that: (a) residual interests are not held by disqualified organizations (as defined in section 860E(e)(5)), and (b) information necessary for the application of section 860E(e) will be made available.

For more information about REMICs see the Instructions for Form 1066, U. S. Real Estate Mortgage Investment Conduit Income Tax Return.

Personal service corporations.—Check this box if the entity is a personal service corporation. An entity is a personal service corporation for a tax year only if

1. The entity is a C corporation for the tax year.

2. The principal activity of the entity during the testing period (as defined in Temporary Regulations section 1.441-4T(f)) for the tax year is the performance of personal service.

3. During the testing period for the tax year, such services are substantially performed by employee-owners.

4. The employee-owners own 10 percent of the fair market value of the outstanding stock in the entity on the last day of the testing period for the tax year.

For more information about personal service corporations, see the instructions for **Form 1120**, U.S. Corporation Income Tax Return, and Temporary Regulations section 1.441-4T.

Other corporations.—This box is for any corporation other than a personal service corporation. If you check this box, enter the type of corporation (such as insurance company) in the space provided.

Other nonprofit organizations.—Check this box if the nonprofit organization is other than a church or church-controlled organization and specify the type of nonprofit organization (for example, an educational organization.)

Group exemption number (GEN).—If the applicant is a nonprofit organization that is a subordinate organization to be included in a group exemption letter under Revenue Procedure 80-27, 1980-1 C.B. 677, enter the GEN in the space provided. If you do not know the GEN, contact the parent organization for it. GEN is a four-digit number. Do not confuse it with the nine-digit EIN.

Line 9.—Check only one box. Do not enter N/A.

Started new business.—Check this box if you are starting a new business that requires an EIN. If you check this box, enter the type of business being started. **DO NOT** apply if you already have an EIN and are only adding another place of business.

Changed type of organization.—Check this box if the business is changing its type of organization, for example, if the business was a sole proprietorship and has been incorporated or has become a partnership. If you check this box, specify in the space provided the type of change made, for example, "from sole proprietorship to partnership."

Purchased going business.—Check this box if you acquired a business through purchase. Do not use the former owner's EIN. If you already have an EIN, use that number.

Hired employees.—Check this box if the existing business is requesting an EIN because it has hired or is hiring employees and is therefore required to file employment tax return for which an EIN is required. **DO NOT** apply if you already have an EIN and are only hiring employees.

Created a trust.—Check this box if you created a trust, and enter the type of trust created.

Created a pension plan.—Check this box if you have created a pension plan and need this number for reporting purposes. Also, enter the type of plan created.

Banking purpose.—Check this box if you are requesting an EIN for banking purpose only and enter the banking purpose (for example, checking, loan, etc.).

Other (specify).—Check this box if you are requesting an EIN for any reason other than those for which there are checkboxes and enter the reason.

Line 10.—If you are starting a new business, enter the starting date of the business. If the business you acquired is already operating, enter the date you acquired the business. Trusts should enter the date the trust was legally created. Estates should enter the date of death of the decedent whose name appears on line 1.

Line 11.—Enter the last month of your accounting year or tax year. An accounting year or tax year is usually 12 consecutive months. It may be a calendar year or a fiscal year (including a period of 52 or 53 weeks). A calendar year is 12 consecutive months ending on December 31. A fiscal year is either 12 consecutive months ending on the last day of any month other than December or a 52-53 week year. For more information

on accounting periods, see **Pub. 538**, Accounting Periods and Methods.

Individuals.—Your tax year generally will be a calendar year.

Partnerships.—Partnerships generally should conform to the tax year of either (1) its majority partners; (2) its principal partners; (3) the tax year that results in the least aggregate deferral of income (see Temporary Regulations section 1.706-1T); or (4) some other tax year, if (a) a business purpose is established for the fiscal year, or (b) the fiscal year is a "grandfather" year, or (c) an election is made under section 444 to have a fiscal year. (See the Instructions for **Form 1065**, U.S. Partnership Return of Income, for more information.)

REMICs.—Remics must have a calendar year as their tax year.

Personal service corporations.—A personal service corporation generally must adopt a calendar year unless:

1. It can establish to the satisfaction of the Commissioner that there is a business purpose for having a different tax year, or

2. It elects under section 444 to have a tax year other than a calendar year.

Line 12.—If the business has or will have employees, enter on this line the date on which the business began or will begin to pay wages to the employees. If the business does not have any plans to have employees, enter N/A on this line.

New withholding agent.—Enter the date you began or will begin to pay income to a nonresident alien. This also applies to individuals who are required to file Form 1042 to report alimony paid to a nonresident alien.

Line 14.—Generally, enter the exact type of business being operated (for example, advertising agency, farm, labor union, real estate agency, steam laundry, rental of coin-operated vending machine, investment club, etc.).

Governmental.—Enter the type of organization (state, county, school district, or municipality, etc.).

Nonprofit organization (other than governmental).—Enter whether organized for religious, educational, or humane purposes, and the principal activity (for example, religious organization—hospital, charitable).

Mining and quarrying.—Specify the process and the principal product (for example, mining bituminous coal, contract drilling for oil, quarrying dimension stone, etc.).

Contract construction.—Specify whether general contracting or special trade contracting. Also, show the type of work normally performed (for example, general contractor for residential buildings, electrical subcontractor, etc.).

Trade.—Specify the type of sales and the principal line of goods sold (for example, wholesale dairy products, manufacturer's representative for mining machinery, retail hardware, etc.).

Manufacturing.—Specify the type of establishment operated (for example, sawmill, vegetable cannery, etc.).

Signature block.—The application must be signed by: (1) the individual, if the person is an individual, (2) the president, vice president, or other principal officer, if the person is a corporation, (3) a responsible and duly authorized member or officer having knowledge of its affairs, if the person is a partnership or other unincorporated organization, or (4) the fiduciary, if the person is a trust or estate.

*U.S. Government Printing Office: 1993 — 343-034/80187

Figure 4-11. Sample EIN application. (Continued)

SCHEDULE C
(Form 1040)

Department of the Treasury
Internal Revenue Service (U)

Profit or Loss From Business
(Sole Proprietorship)

▶ Partnerships, joint ventures, etc., must file Form 1065.

▶ **Attach to Form 1040 or Form 1041.** ▶ **See Instructions for Schedule C (Form 1040).**

OMB No. 1545-0074

19 93

Attachment
Sequence No. **09**

Name of proprietor | Social security number (SSN)

A	Principal business or profession, including product or service (see page C-1)	**B** Enter principal business code (see page C-6) ▶
C	Business name. If no separate business name, leave blank.	**D** Employer ID number (EIN), if any
E	Business address (including suite or room no.) ▶ .... City, town or post office, state, and ZIP code	

F Accounting method: (1) ☐ Cash (2) ☐ Accrual (3) ☐ Other (specify) ▶ ....

G Method(s) used to value closing inventory: (1) ☐ Cost (2) ☐ Lower of cost or market (3) ☐ Other (attach explanation) (4) ☐ Does not apply (if checked, skip line H) | **Yes** | **No**

H Was there any change in determining quantities, costs, or valuations between opening and closing inventory? If "Yes," attach explanation . . . .

I Did you "materially participate" in the operation of this business during 1993? If "No," see page C-2 for limit on losses. . .

J If you started or acquired this business during 1993, check here . . . . ▶ ☐

Part I   Income

1	Gross receipts or sales. **Caution:** If this income was reported to you on Form W-2 and the "Statutory employee" box on that form was checked, see page C-2 and check here . . . . ▶ ☐	**1**	
2	Returns and allowances	**2**	
3	Subtract line 2 from line 1	**3**	
4	Cost of goods sold (from line 40 on page 2)	**4**	
5	**Gross profit.** Subtract line 4 from line 3	**5**	
6	Other income, including Federal and state gasoline or fuel tax credit or refund (see page C-2) . . .	**6**	
7	**Gross income.** Add lines 5 and 6 . . . . ▶	**7**	

Part II   Expenses. **Caution:** Do not enter expenses for business use of your home on lines 8–27. Instead, see line 30.

8	Advertising	**8**		**19** Pension and profit-sharing plans	**19**	
9	Bad debts from sales or services (see page C-3)	**9**		**20** Rent or lease (see page C-4):		
10	Car and truck expenses (see page C-3)	**10**		**a** Vehicles, machinery, and equipment .	**20a**	
11	Commissions and fees. . .	**11**		**b** Other business property . .	**20b**	
12	Depletion.	**12**		**21** Repairs and maintenance . .	**21**	
13	Depreciation and section 179 expense deduction (not included in Part III) (see page C-3) . .	**13**		**22** Supplies (not included in Part III) .	**22**	
				23 Taxes and licenses . . .	**23**	
				24 Travel, meals, and entertainment:		
14	Employee benefit programs (other than on line 19) . . .	**14**		**a** Travel	**24a**	
15	Insurance (other than health) .	**15**		**b** Meals and entertainment .		
16	Interest:			**c** Enter 20% of line 24b subject to limitations (see page C-4) .		
a	Mortgage (paid to banks, etc.) .	**16a**				
b	Other	**16b**		**d** Subtract line 24c from line 24b	**24d**	
17	Legal and professional services	**17**		**25** Utilities	**25**	
18	Office expense	**18**		**26** Wages (less jobs credit) . .	**26**	
				27 Other expenses (from line 46 on page 2)	**27**	

28	**Total expenses** before expenses for business use of home. Add lines 8 through 27 in columns. . ▶	**28**	
29	Tentative profit (loss). Subtract line 28 from line 7	**29**	
30	Expenses for business use of your home. Attach **Form 8829**	**30**	
31	**Net profit or (loss).** Subtract line 30 from line 29.		
	• If a profit, enter on **Form 1040, line 12,** and ALSO on **Schedule SE, line 2** (statutory employees, see page C-5). Fiduciaries, enter on Form 1041, line 3.	**31**	
	• If a loss, you MUST go on to line 32.		
32	If you have a loss, check the box that describes your investment in this activity (see page C-5).		
	• If you checked 32a, enter the loss on **Form 1040, line 12,** and ALSO on **Schedule SE, line 2** (statutory employees, see page C-5). Fiduciaries, enter on Form 1041, line 3.	**32a** ☐ All investment is at risk. **32b** ☐ Some investment is not at risk.	
	• If you checked 32b, you MUST attach **Form 6198.**		

For Paperwork Reduction Act Notice, see Form 1040 instructions.   Cat. No. 15786J   **Schedule C (Form 1040) 1993**

Figure 4-12. Sample Schedule C.

Schedule C (Form 1040) 1993   Page **2**

Part III   **Cost of Goods Sold** (see page C-5)

33	Inventory at beginning of year. If different from last year's closing inventory. attach explanation . .	33
34	Purchases less cost of items withdrawn for personal use	34
35	Cost of labor. Do not include salary paid to yourself	35
36	Materials and supplies	36
37	Other costs	37
38	Add lines 33 through 37	38
39	Inventory at end of year	39
40	**Cost of goods sold.** Subtract line 39 from line 38. Enter the result here and on page 1. line 4 . .	40

Part IV   **Information on Your Vehicle.** Complete this part **ONLY** if you are claiming car or truck expenses on line 10 and are not required to file Form 4562 for this business.

41   When did you place your vehicle in service for business purposes? (month. day. year) ▶ . . . . / . . . . . . / . . . .

42   Of the total number of miles you drove your vehicle during 1993. enter the number of miles you used your vehicle for:

a   Business . . . .   **b** Commuting . . . .   **c** Other . . . .

43   Do you (or your spouse) have another vehicle available for personal use? . . . . ☐ **Yes**   ☐ **No**

44   Was your vehicle available for use during off-duty hours? . . . . ☐ **Yes**   ☐ **No**

45a Do you have evidence to support your deduction? . . . . ☐ **Yes**   ☐ **No**
   b If "Yes," is the evidence written? . . . . ☐ **Yes**   ☐ **No**

Part V   **Other Expenses.** List below business expenses not included on lines 8–26 or line 30.

46 Total other expenses. Enter here and on page 1. line 27	46

Figure 4-12. Sample Schedule C. (Continued)

Department of the Treasury
Internal Revenue Service

1993 Principal Business or Professional Activity Codes for Schedules C and C-EZ (Form 1040)

Locate the major category that best describes your activity. Within the major category, select the activity code that most closely identifies the business or profession that is the principal source of your sales or receipts. **Enter this 4-digit code on line B of Schedule C or C-EZ.** *For example, real estate agent is under the major category of* **"Real Estate,"** *and the code is "5520."*

Note: *If your principal source of income is from farming activities, you should file* **Schedule F** *(Form 1040), Profit or Loss From Farming.*

Agricultural Services, Forestry, Fishing
Code
1990 Animal services, other than breeding
1933 Crop services
2113 Farm labor & management services
2246 Fishing, commercial
2238 Forestry, except logging
2212 Horticulture & landscaping
2469 Hunting & trapping
1974 Livestock breeding
0836 Logging
1958 Veterinary services, including pets

Construction
0018 Operative builders (for own account)

Building Trade Contractors, Including Repairs
0414 Carpentering & flooring
0455 Concrete work
0273 Electrical work
0299 Masonry, dry wall, stone, & tile
0257 Painting & paper hanging
0232 Plumbing, heating, & air conditioning
0430 Roofing, siding & sheet metal
0885 Other building trade contractors (excavation, glazing, etc.)

General Contractors
0075 Highway & street construction
0059 Nonresidential building
0034 Residential building
3889 Other heavy construction (pipe laying, bridge construction, etc.)

Finance, Insurance, & Related Services
6064 Brokers & dealers of securities
6080 Commodity contracts brokers & dealers; security & commodity exchanges
6148 Credit institutions & mortgage bankers
5702 Insurance agents or brokers
5744 Insurance services (appraisal, consulting, inspection, etc.)
6130 Investment advisors & services
5777 Other financial services

Manufacturing, Including Printing & Publishing
0679 Apparel & other textile products
1115 Electric & electronic equipment
1073 Fabricated metal products
0638 Food products & beverages
0810 Furniture & fixtures
0695 Leather footwear, handbags, etc.
0836 Lumber & other wood products
1099 Machinery & machine shops
0877 Paper & allied products
1057 Primary metal industries
0851 Printing & publishing
1032 Stone, clay, & glass products
0653 Textile mill products
1883 Other manufacturing industries

Mining & Mineral Extraction
1537 Coal mining
1511 Metal mining

1552 Oil & gas
1719 Quarrying & nonmetallic mining

Real Estate
5538 Operators & lessors of buildings, including residential
5553 Operators & lessors of other real property
5520 Real estate agents & brokers
5579 Real estate property managers
5710 Subdividers & developers, except cemeteries
6155 Title abstract offices

Services: Personal, Professional, & Business Services
Amusement & Recreational Services
9670 Bowling centers
9688 Motion picture & tape distribution & allied services
9597 Motion picture & video production
9639 Motion picture theaters
8557 Physical fitness facilities
9696 Professional sports & racing, including promoters & managers
9811 Theatrical performers, musicians, agents, producers & related services
9613 Video tape rental
9837 Other amusement & recreational services

Automotive Services
8813 Automotive rental or leasing, without driver
8953 Automotive repairs, general & specialized
8839 Parking, except valet
8896 Other automotive services (wash, towing, etc.)

Business & Personal Services
7658 Accounting & bookkeeping
7716 Advertising, except direct mail
7682 Architectural services
8318 Barber shop (or barber)
8110 Beauty shop (or beautician)
8714 Child day care
7872 Computer programming, processing, data preparation & related services
7922 Computer repair, maintenance, & leasing
7286 Consulting services
7799 Consumer credit reporting & collection services
8755 Counseling (except health practitioners)
7732 Employment agencies & personnel supply
7518 Engineering services
7773 Equipment rental & leasing (except computer or automotive)
8532 Funeral services & crematories
7633 Income tax preparation
7914 Investigative & protective services
7617 Legal services (or lawyer)
7856 Mailing, reproduction, commercial art, photography, & stenographic services
7245 Management services
8771 Ministers & chaplains
8334 Photographic studios
7260 Public relations
8733 Research services

7708 Surveying services
8730 Teaching or tutoring
7880 Other business services
6882 Other personal services

Hotels & Other Lodging Places
7237 Camps & camping parks
7096 Hotels, motels, & tourist homes
7211 Rooming & boarding houses

Laundry & Cleaning Services
7450 Carpet & upholstery cleaning
7419 Coin-operated laundries & dry cleaning
7435 Full-service laundry, dry cleaning, & garment service
7476 Janitorial & related services (building, house, & window cleaning)

Medical & Health Services
9274 Chiropractors
9233 Dentist's office or clinic
9217 Doctor's (M.D.) office or clinic
9456 Medical & dental laboratories
9472 Nursing & personal care facilities
9290 Optometrists
9258 Osteopathic physicians & surgeons
9241 Podiatrists
9415 Registered & practical nurses
9431 Offices & clinics of other health practitioners (dieticians, midwives, speech pathologists, etc.)
9886 Other health services

Miscellaneous Repair, Except Computers
9019 Audio equipment & TV repair
9050 Furniture repair & reupholstery
2881 Other equipment repair, except audio & TV

Trade, Retail—Selling Goods to Individuals & Households
3038 Catalog or mail order
3012 Selling door to door, by telephone or party plan, or from mobile unit
3053 Vending machine selling

Selling From Showroom, Store, or Other Fixed Location
Apparel & Accessories
3921 Accessory & specialty stores & furriers for women
3939 Clothing, family
3772 Clothing, men's & boys'
3913 Clothing, women's
3756 Shoe stores
3954 Other apparel & accessory stores

Automotive & Service Stations
3558 Gasoline service stations
3319 New car dealers (franchised)
3533 Tires, accessories, & parts
3335 Used car dealers
3517 Other automotive dealers (motorcycles, recreational vehicles, etc.)

Building, Hardware, & Garden Supply
4416 Building materials dealers
4457 Hardware stores
4473 Nurseries & garden supply stores
4432 Paint, glass, & wallpaper stores

Food & Beverages
0612 Bakeries selling at retail
3086 Catering services
3095 Drinking places (bars, taverns, pubs, saloons, etc.)
3079 Eating places, meals & snacks
3210 Grocery stores (general line)
3251 Liquor stores
3236 Specialized food stores (meat, produce, candy, health food, etc.)

Furniture & General Merchandise
3988 Computer & software stores
3970 Furniture stores
4317 Home furnishings stores (china, floor coverings, drapes)
4119 Household appliance stores
4333 Music & record stores
3996 TV, audio & electronic stores
3715 Variety stores
3731 Other general merchandise stores

Miscellaneous Retail Stores
4812 Boat dealers
5017 Book stores, excluding newsstands
4853 Camera & photo supply stores
3277 Drug stores
5058 Fabric & needlework stores
4655 Florists
5090 Fuel dealers (except gasoline)
4630 Gift, novelty & souvenir shops
4838 Hobby, toy, & game shops
4671 Jewelry stores
4895 Luggage & leather goods stores
5074 Mobile home dealers
4879 Optical goods stores
4697 Sporting goods & bicycle shops
5033 Stationery stores
4614 Used merchandise & antique stores (except motor vehicle parts)
5884 Other retail stores

Trade, Wholesale—Selling Goods to Other Businesses, etc.
Durable Goods, Including Machinery Equipment, Wood, Metals, etc.
2634 Agent or broker for other firms— more than 50% of gross sales on commission
2618 Selling for your own account

Nondurable Goods, Including Food, Fiber, Chemicals, etc.
2675 Agent or broker for other firms— more than 50% of gross sales on commission
2659 Selling for your own account

Transportation, Communications, Public Utilities, & Related Services
6619 Air transportation
6312 Bus & limousine transportation
6676 Communication services
6395 Courier or package delivery
6361 Highway passenger transportation (except chartered service)
6536 Public warehousing
6114 Taxicabs
6510 Trash collection without own dump
6635 Travel agents & tour operators
6338 Trucking (except trash collection)
6692 Utilities (dumps, snow plowing, road cleaning, etc.)
6551 Water transportation
6650 Other transportation services

8888 **Unable to classify**

Cat. No. 15814Q

*U.S. Government Printing Office: 1993 — 301-628/80237

Figure 4-13. Activity codes for Schedule C.

SCHEDULE C-EZ (Form 1040)	**Net Profit From Business**	OMB No. 1545-0074
	(Sole Proprietorship)	**1993**
Department of the Treasury Internal Revenue Service (O)	▶ Partnerships, joint ventures, etc., must file Form 1065. ▶ Attach to Form 1040 or Form 1041. ▶ See Instructions on back.	Attachment Sequence No. **09A**
Name of proprietor		Social security number (SSN)

Part I   General Information

You May Use This Form If You:	• Had gross receipts from your business of $25,000 or less. • Had business expenses of $2,000 or less. • Use the cash method of accounting. • Did not have an inventory at any time during the year. • Did not have a net loss from your business. • Had only one business as a sole proprietor.	**And You:**	• Had no employees during the year. • Are not required to file Form 4562, Depreciation and Amortization, for this business. See the instructions for Schedule C, line 13, on page C-3 to find out if you must file. • Do not deduct expenses for business use of your home. • Do not have prior year unallowed passive activity losses from this business.

A Principal business or profession, including product or service

B Enter principal business code (see page C-6) ▶

C Business name. If no separate business name, leave blank.

D Employer ID number (EIN), if any

E Business address (including suite or room no.). Address not required if same as on Form 1040, page 1.

City, town or post office, state, and ZIP code

Part II   Figure Your Net Profit

1	**Gross receipts.** If more than $25,000, you **must** use Schedule C. **Caution:** *If this income was reported to you on Form W-2 and the "Statutory employee" box on that form was checked, see* **Statutory Employees** *in the instructions for Schedule C, line 1, on page C-2 and check here* . . . . ▶ ☐	**1**	
2	**Total expenses.** If more than $2,000, you **must** use Schedule C. See instructions	**2**	
3	**Net profit.** Subtract line 2 from line 1. Enter on **Form 1040, line 12,** and ALSO on **Schedule SE, line 2.** (Statutory employees **do not** report this amount on Schedule SE, line 2. Fiduciaries, enter on Form 1041, line 3.) If less than zero, you **must** use Schedule C	**3**	

Part III   Information on Your Vehicle. Complete this part **ONLY** if you are claiming car or truck expenses on line 2.

4   When did you place your vehicle in service for business purposes? (month, day, year) ▶ ..... / ..... / ..... .

5   Of the total number of miles you drove your vehicle during 1993, enter the number of miles you used your vehicle for:

a Business .... **b** Commuting .... **c** Other ....

6   Do you (or your spouse) have another vehicle available for personal use? . . . . ☐ Yes ☐ No

7   Was your vehicle available for use during off-duty hours? . . . . ☐ Yes ☐ No

8a Do you have evidence to support your deduction? . . . . ☐ Yes ☐ No

 b If "Yes," is the evidence written? . . . . ☐ Yes ☐ No

For Paperwork Reduction Act Notice, see Form 1040 instructions.   Cat. No. 14374D   Schedule C-EZ (Form 1040) 1993

Figure 4-14. Sample Schedule C-EZ.

Instructions

You may use Schedule C-EZ instead of Schedule C if you operated a business or practiced a profession as a sole proprietorship and you have met all the requirements listed in Part I of the form.

Line A

Describe the business or professional activity that provided your principal source of income reported on line 1. Give the general field or activity and the type of product or service.

Line B

Enter on this line the four-digit code that identifies your principal business or professional activity. See page C-6 for the list of codes.

Line D

You need an employer identification number (EIN) only if you had a Keogh plan or were required to file an employment, excise, fiduciary, or alcohol, tobacco, and firearms tax return. If you need an EIN, file **Form SS-4,** Application for Employer Identification Number. If you don't have an EIN, leave line D blank. **Do not** enter your SSN.

Line E

Enter your business address. Show a street address instead of a box number. Include the suite or room number, if any.

Line 1—Gross Receipts

Enter gross receipts from your trade or business. Be sure to include any amount you received in your trade or business that was reported on Form(s) 1099-MISC. You must show all items of taxable income actually or constructively received during the year (in cash, property, or services). Income is constructively received when it is credited to your account or set aside for you to use. Do not offset this amount by any losses.

Line 2—Total Expenses

Enter the total amount of all deductible business expenses you actually paid during the year. Examples of these expenses include advertising, car and truck expenses, commissions and fees, insurance, interest, legal and professional services, office expense, rent or lease expenses, repairs and maintenance, supplies, taxes, travel, 80% of business meals and entertainment, and utilities (including telephone). For details, see the instructions for Schedule C, Parts II and V, on pages C-3 through C-5.

If you claim car or truck expenses, be sure to complete Part III.

*U.S.GPO:1993-0-345-200

Figure 4-14. Sample Schedule C-EZ. (Continued)

Form **1040**	Department of the Treasury—Internal Revenue Service **U.S. Individual Income Tax Return** (U) **1993**	IRS Use Only—Do not write or staple in this space.

For the year Jan. 1–Dec. 31, 1993, or other tax year beginning _____, 1993, ending _____, 19 ___ | OMB No. 1545-0074

Label (See instructions on page 12.)

L A B E L H E R E

Your first name and initial | Last name | **Your social security number**

If a joint return, spouse's first name and initial | Last name | **Spouse's social security number**

Use the IRS label. Otherwise, please print or type.

Home address (number and street). If you have a P.O. box, see page 12. | Apt. no.

City, town or post office, state, and ZIP code. If you have a foreign address, see page 12.

For Privacy Act and Paperwork Reduction Act Notice, see page 4.

Presidential Election Campaign (See page 12.) ▶
Do you want $3 to go to this fund? . . . . | Yes | No
If a joint return, does your spouse want $3 to go to this fund? . . . .

Note: Checking "Yes" will not change your tax or reduce your refund.

Filing Status (See page 12.)

Check only one box.

1 ☐ Single
2 ☐ Married filing joint return (even if only one had income)
3 ☐ Married filing separate return. Enter spouse's social security no. above and full name here. ▶ _____
4 ☐ Head of household (with qualifying person). (See page 13.) If the qualifying person is a child but not your dependent, enter this child's name here. ▶ _____
5 ☐ Qualifying widow(er) with dependent child (year spouse died ▶ 19 ___). (See page 13.)

Exemptions (See page 13.)

6a ☐ **Yourself.** If your parent (or someone else) can claim you as a dependent on his or her tax return, **do not** check box 6a. But be sure to check the box on line 33b on page 2 . .
b ☐ **Spouse** . . . .
c **Dependents:**

(1) Name (first, initial, and last name)	(2) Check if under age 1	(3) If age 1 or older, dependent's social security number	(4) Dependent's relationship to you	(5) No. of months lived in your home in 1993

If more than six dependents, see page 14.

d If your child didn't live with you but is claimed as your dependent under a pre-1985 agreement, check here ▶ ☐
e Total number of exemptions claimed . . . .

No. of boxes checked on 6a and 6b ___
No. of your children on 6c who:
• lived with you ___
• didn't live with you due to divorce or separation (see page 15) ___
Dependents on 6c not entered above ___
Add numbers entered on lines above ▶ ☐

Income

Attach Copy B of your Forms W-2, W-2G, and 1099-R here.

If you did not get a W-2, see page 10.

If you are attaching a check or money order, put it on top of any Forms W-2, W-2G, or 1099-R.

7 Wages, salaries, tips, etc. Attach Form(s) W-2 . . . . | 7 |
8a **Taxable** interest income (see page 16). Attach Schedule B if over $400 . . . . . | 8a |
b Tax-exempt interest (see page 17). DON'T include on line 8a | 8b |
9 Dividend income. Attach Schedule B if over $400 . . . . . . | 9 |
10 Taxable refunds, credits, or offsets of state and local income taxes (see page 17) . . | 10 |
11 Alimony received . . . . | 11 |
12 Business income or (loss). Attach Schedule C or C-EZ . . . . . | 12 |
13 Capital gain or (loss). Attach Schedule D . . . . | 13 |
14 Capital gain distributions not reported on line 13 (see page 17) . . . . | 14 |
15 Other gains or (losses). Attach Form 4797 . . . . | 15 |
16a Total IRA distributions . | 16a | b Taxable amount (see page 18) | 16b |
17a Total pensions and annuities | 17a | b Taxable amount (see page 18) | 17b |
18 Rental real estate, royalties, partnerships, S corporations, trusts, etc. Attach Schedule E | 18 |
19 Farm income or (loss). Attach Schedule F . . . . | 19 |
20 Unemployment compensation (see page 19) . . . . | 20 |
21a Social security benefits | 21a | b Taxable amount (see page 19) | 21b |
22 Other income. List type and amount—see page 20 .... | 22 |
23 Add the amounts in the far right column for lines 7 through 22. This is your **total income** ▶ | 23 |

Adjustments to Income (See page 20.)

24a Your IRA deduction (see page 20) . . . . . | 24a |
b Spouse's IRA deduction (see page 20) . . . . . . | 24b |
25 One-half of self-employment tax (see page 21) . . . | 25 |
26 Self-employed health insurance deduction (see page 22) . | 26 |
27 Keogh retirement plan and self-employed SEP deduction . | 27 |
28 Penalty on early withdrawal of savings . . . . . | 28 |
29 Alimony paid. Recipient's SSN ▶ _____ | 29 |
30 Add lines 24a through 29. These are your **total adjustments** . . . . ▶ | 30 |

Adjusted Gross Income

31 Subtract line 30 from line 23. This is your **adjusted gross income.** *If this amount is less than $23,050 and a child lived with you, see page EIC-1 to find out if you can claim the "Earned Income Credit" on line 56* . . . . ▶ | 31 |

Form **1040** (1993)

Figure 4-15. Sample 1040 form.

Form 1040 (1993) Page **2**

Tax Computation	**32**	Amount from line 31 (adjusted gross income)	**32**	
	33a	Check if: ☐ **You** were 65 or older, ☐ Blind; ☐ **Spouse** was 65 or older, ☐ Blind. Add the number of boxes checked above and enter the total here . . . . ▶ **33a**		
(See page 23.)	**b**	If your parent (or someone else) can claim you as a dependent, check here . ▶ **33b** ☐		
	c	If you are married filing separately and your spouse itemizes deductions or you are a dual-status alien, see page 24 and check here . . . . ▶ **33c** ☐		
	34	Enter the **larger** of your: { **Itemized deductions** from Schedule A, line 26, **OR** **Standard deduction** shown below for your filing status. **But if you checked any box on line 33a or b**, go to page 24 to find your standard deduction. If you checked **box 33c**, your standard deduction is zero. • Single—$3,700 • Head of household—$5,450 • Married filing jointly or Qualifying widow(er)—$6,200 • Married filing separately—$3,100 }	**34**	
	35	Subtract line 34 from line 32	**35**	
	36	If line 32 is $81,350 or less, multiply $2,350 by the total number of exemptions claimed on line 6e. If line 32 is over $81,350, see the worksheet on page 25 for the amount to enter .	**36**	
If you want the IRS to figure your tax, see page 24.	**37**	**Taxable income.** Subtract line 36 from line 35. If line 36 is more than line 35, enter -0-	**37**	
	38	Tax. Check if from **a** ☐ Tax Table, **b** ☐ Tax Rate Schedules, **c** ☐ Schedule D Tax Worksheet, or **d** ☐ Form 8615 (see page 25). Amount from Form(s) 8814 ▶ **e** ___	**38**	
	39	Additional taxes (see page 25). Check if from **a** ☐ Form 4970 **b** ☐ Form 4972 . .	**39**	
	40	Add lines 38 and 39 . . . . ▶	**40**	
Credits	**41**	Credit for child and dependent care expenses. Attach Form 2441	**41**	
	42	Credit for the elderly or the disabled. Attach Schedule R . .	**42**	
(See page 25.)	**43**	Foreign tax credit. Attach Form 1116	**43**	
	44	Other credits (see page 26). Check if from **a** ☐ Form 3800 **b** ☐ Form 8396 **c** ☐ Form 8801 **d** ☐ Form (specify) ___	**44**	
	45	Add lines 41 through 44	**45**	
	46	Subtract line 45 from line 40. If line 45 is more than line 40, enter -0- . . . . . ▶	**46**	
Other Taxes	**47**	Self-employment tax. Attach Schedule SE. Also, see line 25 .	**47**	
	48	Alternative minimum tax. Attach Form 6251	**48**	
	49	Recapture taxes (see page 26). Check if from **a** ☐ Form 4255 **b** ☐ Form 8611 **c** ☐ Form 8828	**49**	
	50	Social security and Medicare tax on tip income not reported to employer. Attach Form 4137	**50**	
	51	Tax on qualified retirement plans, including IRAs. If required, attach Form 5329 . . .	**51**	
	52	Advance earned income credit payments from Form W-2	**52**	
	53	Add lines 46 through 52. This is your **total tax** . . . . ▶	**53**	
Payments	**54**	Federal income tax withheld. If any is from Form(s) 1099, check ▶ ☐	**54**	
	55	1993 estimated tax payments and amount applied from 1992 return .	**55**	
Attach Forms W-2, W-2G, and 1099-R on the front.	**56**	**Earned income credit.** Attach Schedule EIC	**56**	
	57	Amount paid with Form 4868 (extension request)	**57**	
	58a	Excess social security, Medicare, and RRTA tax withheld (see page 28) .	**58a**	
	b	Deferral of additional 1993 taxes. Attach Form 8841 . . .	**58b**	
	59	Other payments (see page 28). Check if from **a** ☐ Form 2439 **b** ☐ Form 4136 . .	**59**	
	60	Add lines 54 through 59. These are your **total payments** . . . . ▶	**60**	
Refund or Amount You Owe	**61**	If line 60 is more than line 53, subtract line 53 from line 60. This is the amount you **OVERPAID**. ▶	**61**	
	62	Amount of line 61 you want **REFUNDED TO YOU**. . . . . ▶	**62**	
	63	Amount of line 61 you want **APPLIED TO YOUR 1994 ESTIMATED TAX** ▶	**63**	
	64	If line 53 is more than line 60, subtract line 60 from line 53. This is the **AMOUNT YOU OWE**. For details on how to pay, including what to write on your payment, see page 29 . .	**64**	
	65	Estimated tax penalty (see page 29). Also include on line 64	**65**	

Sign Here Keep a copy of this return for your records.	Under penalties of perjury, I declare that I have examined this return and accompanying schedules and statements, and to the best of my knowledge and belief, they are true, correct, and complete. Declaration of preparer (other than taxpayer) is based on all information of which preparer has any knowledge.

Your signature	Date	Your occupation
Spouse's signature. If a joint return, BOTH must sign.	Date	Spouse's occupation

Paid Preparer's Use Only	Preparer's signature / Date / Check if self-employed ☐ / Preparer's social security no.
	Firm's name (or yours if self-employed) and address / E.I. No. / ZIP code

☆U.S. Government Printing Office: 1993 -- 352-739

Figure 4-15. Sample 1040 form. (Continued)

Form **1120** Department of the Treasury Internal Revenue Service	**U.S. Corporation Income Tax Return** For calendar year 1993 or tax year beginning .... , 1993, ending .... , 19 ... ▶ **Instructions are separate. See page 1 for Paperwork Reduction Act Notice.**	OMB No. 1545-0123 1993

A Check if a:		Use IRS label. Other-wise, please print or type.	Name		B Employer identification number
1	Consolidated return (attach Form 851) ☐				
2	Personal holding co. (attach Sch. PH) ☐		Number, street, and room or suite no. (If a P.O. box, see page 7 of instructions.)		C Date incorporated
3	Personal service corp. (as defined in Temporary Regs. sec. 1.441-4T— see instructions) ☐		City or town, state, and ZIP code		D Total assets (see Specific Instructions) $

E Check applicable boxes: (1) ☐ Initial return (2) ☐ Final return (3) ☐ Change of address

Income	1a	Gross receipts or sales [____] **b** Less returns and allowances [____] **c** Bal ▶	1c
	2	Cost of goods sold (Schedule A, line 8)	2
	3	Gross profit. Subtract line 2 from line 1c	3
	4	Dividends (Schedule C, line 19)	4
	5	Interest	5
	6	Gross rents	6
	7	Gross royalties	7
	8	Capital gain net income (attach Schedule D (Form 1120))	8
	9	Net gain or (loss) from Form 4797, Part II, line 20 (attach Form 4797) . . .	9
	10	Other income (see instructions—attach schedule)	10
	11	**Total income.** Add lines 3 through 10 . . . . ▶	11

Deductions (See instructions for limitations on deductions.)	12	Compensation of officers (Schedule E, line 4)	12
	13a	Salaries and wages [____] **b** Less employment credits [____] **c** Bal ▶	13c
	14	Repairs and maintenance	14
	15	Bad debts	15
	16	Rents	16
	17	Taxes and licenses	17
	18	Interest	18
	19	Charitable contributions (see instructions for 10% limitation)	19
	20	Depreciation (attach Form 4562)	20 [____]	
	21	Less depreciation claimed on Schedule A and elsewhere on return . . .	21a [____]	21b
	22	Depletion	22
	23	Advertising	23
	24	Pension, profit-sharing, etc., plans	24
	25	Employee benefit programs	25
	26	Other deductions (attach schedule)	26
	27	**Total deductions.** Add lines 12 through 26 . . . . ▶	27
	28	Taxable income before net operating loss deduction and special deductions. Subtract line 27 from line 11	28
	29	**Less:** **a** Net operating loss deduction (see instructions) . . . . . 29a [____]	
		b Special deductions (Schedule C, line 20) . . . . . . 29b [____]	29c

	30	**Taxable income.** Subtract line 29c from line 28	30
	31	**Total tax** (Schedule J, line 10)	31
Tax and Payments	32	**Payments: a** 1992 overpayment credited to 1993	32a [____]	
	b	1993 estimated tax payments . .	32b [____]	
	c	Less 1993 refund applied for on Form 4466	32c [____] **d** Bal ▶	32d
	e	Tax deposited with Form 7004	32e
	f	Credit from regulated investment companies (attach Form 2439)	32f
	g	Credit for Federal tax on fuels (attach Form 4136). See instructions . . .	32g [____]	32h
	33	Estimated tax penalty (see instructions). Check if Form 2220 is attached . . . . ▶ ☐	33
	34	**Tax due.** If line 32h is smaller than the total of lines 31 and 33, enter amount owed	34
	35	**Overpayment.** If line 32h is larger than the total of lines 31 and 33, enter amount overpaid	35
	36	Enter amount of line 35 you want: **Credited to 1994 estimated tax** ▶ [____] **Refunded** ▶	36

Please Sign Here	Under penalties of perjury, I declare that I have examined this return, including accompanying schedules and statements, and to the best of my knowledge and belief, it is true, correct, and complete. Declaration of preparer (other than taxpayer) is based on all information of which preparer has any knowledge.		
	▶ _____ Signature of officer	Date	▶ _____ Title

Paid Preparer's Use Only	Preparer's signature ▶	Date	Check if self-employed ☐	Preparer's social security number
	Firm's name (or yours if self-employed) and address ▶		E.I. No. ▶ ZIP code ▶	

Cat. No. 11450Q

Figure 4-16. Sample Form 1120.

101

Form 1120 (1993)　　　　　　　　　　　　　　　　　　　　　　　　　　　Page **2**

Schedule A	**Cost of Goods Sold** (See instructions.)		
1	Inventory at beginning of year	1	
2	Purchases	2	
3	Cost of labor	3	
4	Additional section 263A costs (attach schedule)	4	
5	Other costs (attach schedule)	5	
6	**Total.** Add lines 1 through 5	6	
7	Inventory at end of year	7	
8	**Cost of goods sold.** Subtract line 7 from line 6. Enter here and on page 1, line 2	8	

9a Check all methods used for valuing closing inventory:
- ☐ Cost ☐ Lower of cost or market as described in Regulations section 1.471-4
- ☐ Writedown of subnormal goods as described in Regulations section 1.471-2(c)
- ☐ Other (Specify method used and attach explanation.) ▶ ....

  b Check if the LIFO inventory method was adopted this tax year for any goods (if checked, attach Form 970) . . . . . ▶ ☐

  c If the LIFO inventory method was used for this tax year, enter percentage (or amounts) of closing inventory computed under LIFO **9c**

  d Do the rules of section 263A (for property produced or acquired for resale) apply to the corporation? . . . . . ☐ Yes ☐ No

  e Was there any change in determining quantities, cost, or valuations between opening and closing inventory? If "Yes," attach explanation . . . . . ☐ Yes ☐ No

Schedule C	**Dividends and Special Deductions** (See instructions.)	(a) Dividends received	(b) %	(c) Special deductions (a) × (b)
1	Dividends from less-than-20%-owned domestic corporations that are subject to the 70% deduction (other than debt-financed stock)		70	
2	Dividends from 20%-or-more-owned domestic corporations that are subject to the 80% deduction (other than debt-financed stock)		80	
3	Dividends on debt-financed stock of domestic and foreign corporations (section 246A)		see instructions	
4	Dividends on certain preferred stock of less-than-20%-owned public utilities		42	
5	Dividends on certain preferred stock of 20%-or-more-owned public utilities		48	
6	Dividends from less-than-20%-owned foreign corporations and certain FSCs that are subject to the 70% deduction		70	
7	Dividends from 20%-or-more-owned foreign corporations and certain FSCs that are subject to the 80% deduction		80	
8	Dividends from wholly owned foreign subsidiaries subject to the 100% deduction (section 245(b))		100	
9	**Total.** Add lines 1 through 8. See instructions for limitation			
10	Dividends from domestic corporations received by a small business investment company operating under the Small Business Investment Act of 1958		100	
11	Dividends from certain FSCs that are subject to the 100% deduction (section 245(c)(1))		100	
12	Dividends from affiliated group members subject to the 100% deduction (section 243(a)(3))		100	
13	Other dividends from foreign corporations not included on lines 3, 6, 7, 8, or 11			
14	Income from controlled foreign corporations under subpart F (attach Form(s) 5471)			
15	Foreign dividend gross-up (section 78)			
16	IC-DISC and former DISC dividends not included on lines 1, 2, or 3 (section 246(d))			
17	Other dividends			
18	Deduction for dividends paid on certain preferred stock of public utilities (see instructions)			
19	**Total dividends.** Add lines 1 through 17. Enter here and on line 4, page 1 ▶			

20 **Total special deductions.** Add lines 9, 10, 11, 12, and 18. Enter here and on line 29b, page 1 . . . . . ▶

Schedule E	**Compensation of Officers** (See instructions for line 12, page 1.)					

Complete Schedule E only if total receipts (line 1a plus lines 4 through 10 on page 1, Form 1120) are $500,000 or more.

(a) Name of officer	(b) Social security number	(c) Percent of time devoted to business	Percent of corporation stock owned		(f) Amount of compensation
			(d) Common	(e) Preferred	
1		%	%	%	
		%	%	%	
		%	%	%	
		%	%	%	
		%	%	%	

2 Total compensation of officers . . . .
3 Compensation of officers claimed on Schedule A and elsewhere on return . . . .
4 Subtract line 3 from line 2. Enter the result here and on line 12, page 1 . . . .

Figure 4-16. Sample Form 1120. (Continued)

Form 1120 (1993) Page **3**

Schedule J   **Tax Computation** (See instructions.)

1 Check if the corporation is a member of a controlled group (see sections 1561 and 1563) . . . . ▶ ☐

2a If the box on line 1 is checked, enter the corporation's share of the $50,000, $25,000, and $9,925,000 taxable
   income brackets (in that order):
   (1) $_____   (2) $_____   (3) $_____

b Enter the corporation's share of:
   (1) additional 5% tax (not more than $11,750) $_____
   (2) additional 3% tax (not more than $100,000) $_____

3 Income tax. Check this box if the corporation is a qualified personal service corporation as defined in section
   448(d)(2) (see instructions on page 15) . . . . ▶ ☐ | **3** |

4a Foreign tax credit (attach Form 1118) . . . . | **4a** |
b Possessions tax credit (attach Form 5735) . . . . | **4b** |
c Orphan drug credit (attach Form 6765) . . . . | **4c** |
d Check: ☐ Nonconventional source fuel credit ☐ QEV credit (attach Form 8834) | **4d** |
e General business credit. Enter here and check which forms are attached:
   ☐ Form 3800 ☐ Form 3468 ☐ Form 5884 ☐ Form 6478 ☐ Form 6765
   ☐ Form 8586 ☐ Form 8830 ☐ Form 8826 ☐ Form 8835 . . . . | **4e** |
f Credit for prior year minimum tax (attach Form 8827) . . . . | **4f** |

5 **Total credits.** Add lines 4a through 4f . . . . | **5** |
6 Subtract line 5 from line 3 . . . . | **6** |
7 Personal holding company tax (attach Schedule PH (Form 1120)) . . . . | **7** |
8 Recapture taxes. Check if from: ☐ Form 4255 ☐ Form 8611 . . . . | **8** |
9a Alternative minimum tax (attach Form 4626) . . . . | **9a** |
b Environmental tax (attach Form 4626) . . . . | **9b** |
10 **Total tax.** Add lines 6 through 9b. Enter here and on line 31, page 1 . . . . | **10** |

Schedule K   **Other Information** (See pages 17 and 18 of instructions.)

		Yes	No

1 Check method of accounting: a ☐ Cash
   b ☐ Accrual c ☐ Other (specify) ▶ ....

2 Refer to page 19 of the instructions and state the principal:
a Business activity code no. ▶ ....
b Business activity ▶ ....
c Product or service ▶ ....

3 Did the corporation at the end of the tax year own, directly
   or indirectly, 50% or more of the voting stock of a
   domestic corporation? (For rules of attribution, see
   section 267(c).) . . . .
   If "Yes," attach a schedule showing: (a) name and identifying
   number, (b) percentage owned, and (c) taxable income or
   (loss) before NOL and special deductions of such corporation
   for the tax year ending with or within your tax year.

4 Is the corporation a subsidiary in an affiliated group or a
   parent-subsidiary controlled group? . . . . . .
   If "Yes," enter employer identification number and name
   of the parent corporation ▶ ....
   ....

5 Did any individual, partnership, corporation, estate or
   trust at the end of the tax year own, directly or indirectly,
   50% or more of the corporation's voting stock? (For rules
   of attribution, see section 267(c).) . . . .
   If "Yes," attach a schedule showing name and identifying
   number. (Do not include any information already entered
   in 4 above.) Enter percentage owned ▶..................

6 During this tax year, did the corporation pay dividends (other
   than stock dividends and distributions in exchange for stock)
   in excess of the corporation's current and accumulated
   earnings and profits? (See secs. 301 and 316.) . . . .
   If "Yes," file Form 5452. If this is a consolidated return,
   answer here for the parent corporation and on **Form 851,**
   Affiliations Schedule, for each subsidiary.

7 Was the corporation a U.S. shareholder of any controlled
   foreign corporation? (See sections 951 and 957.) . . .
   If "Yes," attach Form 5471 for each such corporation.
   Enter number of Forms 5471 attached ▶.................

8 At any time during the 1993 calendar year, did the corporation
   have an interest in or a signature or other authority over a
   financial account in a foreign country (such as a bank
   account, securities account, or other financial account)? . .
   If "Yes," the corporation may have to file Form TD F 90-22.1.
   If "Yes," enter name of foreign country ▶ ....

9 Was the corporation the grantor of, or transferor to, a foreign
   trust that existed during the current tax year, whether or not
   the corporation has any beneficial interest in it? If "Yes," the
   corporation may have to file Forms 926, 3520, or 3520-A

10 Did one foreign person at any time during the tax year own,
   directly or indirectly, at least 25% of: **(a)** the total voting power
   of all classes of stock of the corporation entitled to vote, or **(b)**
   the total value of all classes of stock of the corporation? If "Yes,"
a Enter percentage owned ▶.............................
b Enter owner's country ▶...............................
c The corporation may have to file Form 5472. Enter number
   of Forms 5472 attached ▶.............................

11 Check this box if the corporation issued publicly offered
   debt instruments with original issue discount . ▶ ☐
   If so, the corporation may have to file Form 8281.

12 Enter the amount of tax-exempt interest received or
   accrued during the tax year ▶ $ ....

13 If there were 35 or fewer shareholders at the end of the
   tax year, enter the number ▶.........................

14 If the corporation has an NOL for the tax year and is
   electing to forego the carryback period, check here ▶ ☐

15 Enter the available NOL carryover from prior tax years
   (Do not reduce it by any deduction on line
   29a.) ▶ $

Figure 4-16. Sample Form 1120. (Continued)

Form 1120 (1993) Page **4**

Schedule L	Balance Sheets	Beginning of tax year		End of tax year	
	Assets	(a)	(b)	(c)	(d)
1	Cash				
2a	Trade notes and accounts receivable				
b	Less allowance for bad debts	( )		( )	
3	Inventories				
4	U.S. government obligations				
5	Tax-exempt securities (see instructions)				
6	Other current assets (attach schedule)				
7	Loans to stockholders				
8	Mortgage and real estate loans				
9	Other investments (attach schedule)				
10a	Buildings and other depreciable assets				
b	Less accumulated depreciation	( )		( )	
11a	Depletable assets				
b	Less accumulated depletion	( )		( )	
12	Land (net of any amortization)				
13a	Intangible assets (amortizable only)				
b	Less accumulated amortization	( )		( )	
14	Other assets (attach schedule)				
15	Total assets				
	Liabilities and Stockholders' Equity				
16	Accounts payable				
17	Mortgages, notes, bonds payable in less than 1 year				
18	Other current liabilities (attach schedule)				
19	Loans from stockholders				
20	Mortgages, notes, bonds payable in 1 year or more				
21	Other liabilities (attach schedule)				
22	Capital stock: a Preferred stock				
	b Common stock				
23	Paid-in or capital surplus				
24	Retained earnings—Appropriated (attach schedule)				
25	Retained earnings—Unappropriated				
26	Less cost of treasury stock		( )		( )
27	Total liabilities and stockholders' equity				

Note: *You are not required to complete Schedules M-1 and M-2 below if the total assets on line 15, column (d) of Schedule L are less than $25,000.*

Schedule M-1	Reconciliation of Income (Loss) per Books With Income per Return (See instructions.)

1 Net income (loss) per books
2 Federal income tax
3 Excess of capital losses over capital gains
4 Income subject to tax not recorded on books this year (itemize): ....
5 Expenses recorded on books this year not deducted on this return (itemize):
 a Depreciation . . . . $ ....
 b Contributions carryover $ ....
 c Travel and entertainment $ ....
....
6 Add lines 1 through 5

7 Income recorded on books this year not included on this return (itemize):
 Tax-exempt interest $ ....
....
8 Deductions on this return not charged against book income this year (itemize):
 a Depreciation . . . . $ ....
 b Contributions carryover $ ....
....
....
9 Add lines 7 and 8
10 Income (line 28, page 1)—line 6 less line 9

Schedule M-2	Analysis of Unappropriated Retained Earnings per Books (Line 25, Schedule L)

1 Balance at beginning of year
2 Net income (loss) per books
3 Other increases (itemize): ....
....
....
4 Add lines 1, 2, and 3

5 Distributions: a Cash
      b Stock
      c Property
6 Other decreases (itemize): ....
7 Add lines 5 and 6
8 Balance at end of year (line 4 less line 7)

Printed on recycled paper *U.S. Government Printing Office: 1993 — 345-287*

Figure 4-16. Sample Form 1120. (Continued)

Form **8829**	**Expenses for Business Use of Your Home**	OMB No. 1545-1266
	► File only with Schedule C (Form 1040). Use a separate Form 8829 for each home you used for business during the year.	**19 93**
Department of the Treasury Internal Revenue Service (O)	► See separate instructions.	Attachment Sequence No. **66**
Name(s) of proprietor(s)		Your social security number

Part I Part of Your Home Used for Business

1	Area used regularly and exclusively for business, regularly for day care, or for inventory storage. See instructions	1	
2	Total area of home	2	
3	Divide line 1 by line 2. Enter the result as a percentage	3	%

• For day-care facilities not used exclusively for business, also complete lines 4–6.
• All others, skip lines 4–6 and enter the amount from line 3 on line 7.

4	Multiply days used for day care during year by hours used per day .	4		hr.
5	Total hours available for use during the year (365 days × 24 hours). See instructions	5	8,760	hr.
6	Divide line 4 by line 5. Enter the result as a decimal amount . . .	6	.	
7	Business percentage. For day-care facilities not used exclusively for business, multiply line 6 by line 3 (enter the result as a percentage). All others, enter the amount from line 3 . . . . ►	7		%

Part II Figure Your Allowable Deduction

8	Enter the amount from Schedule C, line 29, **plus** any net gain or (loss) derived from the business use of your home and shown on Schedule D or Form 4797. If more than one place of business, see instructions	8	

See instructions for columns (a) and (b) before completing lines 9–20.

		(a) Direct expenses	(b) Indirect expenses	
9	Casualty losses. See instructions	9		
10	Deductible mortgage interest. See instructions . .	10		
11	Real estate taxes. See instructions	11		
12	Add lines 9, 10, and 11	12		
13	Multiply line 12, column (b) by line 7	13		
14	Add line 12, column (a) and line 13			14
15	Subtract line 14 from line 8. If zero or less, enter -0- .			15
16	Excess mortgage interest. See instructions . .	16		
17	Insurance	17		
18	Repairs and maintenance	18		
19	Utilities	19		
20	Other expenses. See instructions	20		
21	Add lines 16 through 20	21		
22	Multiply line 21, column (b) by line 7	22		
23	Carryover of operating expenses from 1992 Form 8829, line 41 . .	23		
24	Add line 21 in column (a), line 22, and line 23			24
25	Allowable operating expenses. Enter the **smaller** of line 15 or line 24			25
26	Limit on excess casualty losses and depreciation. Subtract line 25 from line 15			26
27	Excess casualty losses. See instructions	27		
28	Depreciation of your home from Part III below	28		
29	Carryover of excess casualty losses and depreciation from 1992 Form 8829, line 42	29		
30	Add lines 27 through 29			30
31	Allowable excess casualty losses and depreciation. Enter the **smaller** of line 26 or line 30 . .			31
32	Add lines 14, 25, and 31			32
33	Casualty loss portion, if any, from lines 14 and 31. Carry amount to **Form 4684**, Section B . .			33
34	Allowable expenses for business use of your home. Subtract line 33 from line 32. Enter here and on Schedule C, line 30. If your home was used for more than one business, see instructions ►			34

Part III Depreciation of Your Home

35	Enter the **smaller** of your home's adjusted basis or its fair market value. See instructions . .	35	
36	Value of land included on line 35	36	
37	Basis of building. Subtract line 36 from line 35	37	
38	Business basis of building. Multiply line 37 by line 7	38	
39	Depreciation percentage. See instructions	39	%
40	Depreciation allowable. Multiply line 38 by line 39. Enter here and on line 28 above. See instructions	40	

Part IV Carryover of Unallowed Expenses to 1994

41	Operating expenses. Subtract line 25 from line 24. If less than zero, enter -0-	41	
42	Excess casualty losses and depreciation. Subtract line 31 from line 30. If less than zero, enter -0- .	42	

For Paperwork Reduction Act Notice, see page 1 of separate instructions.   Cat. No. 13232M   Form **8829** (1993)
*U.S.GPO:1993-0-345-468

Figure 4-17. Sample Form 8829.

SCHEDULE SE	Self-Employment Tax	OMB No. 1545-0074
(Form 1040)	▶ See Instructions for Schedule SE (Form 1040).	**1993**
Department of the Treasury Internal Revenue Service (O)	▶ Attach to Form 1040.	Attachment Sequence No. **17**

Name of person with **self-employment** income (as shown on Form 1040)	Social security number of person with **self-employment** income ▶	

Who Must File Schedule SE

You must file Schedule SE if:

- Your wages (and tips) subject to social security AND Medicare tax (or railroad retirement tax) were less than $135,000; **AND**
- Your net earnings from self-employment from other than church employee income (line 4 of Short Schedule SE or line 4c of Long Schedule SE) were $400 or more; **OR**
- You had church employee income of $108.28 or more. Income from services you performed as a minister or a member of a religious order **is not** church employee income. See page SE-1.

Note: *Even if you have a loss or a small amount of income from self-employment, it may be to your benefit to file Schedule SE and use either "optional method" in Part II of Long Schedule SE. See page SE-3.*

Exception. If your only self-employment income was from earnings as a minister, member of a religious order, or Christian Science practitioner, **AND** you filed Form 4361 and received IRS approval not to be taxed on those earnings, **DO NOT** file Schedule SE. Instead, write "Exempt–Form 4361" on Form 1040, line 47.

May I Use Short Schedule SE or MUST I Use Long Schedule SE?

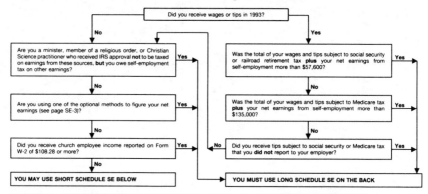

Section A—Short Schedule SE. Caution: *Read above to see if you can use Short Schedule SE.*

1	Net farm profit or (loss) from Schedule F, line 36, and farm partnerships, Schedule K-1 (Form 1065), line 15a	1
2	Net profit or (loss) from Schedule C, line 31; Schedule C-EZ, line 3; and Schedule K-1 (Form 1065), line 15a (other than farming). Ministers and members of religious orders see page SE-1 for amounts to report on this line. See page SE-2 for other income to report	2
3	Combine lines 1 and 2	3
4	**Net earnings from self-employment.** Multiply line 3 by 92.35% (.9235). If less than $400, **do not** file this schedule; you do not owe self-employment tax . . . . ▶	4
5	**Self-employment tax.** If the amount on line 4 is: • $57,600 or less, multiply line 4 by 15.3% (.153) and enter the result. • More than $57,600 but less than $135,000, multiply the amount in excess of $57,600 by 2.9% (.029). Then, add $8,812.80 to the result and enter the total. • $135,000 or more, enter $11,057.40. Also enter on **Form 1040, line 47. (Important:** You are allowed a deduction for **one-half** of this amount. Multiply line 5 by 50% (.5) and enter the result on **Form 1040, line 25.)**	5

For Paperwork Reduction Act Notice, see Form 1040 instructions.   Cat. No. 11358Z   Schedule SE (Form 1040) 1993

Figure 4-18. Sample Schedule SE.

Schedule SE (Form 1040) 1993 | Attachment Sequence No. **17** | Page **2**

Name of person with **self-employment** income (as shown on Form 1040)	Social security number of person with **self-employment** income ▶		

Section B—Long Schedule SE

Part I   **Self-Employment Tax**

Note: *If your only income subject to self-employment tax is church employee income, skip lines 1 through 4b. Enter -0- on line 4c and go to line 5a. Income from services you performed as a minister or a member of a religious order* **is not** *church employee income. See page SE-3.*

A   If you are a minister, member of a religious order, or Christian Science practitioner **AND** you filed Form 4361, but you had $400 or more of **other** net earnings from self-employment, check here and continue with Part I . . . . . ▶ ☐

1	Net farm profit or (loss) from Schedule F, line 36, and farm partnerships, Schedule K-1 (Form 1065), line 15a. **Note:** *Skip this line if you use the farm optional method. See page SE-3*	1	
2	Net profit or (loss) from Schedule C, line 31; Schedule C-EZ, line 3; and Schedule K-1 (Form 1065), line 15a (other than farming). Ministers and members of religious orders see page SE-1 for amounts to report on this line. See page SE-2 for other income to report. **Note:** *Skip this line if you use the nonfarm optional method. See page SE-3*	2	
3	Combine lines 1 and 2	3	
4a	If line 3 is more than zero, multiply line 3 by 92.35% (.9235). Otherwise, enter amount from line 3	4a	
b	If you elected one or both of the optional methods, enter the total of lines 17 and 19 here . .	4b	
c	Combine lines 4a and 4b. If less than $400, **do not** file this schedule; you do not owe self-employment tax. **Exception.** If less than $400 and you had church employee income, enter -0- and continue . ▶	4c	
5a	Enter your church employee income from Form W-2. **Caution:** *See page SE-1 for definition of church employee income*	5a	
b	Multiply line 5a by 92.35% (.9235). If less than $100, enter -0-	5b	
6	**Net earnings from self-employment.** Add lines 4c and 5b	6	
7	Maximum amount of combined wages and self-employment earnings subject to social security tax or the 6.2% portion of the 7.65% railroad retirement (tier 1) tax for 1993	7	57,600 00
8a	Total social security wages and tips (from Form(s) W-2) and railroad retirement (tier 1) compensation	8a	
b	Unreported tips subject to social security tax (from Form 4137, line 9)	8b	
c	Add lines 8a and 8b	8c	
9	Subtract line 8c from line 7. If zero or less, enter -0- here and on line 10 and go to line 12a ▶	9	
10	Multiply the **smaller** of line 6 or line 9 by 12.4% (.124)	10	
11	Maximum amount of combined wages and self-employment earnings subject to Medicare tax or the 1.45% portion of the 7.65% railroad retirement (tier 1) tax for 1993	11	135,000 00
12a	Total Medicare wages and tips (from Form(s) W-2) and railroad retirement (tier 1) compensation	12a	
b	Unreported tips subject to Medicare tax (from Form 4137, line 14) .	12b	
c	Add lines 12a and 12b	12c	
13	Subtract line 12c from line 11. If zero or less, enter -0- here and on line 14 and go to line 15 .	13	
14	Multiply the **smaller** of line 6 or line 13 by 2.9% (.029)	14	
15	**Self-employment tax.** Add lines 10 and 14. Enter here and on **Form 1040, line 47. (Important:** You are allowed a deduction for **one-half** of this amount. Multiply line 15 by 50% (.5) and enter the result on **Form 1040, line 25.)**	15	

Part II   **Optional Methods To Figure Net Earnings (See page SE-3.)**

Farm Optional Method. You may use this method **only** if **(a)** Your gross farm income[1] was not more than $2,400 **or (b)** Your gross farm income[1] was more than $2,400 and your net farm profits[2] were less than $1,733.

16	Maximum income for optional methods	16	1,600 00
17	Enter the **smaller** of: two-thirds (⅔) of gross farm income[1] (not less than zero) **or** $1,600. Also, include this amount on line 4b above	17	

Nonfarm Optional Method. You may use this method **only** if **(a)** Your net nonfarm profits[3] were less than $1,733 and also less than 72.189% of your gross nonfarm income,[4] **and (b)** You had net earnings from self-employment of at least $400 in 2 of the prior 3 years. **Caution:** *You may use this method no more than five times.*

18	Subtract line 17 from line 16	18	
19	Enter the **smaller** of: two-thirds (⅔) of gross nonfarm income[4] (not less than zero) **or** the amount on line 18. Also, include this amount on line 4b above	19	

[1]From Schedule F, line 11, and Schedule K-1 (Form 1065), line 15b.   [3]From Schedule C, line 31; Schedule C-EZ, line 3; and Schedule K-1 (Form 1065), line 15a.
[2]From Schedule F, line 36, and Schedule K-1 (Form 1065), line 15a.   [4]From Schedule C, line 7; Schedule C-EZ, line 1; and Schedule K-1 (Form 1065), line 15c.

⍟ U.S. GOVERNMENT PRINTING OFFICE: 1993 315-000

Figure 4-18. Sample Schedule SE (Continued)

Form **1065** Department of the Treasury Internal Revenue Service		**U.S. Partnership Return of Income** For calendar year 1993, or tax year beginning .... , 1993, and ending .... , 19 .... . ▶ See separate instructions.		OMB No. 1545-0099 **1993**
A Principal business activity	Use the IRS label. Other- wise, please print or type.	Name of partnership		**D** Employer identification number
B Principal product or service		Number, street, and room or suite no. (If a P.O. box, see page 9 of the instructions.)		**E** Date business started
C Business code number		City or town, state, and ZIP code		**F** Total assets (see **Specific Instructions**) $

G Check applicable boxes: **(1)** ☐ Initial return **(2)** ☐ Final return **(3)** ☐ Change in address **(4)** ☐ Amended return
H Check accounting method: **(1)** ☐ Cash **(2)** ☐ Accrual **(3)** ☐ Other (specify) ▶ ....
I Number of Schedules K-1. Attach one for each person who was a partner at any time during the tax year ▶ ....

Caution: *Include **only** trade or business income and expenses on lines 1a through 22 below. See the instructions for more information.*

Income	**1a** Gross receipts or sales	**1a**		
	b Less returns and allowances.	**1b**	**1c**	
	2 Cost of goods sold (Schedule A, line 8)		**2**	
	3 Gross profit. Subtract line 2 from line 1c		**3**	
	4 Ordinary income (loss) from other partnerships and fiduciaries *(attach schedule)*		**4**	
	5 Net farm profit (loss) *(attach Schedule F (Form 1040))*		**5**	
	6 Net gain (loss) from Form 4797, Part II, line 20.		**6**	
	7 Other income (loss) (see instructions) *(attach schedule)*		**7**	
	8 **Total income (loss).** Combine lines 3 through 7		**8**	
Deductions (see instructions for limitations)	**9a** Salaries and wages (other than to partners).	**9a**		
	b Less employment credits	**9b**	**9c**	
	10 Guaranteed payments to partners		**10**	
	11 Repairs and maintenance		**11**	
	12 Bad debts		**12**	
	13 Rent		**13**	
	14 Taxes and licenses		**14**	
	15 Interest		**15**	
	16a Depreciation (see instructions)	**16a**		
	b Less depreciation reported on Schedule A and elsewhere on return	**16b**	**16c**	
	17 Depletion **(Do not deduct oil and gas depletion.)**		**17**	
	18 Retirement plans, etc.		**18**	
	19 Employee benefit programs		**19**	
	20 Other deductions *(attach schedule)*		**20**	
	21 **Total deductions.** Add the amounts shown in the far right column for lines 9c through 20 .		**21**	
	22 **Ordinary income (loss)** from trade or business activities. Subtract line 21 from line 8 . .		**22**	

Please Sign Here Under penalties of perjury, I declare that I have examined this return, including accompanying schedules and statements, and to the best of my knowledge and belief, it is true, correct, and complete. Declaration of preparer (other than general partner) is based on all information of which preparer has any knowledge.

▶ Signature of general partner		▶ Date

Paid Preparer's Use Only	Preparer's signature ▶	Date	Check if self-employed ▶ ☐	Preparer's social security no.
	Firm's name (or yours if self-employed) and address ▶		E.I. No. ▶ ZIP code ▶	

For Paperwork Reduction Act Notice, see page 1 of separate instructions. Cat. No. 11390Z Form **1065** (1993)

Figure 4-19. Sample Form 1065.

Schedule A	Cost of Goods Sold

1	Inventory at beginning of year	1
2	Purchases less cost of items withdrawn for personal use	2
3	Cost of labor.	3
4	Additional section 263A costs (see instructions) *(attach schedule)*	4
5	Other costs *(attach schedule)*	5
6	**Total.** Add lines 1 through 5	6
7	Inventory at end of year	7
8	**Cost of goods sold.** Subtract line 7 from line 6. Enter here and on page 1, line 2	8

9a Check all methods used for valuing closing inventory:

   (i) ☐ Cost

   (ii) ☐ Lower of cost or market as described in Regulations section 1.471-4

   (iii) ☐ Writedown of "subnormal" goods as described in Regulations section 1.471-2(c)

   (iv) ☐ Other (specify method used and attach explanation) ▶ .... ▶ ☐

   b Check this box if the LIFO inventory method was adopted this tax year for any goods *(if checked, attach Form 970)* . . ▶ ☐

   c Do the rules of section 263A (for property produced or acquired for resale) apply to the partnership? . . ☐ **Yes** ☐ **No**

   d Was there any change in determining quantities, cost, or valuations between opening and closing inventory? ☐ **Yes** ☐ **No**
   If "Yes," attach explanation.

Schedule B	Other Information		Yes	No

		Yes	No
1	What type of entity is filing this return? Check the applicable box ▶ ☐ General partnership ☐ Limited partnership ☐ Limited liability company		
2	Are any partners in this partnership also partnerships?		
3	Is this partnership a partner in another partnership?		
4	Is this partnership subject to the consolidated audit procedures of sections 6221 through 6233? If "Yes," see **Designation of Tax Matters Partner** below		
5	Does this partnership meet **ALL THREE** of the following requirements?		
a	The partnership's total receipts for the tax year were less than $250,000;		
b	The partnership's total assets at the end of the tax year were less than $600,000; **AND**		
c	Schedules K-1 are filed with the return and furnished to the partners on or before the due date (including extensions) for the partnership return. If "Yes," the partnership is not required to complete Schedules L, M-1, and M-2; Item F on page 1 of Form 1065; or Item J on Schedule K-1		
6	Does this partnership have any foreign partners?		
7	Is this partnership a publicly traded partnership as defined in section 469(k)(2)?		
8	Has this partnership filed, or is it required to file, **Form 8264,** Application for Registration of a Tax Shelter? . .		
9	At any time during calendar year 1993, did the partnership have an interest in or a signature or other authority over a financial account in a foreign country (such as a bank account, securities account, or other financial account)? (See the instructions for exceptions and filing requirements for form TD F 90-22.1.) If "Yes," enter the name of the foreign country. ▶		
10	Was the partnership the grantor of, or transferor to, a foreign trust that existed during the current tax year, whether or not the partnership or any partner has any beneficial interest in it? If "Yes," you may have to file Forms 3520, 3520-A, or 926		
11	Was there a distribution of property or a transfer (e.g., by sale or death) of a partnership interest during the tax year? If "Yes," you may elect to adjust the basis of the partnership's assets under section 754 by attaching the statement described on page 5 of the instructions under **Elections Made By the Partnership**		

Designation of Tax Matters Partner (See instructions.)
Enter below the general partner designated as the tax matters partner (TMP) for the tax year of this return:

Name of
designated TMP ▶   Identifying
                                                                      number of TMP ▶

Address of
designated TMP ▶

Figure 4-19. Sample Form 1065. (Continued)

Form 1065 (1993)   Page **3**

Schedule K	Partners' Shares of Income, Credits, Deductions, etc.	
	(a) Distributive share items	**(b) Total amount**

Income (Loss)

1	Ordinary income (loss) from trade or business activities (page 1, line 22)	1
2	Net income (loss) from rental real estate activities (attach Form 8825)	2
3a	Gross income from other rental activities **3a**	
b	Expenses from other rental activities (attach schedule) **3b**	
c	Net income (loss) from other rental activities. Subtract line 3b from line 3a	3c
4	Portfolio income (loss) (see instructions): a Interest income	4a
b	Dividend income	4b
c	Royalty income	4c
d	Net short-term capital gain (loss) (attach Schedule D (Form 1065))	4d
e	Net long-term capital gain (loss) (attach Schedule D (Form 1065))	4e
f	Other portfolio income (loss) (attach schedule)	4f
5	Guaranteed payments to partners	5
6	Net gain (loss) under section 1231 (other than due to casualty or theft) (attach Form 4797)	6
7	Other income (loss) (attach schedule)	7

Deductions

8	Charitable contributions (see instructions) (attach schedule)	8
9	Section 179 expense deduction (attach Form 4562)	9
10	Deductions related to portfolio income (see instructions) (itemize)	10
11	Other deductions (attach schedule)	11

Investment Interest

12a	Interest expense on investment debts	12a
b	(1) Investment income included on lines 4a, 4b, 4c, and 4f above	12b(1)
	(2) Investment expenses included on line 10 above	12b(2)

Credits

13a	Credit for income tax withheld	13a
b	Low-income housing credit (see instructions):	
	(1) From partnerships to which section 42(j)(5) applies for property placed in service before 1990	13b(1)
	(2) Other than on line 13b(1) for property placed in service before 1990	13b(2)
	(3) From partnerships to which section 42(j)(5) applies for property placed in service after 1989	13b(3)
	(4) Other than on line 13b(3) for property placed in service after 1989	13b(4)
c	Qualified rehabilitation expenditures related to rental real estate activities (attach Form 3468)	13c
d	Credits (other than credits shown on lines 13b and 13c) related to rental real estate activities (see instructions)	13d
e	Credits related to other rental activities (see instructions)	13e
14	Other credits (see instructions)	14

Self-Employment

15a	Net earnings (loss) from self-employment	15a
b	Gross farming or fishing income	15b
c	Gross nonfarm income	15c

Adjustments and Tax Preference Items

16a	Depreciation adjustment on property placed in service after 1986	16a
b	Adjusted gain or loss	16b
c	Depletion (other than oil and gas)	16c
d	(1) Gross income from oil, gas, and geothermal properties	16d(1)
	(2) Deductions allocable to oil, gas, and geothermal properties	16d(2)
e	Other adjustments and tax preference items (attach schedule)	16e

Foreign Taxes

17a	Type of income ▶ .... b Foreign country or U.S. possession ▶	
c	Total gross income from sources outside the United States (attach schedule)	17c
d	Total applicable deductions and losses (attach schedule)	17d
e	Total foreign taxes (check one): ▶ ☐ Paid ☐ Accrued	17e
f	Reduction in taxes available for credit (attach schedule)	17f
g	Other foreign tax information (attach schedule)	17g

Other

18a	Total expenditures to which a section 59(e) election may apply	18a
b	Type of expenditures ▶..............	
19	Tax-exempt interest income	19
20	Other tax-exempt income	20
21	Nondeductible expenses	21
22	Other items and amounts required to be reported separately to partners (see instructions) (attach schedule)	

Analysis

23a	Income (loss). Combine lines 1 through 7 in column (b). From the result, subtract the sum of lines 8 through 12a, 17e, and 18a	23a

b Analysis by type of partner:	(a) Corporate	(b) Individual		(c) Partnership	(d) Exempt organization	(e) Nominee/Other
		i. Active	ii. Passive			
(1) General partners						
(2) Limited partners						

Figure 4-19. Sample Form 1065. (Continued)

Note: If Question 5 of Schedule B is answered "Yes," the partnership is not required to complete Schedules L, M-1, and M-2.

Schedule L — Balance Sheets

Assets	Beginning of tax year (a)	(b)	End of tax year (c)	(d)
1 Cash.				
2a Trade notes and accounts receivable				
b Less allowance for bad debts				
3 Inventories.				
4 U.S. government obligations				
5 Tax-exempt securities				
6 Other current assets (attach schedule)				
7 Mortgage and real estate loans				
8 Other investments (attach schedule)				
9a Buildings and other depreciable assets				
b Less accumulated depreciation				
10a Depletable assets				
b Less accumulated depletion				
11 Land (net of any amortization)				
12a Intangible assets (amortizable only).				
b Less accumulated amortization				
13 Other assets (attach schedule)				
14 Total assets				
Liabilities and Capital				
15 Accounts payable				
16 Mortgages, notes, bonds payable in less than 1 year.				
17 Other current liabilities (attach schedule)				
18 All nonrecourse loans				
19 Mortgages, notes, bonds payable in 1 year or more.				
20 Other liabilities (attach schedule)				
21 Partners' capital accounts				
22 Total liabilities and capital				

Schedule M-1 — Reconciliation of Income (Loss) per Books With Income (Loss) per Return (see instructions)

1 Net income (loss) per books

2 Income included on Schedule K, lines 1 through 4, 6, and 7, not recorded on books this year (itemize): ....

3 Guaranteed payments (other than health insurance)

4 Expenses recorded on books this year not included on Schedule K, lines 1 through 12a, 17e, and 18a (itemize):
a Depreciation $ ....
b Travel and entertainment $ ....

5 Add lines 1 through 4

6 Income recorded on books this year not included on Schedule K, lines 1 through 7 (itemize):
a Tax-exempt interest $ ....

7 Deductions included on Schedule K, lines 1 through 12a, 17e, and 18a, not charged against book income this year (itemize):
a Depreciation $ ....

8 Add lines 6 and 7

9 Income (loss) (Schedule K, line 23a). Subtract line 8 from line 5

Schedule M-2 — Analysis of Partners' Capital Accounts

1 Balance at beginning of year.

2 Capital contributed during year

3 Net income (loss) per books

4 Other increases (itemize): ....

5 Add lines 1 through 4

6 Distributions: a Cash
b Property

7 Other decreases (itemize): ....

8 Add lines 6 and 7

9 Balance at end of year. Subtract line 8 from line 5

 Printed on recycled paper   ☆ U.S. GPO:1993-345-264

Figure 4-19. Sample Form 1065. (Continued)

is due under the law. You are liable only for the correct amount of tax. The purpose of the IRS is to apply the law consistently and fairly.

You have the right to have your tax matters kept confidential. Under the law, the IRS must protect the privacy of your tax information. However, if a lien or lawsuit is filed, certain aspects of your tax matters will become public record. People who prepared your return or represent you must also keep your information confidential.

You also have the right to know why the IRS is asking you for information, exactly how they will use it, and what might happen if you do not give it.

An IRS examination usually begins when the IRS notifies you that your return has been selected. The IRS will tell you which records you will need. If you gather your records before the examination, it can be completed with the least amount of effort. Take to the examination meeting only those items that the IRS has requested. Do not volunteer anything.

The IRS selects returns for examination by several methods. A computer program called the *Discriminant Function System* (DIF) is used to select most returns. In this method, the computer uses historical data to give part of the return a score. IRS personnel then screen the return. Returns most likely to have mistakes are selected for examination. The IRS considers the amount of income and tax and determines a "return on investment" by which the IRS will expend its auditing resources so as to receive the largest dollar yield from auditing the particular return. Because only a small percentage of returns are audited each year (less than 2 percent, the IRS determines which returns represent the highest dollar tax receipts as the result of a successful audit.

Some returns are selected at random. In addition, the IRS selects returns by examining claims for credit or refund and by matching information documents, such as Forms W-2 and 1099, with returns. The IRS also selects returns on the basis of relationships to other returns that have been examined. For example, if the examination of one of your customers or suppliers were to reveal inconsistencies, the IRS would determine that taxpayer's business relationships and evaluate those taxpayers for return examination. The IRS offers a reward to individuals who inform on taxpayers who they believe may be breaking certain tax laws. The IRS, if it believes such action is warranted, will examine the returns of those taxpayers who have been cited. If the IRS recovers additional taxes as the result of an informant-instigated examination, the informant will receive a negotiated percentage of the penalties levied and collected by the Internal Revenue Service.

Many examinations are handled by mail. If the IRS gives you notice that your examination is to be conducted through a personal interview, or if you request such an interview, you have the right to ask that the examination take place at a reasonable time and place that is convenient for both you and the IRS. If the time or place suggested by the IRS is not convenient, the examiner will usually try to work out something more suitable. However, as in most dealings with the IRS, the IRS will make the final determination on how, when, and where an examination takes place.

Generally, your individual return is examined in the IRS district office nearest your home or business. However, not all offices have examination facilities. Your business return is examined where your books and records are maintained. If the place of examination is not convenient, you may ask to have the examination held in another office or transferred to a different district.

Representation

Throughout the examination, you may represent yourself, have someone else accompany you, or, with proper authorization, have someone represent you in your absence. If you want to consult an attorney, a C.P.A., an enrolled agent, or any other person permitted to represent a taxpayer during an examination, the IRS will reschedule the interview. The IRS cannot suspend the interview if you are there on an IRS summons. The IRS may issue summonses to third-party recordkeepers (banks, brokers, accountants, etc.) for the production of records concerning the business transactions or affairs of a taxpayer. A point to keep in mind is that any communications between you and your accountant (whether a CPA or not) is not treated as a confidential communication in the way your communications and conversations with an attorney are treated. Whatever you say to your accountant can be used as testimony against you in a court of law or proceedings with the IRS. It is for this reason that many taxpayers employ the services of a tax attorney. At all times, do not attempt to represent yourself. Seek qualified counsel to protect your interests. A tax attorney experienced with examinations would be a good choice. Be sure your counsel has experience in tax law and can provide appropriate and capable representation. Another caveat: If the IRS agent identifies himself or herself as a "special agent," take special precautions. A special agent is concerned primarily with criminal fraud, and the presence of such an agent on your doorstep could signify big trouble. Say nothing to the agent, and contact your counsel as soon as possible. The agent will probably read you your rights, namely, that you do not have to say anything without an attorney or other counsel present. Listen to and heed the warning.

Recordings

You can generally make an audio recording of an interview with an IRS examination officer. Your request to make the recording should be made to the IRS in writing. You must notify the IRS 10 days before the meeting and bring your own recording equipment. The IRS can also record an interview. If the IRS initiates the recording, it will notify you 10 days before the meeting, and you will be able to get a copy at your own expense.

> Death is not the greatest loss in life. The greatest loss is what dies inside us while we live.
>
> Norman Cousins

Chapter 5

Using Information Management to Handle The Info-Glut

DESIGNING AN INFORMATION MANAGEMENT STRATEGY

If you are like most entrepreneurs, you try to digest every fact, every figure, every loose Post-It note, and every software program that you think might assist you in your quest. You are probably reading this book so that you can use your PC to digitize the free world, as we know it, by putting every detail at the beck and call of a mouse click or a few keystrokes. But, as often happens, our appetite for information often exceeds the size of our data digestive tract. This situation is known as *info-glut*.

There is a great deal of software that takes a stab at coping with and mastering this info-glut. *Personal information managers* (PIM) and *contact managers*, two surging Windows categories, work at getting a handle on all this information. The trouble is, no single program is perfect for every business user. You can't put one program on your hard disk, turn away, then look back to see that it has organized your day and tracked every item of your business.

You need an *information management strategy*. You need to know what various software programs can do for you, what they can't do, and, in some cases, what combination of programs most easily transmute into a comprehensive system that dovetails with the way you want to work.

INFORMATION MANAGERS VERSUS CONTACT MANAGERS

Information management for you and your business is best done with PIMs and contact managers. Typically, these applications are rooted in a specialized, predesigned database that stores names, addresses, phone numbers, and other pieces of personal data. When you have a modem attached to a PC, the software dials phone numbers from the database, then records the result. A calendar and a to-do list maker, along with their accompanying scheduling tools, join the database so you can track your own actions, not just those of others. And at least some note-taking capability is available in all such software. These are the basics of a PIM.

Contact managers go further. These software packages, which evolved from tools for sales professionals, either include an adequate, albeit limited, word processor for writing letters and memos, or link with an outside word processor for the same jobs. Call-backs are typically tracked automatically, and alarms sound to remind you of what to do and when to do it. The generation of reports, another important feature of a contact manager, lets you produce proof that you worked hard. Peripheral modules, such as expense account recorders and telemarketing sales script makers, are often included.

The difference between a PIM and a contact manager is that the former is part of a suite of software, whereas the latter tries to keep you staring at its screen most of the day. Your computer becomes *activity-driven* instead of *application-driven*. The PIM features manage critical details—scheduling meetings, creating to-do lists, finding names and addresses, making phone calls, tracking conversations, and writing personal notes—and some allow customization of the desktop as in PackRat, which allows you to arrange your PC to work the way you do. Enhanced integration capabilities let you store and run other popular Windows applications within the information manager. You'll have complete flexibility in organizing your desktop, with instant access to the applications and tools you need most.

Information management is one of the fastest-growing software categories today. An increasing number of professionals are looking for a more effective way to manage their business information. They have to meet today's demand for quality, service, and a higher degree of productivity. A powerful information manager helps them perform to the best of their abilities by making their data available instantly. With the proliferation of Microsoft Windows, more people can now run their information manager and their favorite applications simultaneously and move information instantly between applications.

A full-featured information manager will store and coordinate all the diverse information within your computer, and will organize your computing desktop, including:

- Contact names, addresses, phone and fax numbers, and conversation logs;
- Calendars and schedules;
- Tasks and to-do lists;
- Files from word processors or other Windows software;
- Financial records;
- Project management features;
- Audible on-screen alerts;
- Time management and billing capabilities;
- Resource scheduling;
- Personalized databases; and
- Desktop applications and accessories.

An information manager gives you all the recognized features of a contact manager in a completely customizable format, while fully integrating with all the elements of your PC. Some contact managers claim to be information managers, but are not. Unlike a contact manager that can process only limited types of information, such as names, notes, phone books, and conversation logs, an information manager offers a way to manage all forms of information and organizes your entire computer into familiar, easily accessible work spaces.

Think of PackRat 5.0 as the central control function for all of the information in your PC. It stores data in customizable folder work spaces on your desktop. PackRat lets you add all of the features you want and remove all of those you don't. Just place an Application Window object on any folder work space, and select that work space to open and run that application from within PackRat. Then each time you access a folder, all of its related applications will be open and ready when you are. As you work, PackRat will step in as usual with alerts to keep you on top of important appointments and deadlines. You'll also have instant access to your most frequently used commands, scripts, and macros by adding ActionButtons to your work spaces. ActionButtons automate complex tasks, such as setting up letters and faxes, with just a click of the mouse.

A good information manager lets you make better use of the information that's already at your fingertips, inasmuch as data is quickly stored and easily retrieved. It is not necessary to enter information more than once, because files are automatically updated. You'll be able to focus on the information you need and the ways in which you use it. Most businesspeople spend hours processing information. For them, the ideal information manager would handle all information with equal ease, whether it comes from the telephone, via fax, through E-MAIL, or from other software applications.

A good information manager boosts personal productivity. For example, Raoul, a salesperson responsible for customers in the Sunbelt region wants to send a letter to every customer who bought a widget in the last six months, urging these customers to buy a widget add-on or a super widget. He quickly accesses his word processing document on his PackRat work space. By clicking on an ActionButton, he initiates a search and performs a mail merge to insert each customer's personal information into the letter. Having generated the letters and envelopes automatically in a matter of minutes, Raoul is now free to focus on an important project: initiating a new sales strategy designed to double his existing customer base.

Performing the same task manually (looking up addresses, typing them in, searching through files for customer purchasing patterns, and writing reminder notes) might have otherwise taken him all day.

Carole, a businessowner, uses PackRat to plan and run her day. She customizes her folder work spaces, naming them Calendar, Phone Book/Log, and Project Manager. In her Phone Book/Log folder, she includes a series of ActionButtons that automate the searches she performs every day when calling different important suppliers. Recurring conference calls with key vendors or salespeople are set up automatically, and she can log notes about each call and see records of earlier calls at the touch of an ActionButton. She also uses ActionButtons to print out labels for customer mailings. Her Calendar folder can print out daily, weekly, or monthly overviews for her day-planning book so that she can stay up to date when she's not near her computer. Audible alerts sound and appear in dialog boxes on her screen to remind her of meetings, no matter which Windows application she is using. Her Project Manager folder includes several Lotus 1-2-3 spreadsheets, so she can quickly see how much money each particular project is going to require.

Before you assemble a system, you need to know the essential strategies you can use to wage war on the information glut. The fastest, and usually least expensive, way to handle information is with a specialized, single-purpose PIM. But though most PIMs offer a blizzard of features, their information-processing abilities don't stray far from a foundation of contact database, calendar, and notetaker. This strategy doesn't solve all your needs, for it relies on other software—primarily a word processor—to handle large bites of text-based information.

Contact managers promise a more integrated solution to the problem, as they typically include a text tool of some sort, the ability to bring in information already stored in other forms—particularly text files—and some type of macro function. Unfortunately, contact managers can't match a full-featured word processor in document creation work, nor are they usually set up to manage large numbers of documents.

Ultimately, the most comprehensive, and thus the most successful, strategy depends on using multiple packages to create a complete information management system. By matching a program that's strong on contacts with one that excels at retrieving other information, you can create a rock-solid system. This strategy is not for everyone, however, because it not only costs more to assemble, but also takes more time to operate.

A PC AND THE RIGHT SOFTWARE WON'T PERFORM MIRACLES

No product will organize you—instead, you must use products to organize yourself. Once you know how you want to organize a particular task, then consider the available software and organizers. If you don't have the right equipment, you are making your work life unnecessarily difficult. By equipping yourself with the right products, you'll save time and money, and you'll improve the service you give your customers or clients. We will discuss hardware, software, and operating system requirements in more depth in the next two chapters.

THE MOST COMMON PIMS AND CONTACT MANAGERS AVAILABLE

OnTime

Published by: Campbell Services, Inc.
21700 Northwestern Highway
Suite 1070
Southfield, MI 48075
313-559-5955 FAX 313-559-1034

People in business have reported that time wasted in scheduling meetings is one of their greatest frustrations. Probably an even bigger waste of time is attending most of the meetings. OnTime can't help with the content of the meetings, but it provides a PC calendar that schedules individual and group meetings quickly, easily, and cost-effectively. OnTime distinguishes itself because it was built with the individual in mind. If the user doesn't buy in, the system won't work. In order to serve the needs of the group, OnTime must first serve the needs of the individual, with a calendaring/group scheduling system that:

- Is easy to use;
- Provides the personal benefits of the stand-alone calendar that was awarded *PC Week's* Analyst's Choice and *PC World's* Best Buy awards; and
- Allows you to work in the operating environment you're comfortable with (DOS or Windows).

Ease of use is critical to achieve maximum participation. That's why OnTime for Networks is simple enough for every person in every department or function within your business, from the shipping dock to the front office. With this system, it is just as easy to schedule use of conference rooms and delivery trucks as it is to set up a major multidepartment meeting.

OnTime doesn't bog you down with unnecessary bells and whistles. The program does one thing and does it extremely well—it manages your calendar.

Lotus Organizer for Windows Release 1.1

Published by: Lotus Development Corporation
55 Cambridge Parkway
Cambridge, MA 02142
1-800-343-5414 (Canada) 1-800-GO-LOTUS

It's never been easier to schedule appointments and manage your work load, whether you work alone or in a group. Lotus Organizer now offers group scheduling on cc:Mail. This on-screen book has tabs for each section and pages that turn, just like most paper systems. So you'll feel at home, right from the start.

You can schedule appointments and confirm meetings with colleagues around the corner or around the world in the Calendar. Create your color-coded priority list under the To-Do tab. Block out major events in the 12-month Planner. Look up and dial phone numbers in the Address book. Make notes or import files in the Notepad, and mark important dates in the Anniversary section. Organizer shows its true power once you create links between entries stored in different sections. For example, you can link an appointment in Calendar to a task in your To-Do list, to a letter stored in the Notepad, and then move freely between linked entries.

Moreover, Lotus Organizer with group scheduling makes it fast and easy to set up a meeting among a large group of people—no matter where they're located. Organizer has won top awards from leading publications all around the world, including the Award of Distinction for 1992 from *BYTE* magazine, the "Best of 1992" from *PC Magazine*, and an MVP Finalist Award from *PC Computing*. Even more important, thousands of users are engaging Organizer to clear their desks and simplify their lives.

With Lotus Organizer, you'll spend less time juggling your schedule and more time doing your job or running your business. You'll never forget a meeting, because Calendar lets you set alarms to remind you of upcoming commitments—no matter what Windows application you're in. Plus you can trigger applications to run automatically at appointed times. If you need to retrieve information and can't remember what section it's in, Organizer will find it for you instantaneously, wherever it is. You can also show events from your Planner and To-Do list in Calendar to integrate all your business and personal commitments, then print a hard copy to take with you while you're on the road.

Lotus Organizer lets you access up to 65,000 names, addresses, and phone numbers—in an instant. You can browse through the Address section in a flash. Then, anytime you want to select a specific group of people, use the filter to choose just the records you need. You can easily sort your contacts by name, company, zip, or type of record; print listings to use while you're away from the office; create mailing labels; and export data for mail-merge letters. The Address section lets you dial telephone numbers through a modem, keep track of your calls, and redial unanswered phone numbers, thus saving you time and money.

The Notepad section of Lotus Organizer is more than a convenient place to jot down free-form ideas. You can create links to other applications and import files including text, numbers, and graphics. In addition, the Notepad automatically generates a table of contents, so you can go directly to the page you're looking for. You can then view your page in a single-page format or fold it out for better viewing of spreadsheets, charts, and diagrams.

ClientWorks

Published by: IMS, Inc. (Information Management Services)
P.O. Box 1471
Cary, NC 27512
1-800-298-3674 FAX 407-339-6520

ClientWorks states that "your contacts ARE your career." To assist with your client contacts, IMS, Inc. has produced a program that is effective and ready to run without any additional programming. It allows you to organize and maintain connections with all your professional, business, and personal contacts. This is an innovative approach to dealing with your clients, friends, customers, and associates. ClientWorks simplifies tasks to just one click of the mouse. Print an envelope, sort client records, copy to the clipboard, jot down notes, merge names into labels or letters, dial a client's phone number, find and create a list—all with just on click.

ClientWorks automatically organizes and maintains Mailing Lists, Notes, and Contact Lists with no programming. Perform a professional quality mail-merge using ClientWorks's built-in text editor, print labels automatically, keep unlimited notes, create your own reports in a snap, and integrate your client information with other Windows software. The system is ready to run, right out of the box—with a quick Windows setup.

A VCR control panel for easy browsing, one of the fastest, easiest report-writing tools on the market, prints summaries of Client

History, Last Contact, Next Contact, and Mail Codes. The retail price is surprisingly low, and the file performance of ClientWorks will equal or surpass most products at higher prices, so there is tremendous "headroom" for processing demands with a low-cost entry point.

PackRat 5.0

Published by: Polaris Software, Inc.
15175 Innovation Drive
San Diego, CA 92128
(619) 592-7400 FAX (619) 592-7430

Polaris PackRat 5.0 represents a new level of information management by combining work space organizing features with PIM functionality. PackRat 5.0 offers multiple, customizable work spaces on the Windows desktop. Each work space reflects the way the user works, thinks, and organizes information. With PackRat 5.0, users can streamline their Windows desktop, launch programs, integrate information and objects from diverse locations, and alter the appearance of a work space to best meet their needs and boost productivity. PackRat's PIM features include contact management, scheduling, multiple calendar views, task management, time management and billing, and document and file management.

PackRat 5.0 was developed in response to users' growing demands for a flexible, easy-to-learn information management program. With Polaris's exclusive SmartStart installation, users can begin working in PackRat immediately. PackRat automatically provides a customized "starter set" of work spaces, geared to the professional category specified by the user during installation. Once up and running, the work spaces can be used "as-is" or further customized. Users can customize existing work space folders by adding, editing, or removing tools, or they can create entirely new folders. Instant Options provides users with an easy point-and-click method to access the customizing function for each of PackRat 5.0's many object-oriented tools.

Polaris's software program is a twofold productivity tool. Functioning as a software manager, it streamlines the Windows desktop for maximum efficiency, allowing users to perform most PC functions without ever leaving PackRat. It also organizes the user's crucial business and personal information—from major projects to critical details—so that she or he is free to concentrate on important projects and goals.

An important factor in the growth of information managers has been the popularity of Microsoft's Windows platform. According to International Data Corporation, roughly 27 million PCs—about 37 percent of all PCs installed in the United States—are expected to be equipped with Windows by 1995. Windows-based information managers, with easy-to-use interfaces and the ability to serve as the information hub of the PC, will work naturally in conjunction with other Windows applications.

Keeping on top of all the tasks necessary to operate a business by using cumbersome manual methods would have once required, if not a small office staff, at least a lot of time. The combination of the PC and the flexible Windows environment, which allows people to switch easily between one application and another, can, however, turn the personal computer into an effective automation tool that allows busy people to work quickly and more efficiently than ever before.

The increasing volume of information pouring into and out of today's PCs demands a way of managing and maintaining control. Effective information management prevents users from becoming swamped. It can also help people to see new opportunities as information is linked together. The need to combine information from different sources has also grown with the advent of the telephone and fax capabilities that turn personal computers into centers for incoming and outgoing information.

To manage information in your Windows-based PC, Polaris's PackRat 5.0 will help you customize your PC to organize details, integrate applications, and link information from different sources, freeing up your time so that you may tackle important projects. Polaris Software's mission is to liberate users from manual organizational methods by providing powerful, easy-to-use personal and group information management software that substantially increases productivity. PackRat is more than just a contact and time manager. Its powerful features and intuitive design allow it to handle a full spectrum of business and information needs, such as document tracking, financial management, meeting and task scheduling, calendars, phone books, and more.

Polaris is committed to software innovation, and is investing in the technology that will make it possible. Polaris believes that an information manager should not only automate otherwise manual tasks, but should fulfill the promise of computers to make people more capable in their businesses. Enhanced productivity doesn't spring from performing tasks the same way day after day; it comes from examining the optimal flow of information and developing technology to implement more efficient ways of working.

The technology that will produce the next generation of information managers is available today. Some of it is in the form of established standards, such as the use of *dynamic data exchange* (DDE), *object linking and embedding* (OLE), and *messaging APIs*. Much of the integration is available through the PackRat Integration Library, a companion application that allows users to access PackRat data from within other Windows applications. PackRat 5.0 users have the advantages of database and E-mail compatability and enjoy the option of adding third-party enhancement tools that further expand PackRat's capabilities.

In December 1993, Polaris Software announced that it had opened its own forum on the CompuServe on-line information service, whereby PackRat users can receive prompt assistance with technical issues, access product news, and interact with other users. Previously, Polaris had maintained a small section on CompuServe as part of the Windows Third-Party Applications forum.

To access the Polaris forum, type GO POLARIS at the CompuServe prompt. Users have the option of exploring forum sections dedicated to PackRat 5.0 technical support, macros, third-party hardware and software, and customer service. There is also a section called The North Star Lounge, where users may gather and socialize in a casual atmosphere.

San Diego-based Polaris Software is a pioneer in the field of information management software. PackRat, designating the company's flagship products, has won numerous awards for excellence, including *PC Magazine's* Editor's Choice, *Windows Magazine's Reader's Choice, InfoWorld's Buyers Assurance, Window Magazine's Win 100,* and *PC World's World Class Award.*

Timeslips 5.0 for Windows

Published by: Timeslips Corporation
239 Western Avenue
Essex, MA 01929
800-285-0999 FAX 508-768-7660

Founded in January 1985, Timeslips Corporation is the recognized leader in time tracking, cost recovery, and professional billing software. Timeslips Corporation is the developer and distributor of Timeslips, the most efficient and cost-effective time and expense tracking system available. This system has been implemented on DOS, Windows, and Macintosh platforms, with a compatible paper tracking system available through Safeguard Business Systems, a leader in One-Write paper forms. NEBS (New England Business Service) selected Timeslips Corporation as its strategic software partner in the development and distribution of Timeslips 5.0 software to their one million customers.

Timeslips Corporation has built a force of more than 300 certified consultants, who are tested periodically for competence in knowledge of product line. This group of consultants has been instrumental in launching new products, and presenting the software and the company at regional trade shows and professional organizations. The Certified Consultant program has been the cornerstone of the corporation's marketing strategy for the past several years.

Never again will you have to worry about billable time going unrecorded. With Timeslips 5.0 for Windows, every moment you spend on each client can be recorded and tracked automatically. Bills can be processed swiftly and accurately; substantiation for time and charges is accurate and complete; and you'll have a clear idea of your own productivity at all times.

A major enhancement to one of the most popular time and billing software systems, Timeslips 5.0 for Windows is easy to use. Many powerful features streamline recordkeeping, perform complex analyses swiftly and expertly, and facilitates customized bills with a choice of fonts and graphics.

This is the most versatile system for tracking time and expenses and assigning charges. Just click your mouse, and an on-screen "stopwatch" in the TSTimer window starts keeping time for the job you're working on. You can enter clients, activities, users, and transactions—even browse through a series of records—without leaving the window. You can track your time by individual or project/matter, while consolidating information and billing at the client level.

Choose from up to six predetermined billing rates for each user, client, and activity. Sophisticated rate tables let you automate rate assignments as you track each event. The program also makes it easy to track services by hourly rate or flat fee, as well as compute and record interest on overdue invoices.

You have complete capability for management of accounts receivable. For example, you can maintain separate billing, accounts receivable, and payment history files—by client or by project/matter. You can also set up and maintain retainer accounts—for client retainer, trust, and escrow monies—without affecting the client's regular payment balance.

More than 40 different reports help you manage your business more profitability. With just a few clicks of the mouse, Timeslips 5.0 for Windows generates up-to-the-minute reports, graphs, and detailed analyses of time and billing activities. Included are practice management reports such as accounts receivable, aged work in progress, client investment, flat fee analysis, budgeting, and hourly rate analysis.

Check the aged accounts receivable reports to find out what is owed and to learn the status of any overdue balances. Scan a time and expense analysis and you'll see exactly where the time is going and how it's affecting profitability.

An easy-to-use layout tool gives your bills a professional look, which makes them appear more important and impressive. Modeled after desktop publishing programs, the layout tool lets you use eye-catching fonts and graphics to customize headers and footers on any page of a bill. It can also draw lines to highlight special sections.

Timeslips 5.0 for Windows makes it simple to customize each client's bill according to the amount of detail required. For example, you can break out daily hours, show weekly summaries by employee, project, or activity, or consolidate multiple projects in one invoice and include a billing summary. What's more, you can set a different format for each client. Special messages may be included, such as holiday greetings, an overdue balance reminder, or payment policy note.

The Timeslips Navigator—with its icon button menu bar and color-coded procedures maps—provides a new interface metaphor that takes "ease-of-use" to an even higher level. It allows the user to quickly access commands and program functions from a graphical format. This means you can click on icons, rather than having to search through menus; quickly perform desired tasks; or move around within the program.

Previously, time and billing procedures were difficult to learn and follow. Now, with the Timeslips Navigator, each step is clearly illustrated. Almost every aspect of office management is virtually effortless. The Timeslips Navigator delivers on the promise of truly automating business procedures—as well as the tasks related to firm management.

The program enhances the user's flexibility in how work can be done. A really flexible aging system means that aging periods can be assigned in one-day increments, up to 250 days. New Canadian GST (Goods and Services Tax) laws are fully supported down to the provincial level. In addition, data entry has been streamlined. Payments and other transactions can now be entered in a batch format. Moreover, instead of having to return to the master client list on the menu bar, you can now enter daily payments and transactions on a single screen.

TAL (Timeslips Accounting Link) extends the power of Timeslips 5.0. It provides customized income reports and links the billing and payment data from Timeslips 5.0 to many accounting software programs. Whether TAL links directly to the accounting program or transactions are posted manually, the Transfer Register report details the account breakdown for each transaction. TAL is available for both Windows and DOS platforms.

Timeslips 5.0 for Windows also seamlessly links with TimeView, Timeslips Corporation's newest DOS program. TimeView is a time management, calendaring, and scheduling program. The two programs work together to perform as a highly efficient, single-entry scheduling and billing system that can cut data entry time by up to 50 percent. Once a billable event has been completed in TimeView, it can be sent directly to Timeslips 5.0 for billing. And when a client, user, or activity is created in one program, the database is automatically updated in the other program.

Combined with clearly written documentation and excellent technical support, Timeslips 5.0 for Windows provides a most comprehensive, yet easy-to-use, time and billing system.

> One should accept the truth from whatever source it proceeds.
>
> Maimonides

Chapter 6

Computerizing Your Business—Choosing the Right Hardware and Operating System

WHY COMPUTERIZE?

Consider your position in regard to the use of computers in your business. You either use them or you don't. If you don't, rest assured that you may eventually face the possibility of losing your business. This is not a baseless threat, but a stark reality. Sooner or later, computerization will be essential to your business's ability to maintain or improve its position in an intensely (and increasingly) competitive market. Computerization can drastically decrease the amount of time required to gather information and put it into an organized, easy-to-read format (i.e., recordkeeping, paper management, and bookkeeping). The result is a quantum increase in readily available information, enabling you to make better-informed decisions and, by quickly pinpointing the sources of existing or potential problems, alerting you to action. However, computerizing your business requires a great deal of forethought and planning. Ill-conceived plans can prove to be very costly in terms of money spent, time invested, and unrealized potential, not to mention the havoc a computerized mess can visit upon a business.

You must commit yourself to the concept of computerization and then enlist your staff (if any) to make the switch to a successful computerized business. The implementation of any computer system will require an initial investment of time to get it "up and running," and the normal daily operation of your business must continue while you are involved in the conversion. There is no particular "good time" to begin the new system, but there are some very bad times, which include your busiest periods as well as holidays. If a company chooses such times, the resultant resentment of staff who would rather be with their families than struggling with the new computer system may be carried over to a generally negative attitude toward the computer system. You simply must make the time to do it. A failure to formulate an implementation strategy has left many businessowners with new computers unused in their offices for months at a time, the packages and boxes still sealed and all well-intentioned efforts frustrated. "We're too busy right now," they say. "We don't have the time." If you are that busy, you may need a computer more than you realize.

When computerizing, it makes sense to automate as many processes as possible in order to use the computer to its fullest potential. As a result, your business will probably encounter some stumbling blocks, because resistance to change has historically been a barrier to progress. However, the initial inconvenience of getting accustomed to new or modified procedures will be more than offset by the long-term benefits derived from computerization. There is also a very real fear of computers among those who have little or no experience with them. This *computerphobia* is sometimes intertwined with the resistance to change.

(Incidently, a computer won't replace a good employee or take anyone's job. But it will give these same people more time to focus on tasks more important than some of the tedious and mundane functions that, although absolutely necessary, are easily automated.) The only answer to this fear is information, persuasion, and hands-on experience. You might keep in mind this acrostic for FEAR—False Evidence Appearing Real.

RESEARCH SOFTWARE BEFORE PURCHASING THE HARDWARE

The first step is to research the software programs available. (You'll find a discussion of the different types of accounting software available in Chapter 7). The *software* is the "brains" of the system, and its selection is the most critical decision to be made in computerizing your business. Shop around. Consult your trade group if one exists for your industry. If you haven't yet found a trade organization, start looking right away. A good place to start is with your neighborhood library. Ask the librarian for assistance; there is an *Encyclopedia of Associations* as well as other reference materials available. Through contacting such an organization you may learn of specific computer systems tailor made for your particular business, which will save a considerable amount of searching. Although your direct competitors will be unlikely to share information with you, perhaps you can locate other businesses like yours in another part of the country. Ask them what they think about the software you are considering or to suggest another software package, even one that you have not yet heard of. It's amazing how honest and forthcoming people will be when asked this type of question.

This phase is an education process, during which you will learn all the facts necessary to make an informed purchase. Ask as many questions as you can. There are innumerable acronyms and buzzwords inside the computer industry, most of which have no meaning to outsiders. If a computer salesperson or consultant talks to you in terms you don't understand, stop the conversation and ask for an explanation. Make that person make it clear to you. Another helpful strategy is to get key people in your business involved in the selection process. Solicit their opinions when evaluating software programs, because they are likely to be the actual operators of the computer. The input of staff members can be invaluable, and their involvement can help alleviate any resistance to, and fear of, computerization. Through their inclusion in the decision-making process, they should gain some of the knowledge required to operate the system chosen.

One of the best ways of selecting the ideal software for your business is to look for software that works closest to the way your business works now. At the same time, keep an eye to the future. Some software features may seem superfluous for the smaller, growing business, and indeed they may be—today. Yet those same features may be invaluable to the business anticipating future expansion. Look for software that you can easily grow into, and not something you'll soon grow out of. Modifiability is an important consideration, and access to source code could prove invaluable. By considering these needs in your buying decision, you can greatly enhance the future usefulness of your computer investment. We will discuss the software packages available to you in detail in the next chapter.

CHOOSING THE RIGHT HARDWARE FOR YOUR NEEDS

Once you have chosen the software package(s) you feel most comfortable with, find the hardware that will allow you to use it. Each software package and its descriptive literature have a section on *minimum hardware requirements*, which enumerates the specifications of the hardware needed for that particular software to operate properly. Don't be alarmed if you don't have any idea what it says. Simply show it to the salesperson at the computer sales facility, and you will be directed to the correct hardware. Usually, each computer has a features list that you can check the software requirements against. A choice of operating system will have to be made prior to purchasing your computer. Most PCs operate under MS-DOS and Windows under that system, or under OS/2. The UNIX operating system will require other hardware, and the Apple Macintosh will run System 7 software. Operating systems are discussed in a later section of this chapter.

Once you know what kind of hardware you need, you'll have to determine how much you need. The size of your business should dictate how many people will operate the computer (single-user or multiuser), which in turn should indicate how many terminals (or work stations) will be required. The minimum single-user hardware setup will consist of the computer (known as the CPU or *central processing unit*, also referred to as the *box*), the *keyboard*, the *display monitor*, and a *printer*. Here too, shopping around can save you money. Look closely at the warranties and note the locations of service outlets. If your hardware fails, where can you get it fixed? Many dealerships are authorized service locations as well. If your computer store is not one of these, find out where the nearest service center is. Prices fluctuate a great deal. Shop the advertisements in the computer magazines (available at most newsstands and computer stores) and check the prices of the large reputable mail-order computer dealers. Computer superstores that have their own service departments have contributed to driving prices down and offer a large selection. Do not overlook the smaller computer stores, especially those that have been recommended by knowledgeable friends.

WHAT TO LOOK FOR WHEN BUYING YOUR IDEAL COMPUTER SYSTEM

The PC that you purchase for your business today will have to see you through the next three to five years. Therefore, you want a system that meets your current needs but can also handle your future expectations. Although the perfect computer for your business depends on many factors, the following suggestions for the ultimate small business computer will aim you in the right direction. Keep in mind, while reading this book, that there is an approximate one-year process of writing and publishing a book. It is for this reason that prices are not given for particular hardware systems, inasmuch as the trend has been rapid price reduction and more features for less cost. It has been said that if the automobile industry had experienced the same price-value compression that has been true of the computer industry, you would be able to buy a new midrange automobile for about $29.95. Think back to the days, not so long ago, when computers were housed in glass-cnclosed, temperature-controlled rooms and cost millions of dollars. The computing power of those machines was equal to or less than today's PCs selling for a few thousand dollars.

Rather than specifying a real-life computer system by brand name and model number, I'll describe the basic features that are all available. Whatever your dream machine, it takes the right information and some effective shopping to turn your imagination into reality.

Easy Expansion and Space-Saving Design

Although it sports about the same number of expansion slots as a desktop computer (seven or eight), a *minitower* or *tower* usually offers a few more front-accessible drive bays for easy access when installing peripherals such as CD-ROMs. About $150 more than the price of desktop buys a system that provides somewhat more convenient access to internal slots and system memory. Because it sits on the floor, a minitower is a natural for those with limited desk space.

High-Speed Processing

Go for one of the highest-performance processors, the 66-MHz 486DX2. For the budget minded, one 33-MHz 486DX system, which costs $500 to $1,000 less than a DX2/66, is at the entry level for comfortably running everything from Windows-based word processors to graphics programs and spreadsheets. Unlike Intel's lower-end 486SX chip, all 486DX and 486DX2 chips have built-in math coprocessors, making them a better choice for accounting systems and other number crunchers.

Future Features

Don't consider a system that will not let you upgrade to a faster processor. Look for a PC with an Intel OverDrive Processor socket.

Plugging Intel's forthcoming Pentium Processor OverDrive chip into that socket will likely boost the performance of a 486DX2/66 system by 40 to 70 percent.

Sweet, Sweet Memory

Having too little *system memory* (RAM) will only get more frustrating as more software advances are made over the next few years. More systems—even notebooks—come with a minimum of 8 MB of RAM. You'll work most efficiently under Windows with 16 MB (about $300 to $400 more up front than you'll pay for 8 MB). Prepare yourself for the future's sound and video-laden software by ensuring that total RAM is expandable to at least 32 MB.

Performance Booster

Instead of taking a slow boat to system memory, a RAM cache picks up the tempo by storing and promptly delivering the data and instructions that applications will likely need next. The 486DX processor family is built with only 8 K of internal cache; to really have an impact on performance, get an extra 256 K *external cache* (about $100).

Backward Compatibility

Just about every PC comes with a high-density, 1.44-MB, 3.5-inch *floppy drive*, and almost every program comes shipped in that format. But if you have disks in the older 5.25-inch format, or expect to receive some from clients or suppliers, spend the extra $80 or so for a 1.2-MB, 5.25-inch drive too.

Expansion Room

With Windows applications taking upwards of 20 MB of space on your hard disk, don't dare to skimp on storage size—in fact, a 200-MB IDE (integrated drive electronics, the current standard for small business use) drive is the smallest recommended and a 340-MB IDE is better yet. Performance is also important. You'll see systems vendors quoting seek times between 10 and 15 milliseconds (ms); in general, the lower the number, the faster the drive. Expect to pay about $110 more for a 13-ms, 340-MB IDE hard disk than for a 200 MB drive. (The definition of millisecond is that amount of time between a New York traffic signal changing to green and the first horn blast from a taxicab driver).

Raising the Speed Limit

A VESA (*Video Electronics Standards Association*) VL-Bus local bus means life in the fast lane, not an alternative to car pooling. System information, to get to and from the processor, rides hardware known as an expansion bus—usually the ISA (*Industry Standard Architecture*) bus. Regardless of your processor's clock speed—whether it's 15 MHz or 66 MHz—the ISA bus transfers information at only 8 MHz, a snail's pace compared with the VESA VL-Bus, which runs up to five times faster. A VL-Bus system supports up to three local bus slots; cards that sit in these slots, such as video cards or hard-disk controllers, perform at peak levels. (VESA local bus systems also include standard ISA bus slots.) VL-Bus is the current industry standard, and there are many VL-Bus peripherals on the market. Clock speed is analogous to the RPMs of an engine. Many ISA systems allow you to adjust the clock speed of their expansion buses so you can eke the most performance from your expansion boards. Higher speeds (lower divisors) can deliver more performance, but rates above 12 MHx may sacrifice reliability. In binary synchronous communication, the computer uses the clock pulses to control synchronization of data and control characters.

Video Capabilities

Your *system processor* is a very busy chip, especially under Windows, and anything that can take over some of its responsibilities will improve performance. Video cards fitted with an *accelerator chip* (such as S3's or 86C928 or ATI's Mach 32 chips) are speed boosters; they take some of the processing burden off the CPU by handling common graphics functions, such as line draws and area fills. In addition, an *accelerator card* that uses VRAM is typically faster than one that uses DRAM. The amount of RAM on the video card affects the number of colors it displays on-screen at various resolutions. One megabyte is usually a good choice, letting you display 65,000 colors in Super VGA (800 by 600) resolution and 256 colors at 1,024 by 768 resolution. For such a card, expect to pay between $150 and $400.

Clear Windows

To make the most of Windows, a *monitor* with a flat-square screen and a 0.28-mm dot pitch provides some of the sharpest images available. Look for a 15-inch monitor ($500 to $750) that provides an 800 by 600 resolution under Windows (so that you can display more information on-screen) at refresh rates of 72 Hz or higher to reduce flicker. Also be sure to get a monitor that meets the Swedish MPR II specifications, which limit harmful emissions.

Multimedia

To take advantage of multimedia and the increasing number of business applications on *CD-ROM*, a CD-ROM drive is a smart investment. On the high end, a fast, double-speed drive that operates at 300 K per second sells for about $450. Not surprisingly, the older, single-speed (150 K) drive is nearly half the price. Look for a drive with an average *access time* of less than 350 ms. Desktop publishers, in particular, might look for a drive that reads multisession Kodak photo CDs.

Stereo Sound

To attach voice notes to spreadsheet cells or to add music to your presentations, you will need a *sound card*, a basic microphone ($15), and speakers ($30). It makes sense to choose a 16-bit sound card ($250 to $350) for its superior CD-quality audio.

Data Protection

A hard-disk crash can be scary, but you will be safe if you have backed up your data. A tape drive stores data on a cassette, instead of on a large number of floppies. A good choice is a quarter-inch drive ($250) that uses DC-2000 minicartridges, storing up to 250 MB.

On-Line Services

Prices for high-speed fax/modems are falling fast. For brisk communications and fast downloads, select an internal error-correcting and data-compressing 14,400-bps V.32 bis fax/modem ($225 to $400). Note that fax transmission is usually conducted at 9600 bps, even on 14,400 bps devices, because that's the rate at which most fax devices receive.

Ergonomics

For working in Windows, nothing feels better than an ergonomic mouse that's shaped to fit a cupped human hand. Some manufacturers offer this type with their systems; if the one you have selected does not, you can purchase such a mouse for approximately $100 to $150.

CHOOSING BETWEEN IBM-COMPATIBLE PCS AND MACINTOSH COMPUTERS

Today, with the wide availability of low-cost PC compatibles, coupled with the emergence of Microsoft Windows as the de facto standard, many small business computer buyers are confused. The major selling point for Macintosh was the graphical user interface, but with Windows, both Macintosh computers and PCs now offer one.

Why buy a Macintosh? According to Apple Computer, the developer and manufacturer of Macintosh, the short answer is this: People prefer Macintosh, are more productive with Macintosh, and are more satisfied with Macintosh. Apple believes that there are a number of reasons and specific cases in which Macintosh would prevail.

The cold facts simply do not support Apple's claims, because the reality is that IBM-compatibles comprise more than 85 percent of the computer population. Many more applications are available for PCs than for Macintosh.

According to independent studies commissioned by Apple Computer, Inc., a claim is made that people prefer Macintosh and feel they accomplish more with it.

When people who use both Macintosh and Windows systems were surveyed in June 1992 by Evans Research, Macintosh was preferred by nearly two out of three people. A wide variety of people who use both systems were surveyed: MIS managers, users in small and large businesses, and home users. In every category, people preferred Macintosh by a margin of almost two to one.

June 1992 study conducted by Evans Research Associates.

In addition, when asked on which system they feel they accomplish more for the time and effort spent, a clear majority of people said Macintosh. People who use both Macintosh and DOS without Windows also preferred Macintosh and said that they accomplished more with Macintosh, by an even wider margin.

That certainly sounds impressive. But look into the composition of the group surveyed. The universe sampled for the survey is composed of users of both PCs with Windows and Macintosh. Inasmuch as only 15 percent of the computer population uses the Macintosh and a smaller and undetermined number of that 15 percent use both computers, we are dealing with a very small segment of the total computer-user population, and probably not the average users because the typical user has one computer rather than both. The user who has both computers and uses both is probably fairly specialized, having gotten the Macintosh primarily for the graphics and the PC for the vastly greater availability of software.

A user satisfaction survey in the personal computer industry was conducted by the prestigious J.D. Power and Associates (of automobile research fame) for two years. In both years, it ranked Apple highest among personal computer companies in overall customer satisfaction.

This is all fine, but, pardon the expression, we're comparing apples to PCs. Although Macintosh users were quite satisfied with their computers, the results do not reflect the almost seven-fold number of PC users who were not sampled in the survey. (In the J.D. Power and Associates 1991 and 1992 Computer End User Satisfaction Studies, the 1992 study was conducted over only 2,555 business end users at 1,145 business sites.) You must decide which system will use the operating system and software programs in a way best suited to your needs. The following discussions on both operating systems and software should help you in making that decision.

After reviewing what independent research firms have said about using the Macintosh, it is apparent that there might be advantages to choosing Macintosh over a lower-cost PC running Microsoft Windows in your particular business. But don't just take someone's word for it. Investigate. Visit some computer dealers. Try a hands-on approach with various Macintoshes and IBM-compatible PC running Windows, and make some comparisons for yourself. Once you've actually experienced the difference, you can make your own decision.

OPERATING SYSTEMS

Disk operating system, or DOS, is a software program necessary to translate your commands to make your computer perform specific tasks. All personal computers need one. An operating system does three basic things:

1. It allows you to communicate with your *peripheral devices* (such as your printer, monitor, and hard drive).
2. It allows you to execute your software programs.
3. It allows you to store and retrieve information on your hard and floppy disks.

Without an operating system to manage your peripherals, programs, and data, your computer can't understand you. "Without an operating system, you would absolutely have to be able to program [in order] to talk to your computer," said Eric Straub, program manager at Microsoft Corporation. In the early days of microcomputers, a programmer had to write a program for each job she or he wanted the computer to perform—to solve a complex mathematical equation, for example. And those computers were not *interactive*, meaning that they couldn't react immediately to instructions. As a result, programmers sent their instruction messages to the computer on hole-punched cards or paper tape. The holes were punched in a code, or *programming language*, that the computer could understand.

The History of Operating Systems

One of the earliest true personal computers was released in 1975. It was called the *Altair*. It didn't have an operating system, but electronics hobbyists loved it. Bill Gates and Paul Allen, of Microsoft Corporation, were commissioned to write a computer language for the Altair. First, they wrote a language called *BASIC*, which they loaded into the computer from paper tape. The BASIC language was not an operating system but a language that could be used to create an operating system. When the Altair acquired a floppy disk drive, Gates and Allen wrote a disk-based version of BASIC, which they loaded into the computer from a floppy disk. It was the first computer language for a commercial computer with a floppy disk. That was in 1976.

Throughout the mid to late 1970s, an operating system called *CP/M* grew to be the standard for small computers. Many hardware and software companies developed products based on this system, and many of the original computer aficionados still speak affectionately of CP/M.

In 1980, International Business Machines Corporation (IBM), a company famous for its electric typewriters as well as its mainframe computers, decided it was time to build a personal computer. IBM asked Microsoft to write an operating system for its proposed machine. Microsoft and Seattle Computer Products collaborated to develop such an operating system. In 1981 the first version of *PC-DOS* was released with the first IBM-PC.

When DOS is discussed, don't be confused by the terms MS-DOS and PC-DOS. MS-DOS and PC-DOS are virtually the same product, developed jointly by IBM and Microsoft but marketed separately. Microsoft sells MS-DOS and IBM sells PC-DOS, just as Del Monte and Chiquita both sell pineapples—the product is the same no matter what its brand. Despite a few cosmetic differences, for the end user MS-DOS and PC-DOS are virtually identical.

Other operating systems exist, but DOS has become the standard operating system for IBM-compatible machines. More than 70 million PCs around the world have installed DOS as an operating system. Although it's not the most powerful operating system (and power computer users sometimes complain), DOS dominates for two reasons: First, after the success of the IBM machine, other computer manufacturers began building *IBM clones* (computers that closely resembled the IBM-PC), and these clones all used DOS as an operating system. Second, software companies realized that if they wanted to make money, they should write their programs for all the computers outfitted with this operating system.

Anyone with an IBM or compatible computer can use DOS. This system is inexpensive, it doesn't take up much memory space, and it doesn't have a lot of hardware requirements. Survival of the fittest is not always a matter of power; it's often a matter of convenience.

Operating System Versions

DOS has gone through a number of *versions*, or changes, since its introduction in 1981. Every time DOS software changes, it gets a new *version number*. The first version was 1.00. The most common version of DOS today is 6.2.

Software programs are like books. They need to be updated from time to time. Each "edition" or version of a software program also receives a version number. Software version numbers have two parts, the major revision number and the minor revision number. The *major revision number*, to the left of the decimal point, indicates a major change in the program. The *minor revision number*, on the right side of the decimal point, indicates only minor changes. It's simple to find out which version of DOS your computer is using. Just follow these steps:

- Begin at any DOS prompt. If you have a hard disk, go to the C prompt. (It looks like this: C).
- Type *VER*. This is called the VER command (for VERsion). The command will look like this: Cver.
- Press the ENTER key.

You'll receive a message such as "MS-DOS Version 6.2," and you'll be back at the C prompt (C). You can also perform the VER command on a disk in your floppy disk drive. It should look like this: Aver.

The Development of the Hard Disk

Before the release of Version 2.0 in 1983, DOS had no concept of a *fixed disk*, which is a fancy name for *hard disk*. You had to *boot*, or start, your computer with DOS on a floppy disk every time the computer was started. An analogy is the use of a hand crank before the advent of starters in automobiles.

Directories Let the User Sort Files

DOS 2.0 also introduced the concept of *hierarchial directories*. Hierarchial directories are logical divisions on a disk that allow you to group the files on your computer, similar to the way you sort your papers into separate file folders in a filing cabinet. The directories are called "hierarchial" because there's one *master directory* at the top that contains all the other directories. These other directories, in turn, can contain directories as well as files. You can move files among directories, and you can create and remove directories. This hierarchial structure is called a *tree structure* because it looks like an upside down tree, or like a family tree. That is why the top level directory, the master directory, is called the *root directory*.

In DOS 2.0, the DIR command became meaningful. In the original version of the operating system, you could type the DIR command and you would see a simple list of files. Starting with DOS 2.0, typing DIR at the C prompt displayed directories as well as files. The command also began displaying the volume label of a disk and the amount of space remaining on the disk.

New DOS Commands Add Versatility

New commands in DOS 2.0 included BACKUP and RESTORE. With BACKUP you could make a copy of the information on your hard disk. Then, if you somehow lost the information on your hard disk, you could use RESTORE to return the data to your hard disk. Before version 2.0, you had to use the COPY command to make more backups. You copied your data from one floppy disk to another.

Another new command was CLS. This command clears the screen and gives you a fresh start at your DOS prompt. Before this command was available, you simply couldn't clear your screen. The CLS command was evidence that DOS was growing to be less and less of a "programmer's only" operating system. FDISK, yet another new command, allows you to partition your hard disk. To *partition* a hard disk is to divide it into sections. Experienced users sometimes partition their disks in order to install different operating systems in each section.

Networking and Expanded Memories Offer More Power

The possibilities of networking arrived with version 3.0 in 1984. Then in 1988 came version 4.0, which was the first version of DOS to offer a graphic, menu-based shell. A shell provides an alternative way to use your operating system. At the C prompt, you can type a command and go to a new screen with a menu at the top. You can select commands from the menu to do such things as copy files and format disks. You can still type commands at the DOS prompt, but the shell is supposed to make things easier. The most important changes in DOS 4.0 had to do with memory management. DOS has a problem with memory, in that DOS can recognize only 640 kilobytes of *random-access memory*, or RAM. RAM is the temporary memory space that DOS uses to process software program instructions and user input. Users were complaining because they wanted to use larger and more sophisticated software programs that needed more than 640 KB of RAM.

In version 4.0, DOS was improved so it could emulate what is called *expanded memory*. Expanded memory is additional random-access memory. The newer features gave more power to users who owned computers based on the 80386 microprocessor. Users could then install additional memory in their computers, and DOS would perform memory swapping in order to access this expanded memory.

Microsoft DOS 6.2 comes with advanced memory management and new Windows utilities. DOS 6.2 is clearly tailored for the Windows market, with memory management features optimized for Windows and other Windows utilities to help optimize and manage the system. Its EMM 386.EXE memory manager, for example, can recover up to 200 KB of upper memory automatically. It also allocates XMS and EMS memory from a shared pool, which enables you to run applications requiring either type of memory without configuration changes having to involve CONFIG.SYS.

If you're a typical user of the Microsoft Windows operating system, chances are that your computer's hard disk is full or rapidly getting to that point. In one sense, that's a good sign: your computer's duties are growing, helping you work more efficiently. But meanwhile, you're faced with a pressing concern, how to increase your computer's storage capacity.

The Microsoft MS-DOS 6.2 operating system addresses hard-disk storage problems, and much more, through a series of safe, easy-to-use features that make the product essential for users of Windows. *Integrated disk compression* in the system can increase your computer's hard disk capacity by as much as two times (depending on your computer's configuration), creating more space for Windows-based applications.

A full hard disk is a sign that you're demanding more from your computer. Most likely, you've added applications, possibly spreadsheets and work processing programs, which require a lot of disk space. Easy-to-use features in MS-DOS 6.2, such as integrated disk compression, let you optimize disk storage whether you're a beginner or a power user.

DOS has an extremely large base of applications that millions of users depend on, and the fact is that those of us with IBM-compatible computers didn't have much choice of an operating system until the advent of IBM's OS/2 operating system.

OS/2 Offers Multitasking with Virtual Memory

IBM Corporation's *OS/2* 2.1 is a true preemptive multitasking operating system with virtual memory. Its design, which is a 32-bit extension of the original OS/2 1.0 design, is far more sophisticated than that of DOS. It also provides advanced features for Windows applications, such as application isolation, overlapped I/O, paged virtual memory, and multiple *virtual DOS machine* (VDM) support.

Application isolation is a function of OS/2's protected memory design, in which each program in the system executes in a special memory address space. This prevents one program from inadvertently accessing memory belonging to another. Because Windows programs were not designed to work this way, by default, OS/2 has all Windows programs share a single address space provided by a single instance of a VDM. However, it offers an option that allows you to get around this problem in a way that Windows 3.1 and Windows NT do not.

OS/2 can run each Windows program in a separate VDM, effectively isolating it from interference from any other program (and preventing it from interfering with any other program). The overhead required to use separate VDMs for each application will eat up system memory and slow down performance, but the ability to run each Windows program in its own address space makes OS/2 a superior platform for mission-critical work.

Preemptive multitasking allows the OS/2 operating system to allocate time to applications, rather than having applications allocate time to each other. That means that programs that get stuck won't take over the computer, because the operating system is always in control. It also provides a way to ensure that time-sensitive programs are allocated the time that they require.

Pentium and Power PC-Based Computers Offer Speed—The Future of Operating Systems

You should now be able to buy a PowerPC-based computer that will run Windows software as fast as a 486PC, Mac software as fast as a Quadra 700, and native Unix software as fast as a Sun SparcStation 10. The high-speed RISC (Reduced Instruction-Set Computing) chips, system software, and breakthroughs in emulation technology that make this possible are coalescing under an umbrella known as the *PowerOpen Environment*. The ambitious goal of PowerOpen is to support a scalable PowerPC-based platform that lets users choose from several different libraries of applications software running with the most popular user interfaces.

Announced in 1991 by IBM, Motorola, and Apple, PowerOpen is in the hands of the PowerOpen Association (Billerica, Massachusetts), an independent corporation whose founding members also

149

include Groupe Bull, Thomson-CSF, Harris, and Tadpole Technology. The seven founders are recruiting additional members, who together will promote PowerOpen and guide its future evolution. You won't actually be able to buy a product called PowerOpen; this is a term designating the compliant operating systems sold by the members of the association.

A microprocessor embodies the underlying design philosophy and capabilities of the PowerOpen architecture. The architecture includes such design decisions as the number and size of the instruction registers, the manner in which instructions and data are moved to and from memory, whether floating-point numbers are a standard data type, and so on. The architecture is the ultimate determinant of the microprocessor's capabilities—and how fast it performs those capabilities. CISC and RISC represent two different microprocessor architectures, and thus two different sets of capabilities. The history of these architectures provides a foundation for examining the pros and cons of Pentium and PowerPC.

CISC stands for *complex instruction set computing.* All of today's personal computers are built on CISC microprocessors. To understand why CISC architectures rose to prominence in the 1970s, we need to look at the market conditions that prevailed then. Current CISC architectures were originally developed in the 1960s and 1970s, when a typical computer's available random-access memory was both limited and expensive. Many of the processor design decisions made at the time were based on minimizing program memory requirements. One way to reduce these requirements was to simplify software as much as possible by building more complexity into the processor. Although increasing the complexity of the processor had a negative impact on processor performance, this trade-off was reasonable at the time. After all, it didn't matter how fast a processor could run if there wasn't enough memory left to load data and run programs.

As the price and availability of random-access memory improved dramatically during the 1980s and into the 1990s, processor designers reexamined performance and complexity trade-offs. An architecture that made sense in the 1970s, when a computer might have only 16 or 32 kilobytes of memory, was not necessarily an optimal architecture in the 1990s. An optimal architecture today is RISC (*reduced instruction set computing*), which takes advantage of the 4 to 8 megabytes of memory that are now standard in most personal computers.

The goal of a RISC architecture is to enable instructions to be executed as fast as possible. One way to accomplish this goal is to simplify the type of instructions the processor executes. The shorter and simpler "reduced" instructions of a RISC processor can run faster than the longer and more complex instructions of a CISC processor. RISC architectures enable higher performance through the use of pipelining and superscalar execution, techniques that allow more than one instruction to be executed at a time. This design requires more money and more advanced compiler technology.

By the mid-1980s, RISC processors were commonly used in high-performance work stations, in which the cost of memory was not an important issue. Now, in the 1990s, memory is quite affordable and advanced compilers are common, so high-performance RISC processors make sense for personal computers.

The largest computer manufacturers in the world (including Cray, IBM, Digital Equipment, Hewlett-Packard, Apple, and Sun), in all categories of computing—supercomputers, mainframes, minicomputers, work stations, and personal computers—have made a commitment to RISC, despite the fact that they have all risen to their current positions by making and selling CISC-based computers.

In comparing CISC and RISC chips, two key features illustrate their differences:

Speed. In general, RISC chips use pipelines to execute instructions that have been broken into segments of equal length. The pipelines process these instructions in stages, which allows RISC chips to process information at a faster rate than CISC chips. Although some recent CISC processors include pipelines, a RISC architecture is better suited to pipelining techniques because of its simpler, fixed-length instructions. This faster processing speed is one of the main reasons that RISC chips are used in most servers and work stations, where computation rates are of primary importance.

Number of transistors. For a given level of performance, CISC microprocessors typically have a higher transistor count than RISC processors. A higher number of transistors will generally translate to a larger die size and higher thermal output. Die size directly affects the cost of producing a microprocessor, and higher thermal output can necessitate special additions to the computer. Systems based on large chips, such as Pentium, may require complex heat sinks or cooling fans, thus increasing costs.

The architectures of the Pentium and PowerPC microprocessors are fundamentally different—Pentium is based on a CISC architecture, whereas PowerPC is a RISC architecture. Pentium is the most recent implementation of Intel's 80 × 86 CISC-based processors, which evolved indirectly from the simple 4004 calculator chip in the early 1970s.* The foundation for the Intel 80 × 86 architecture was set in place by the 8080 chip more than 20 years ago, in 1972. And the follow-on 8086 chip provided the blueprint for the 80 × 86 architecture. The architecture has expanded since then, but for Intel to maintain complete backward compatibility with older 80 × 86 software, the basic 80 × 86 architecture must remain unchanged.

Paradoxically, the feature that seems to give Pentium an advantage in the market is also the key to many of its weaknesses. Because Pentium must maintain complete register-level compatibility with all previous 80 × 86 processors, Intel must work within the restrictions of this older design. Although current and future-generation RISC processors can incorporate the many architectural and design advances made over the last 15 years, Intel—because it must continue to support the 80 × 86 architecture—may be limited in the number of advances it can incorporate into Pentium and follow-on processors. This has not yet been a significant competitive weakness, but the compatibility requirement may make it difficult for Intel to keep up with the performance of current and future RISC competitors.

PowerPC, a RISC architecture, incorporates technology developed in the 1980s and 1990s. The IBM POWER (Performance Optimization with Enhanced RISC) architecture that forms the basis

---

*(Fulcher, John. *An Introduction to Microcomputer Systems: Architecture and Interfacing*, Sydney, Australia: Addison-Wesley Publishing, 1989, pages 64–65).

for the PowerPC chip takes advantage of modern implementation techniques, such as superscalar execution and deep pipelining, to increase performance. And it uses such RISC architectural features as fixed-length instructions, large register sets, and a minimal number of memory addressing modes.

The POWER architecture was specifically designed for use in high-performance computers, such as high-end work stations and servers. PowerPC is a cost-reduced adoption of this architecture, developed jointly by Apple, IBM, and Motorola. PowerPC was designed for use in desktop computers, servers, and notebook computers.

SUMMARY

Now that you know the basics of computer hardware, it's time to decide on what software packages will best suit your needs. The next chapter is dedicated to the types of software available to the self-employed. Keep in mind that you should obtain all the information that you can from both software and hardware manufacturers before deciding on any one product. This book is designed as a guide to what is available to the self-employed. Space and time limit us from going into great detail about every hardware and software product. Shop around and get as much information as you can before making your purchase.

> If you are going to do something
> wrong, at least enjoy it.
>
> Yiddish Folk Saying

Chapter 7

Deciding What Software Programs Are Right for You

We begin this chapter with a discussion of the accounting software available to small businessowners, but accounting is only one aspect of recordkeeping. Word processors, databases, spreadsheets, and all sorts of graphics can aid you in managing the financial and clerical aspects of your business. We will discuss these programs in greater detail at the end of the chapter.

THE BENEFITS OF A COMPUTERIZED ACCOUNTING SYSTEM

Now that you know why it's important to computerize your business, we can look at the types of accounting software that will best meet your needs.

There is probably no area of greater confusion to the self-employed businessperson than the true costs and benefits of installing and using a computerized accounting system. Such business-owners frequently have an inflated picture of the benefits of computerized accounting and an incomplete understanding of the costs. Some computer resellers and systems installers are unwilling to point out these conceptual errors, which often results in some unpleasant surprises and bad feelings.

First and foremost, computerized accounting is *not* simpler than manual accounting. Even the very best accounting system will not magically convert a clerk into a bookkeeper. In fact, many full-charge bookkeepers insist that computerized accounting requires sharper bookkeeping skills than a manual system. Manual systems generally break tasks down into simple steps. Errors are not automatically carried into other accounts. Second, if you are going to bring your accounting in-house, you need to realize that a computerized accounting system is not going to straighten out a manual accounting mess. Small, rapidly growing businesses, faced with limited capital and cramped cash flows, often put off establishing proper accounting procedures until a sunnier day. A manual accounting system verging on a bad dream can become an almost impossible nightmare when computerized. To "go onto" a computerized accounting system, your books have to be in perfect order. Accounts receivable and payable have to be exact and up-to-date, and beginning balances must be accurate.

Moreover, where staff is already stretched, part-time help may be required, because the two systems should be run in parallel for at least two months. In this way, mistakes are more easily caught and corrected and the business need not rely on the new system to provide accurate data. Your staff simply must have time to learn the new system. Expect three to six months to return to earlier efficiency.

The system you purchase will not do everything exactly as you want it. Some modifications may be needed to produce the output you need; these won't be free. Plan on involving an accountant in this task. Don't expect the package seller to provide advice only an accountant should provide. And some tasks simply do not lend themselves to easy, efficient transfer to computers. Computers are only tools.

Finally, let's look at the support issue squarely. Support includes all the services necessary to get and keep your computer system up and running and as productive as possible. These services include instruction, education and maintenance both under warranty and other. Some resellers include preventive maintenance to service your computer before it stops working. The accounting package reseller probably captures a gross margin of 20 percent to 40 percent of the accounting package retail price. Out of that margin, sales commissions and all overhead expenses must be paid. Most support requires not only a thorough knowledge of the package, but a sound grounding in standard accounting procedures. Well-trained and equipped support personnel normally need to charge at least $60 to $75 per hour to make a reasonable profit. Therefore, on average, one should probably not expect more than one hour of qualified support "free" for each $1,000 of purchase price. Free, unqualified support generally costs you more than you can afford.

If you've read this far, you may begin to wonder, "Why bother?" The answer is that there are some very substantial benefits to a well designed and implemented accounting system. Computerized systems can provide more data, more quickly, and in more flexible formats than could possibly be handled by a manual system. Long-term benefits can substantially outweigh the costs.

A good accounting system should allow you to call for interim financial statements and reports, virtually on a moment's notice. Month-end financial reports and other reports should appear near the beginning of the very next month; not two months later. Dated information is good for tax returns, but little else. Current data is needed to run today's business successfully. The well-known author Tom Peters emphasizes the necessity for such change in his bestseller, *Thriving on Chaos* by Tom Peters and published in 1987 by Alfred A. Knopf, Inc. The importance of timely information simply cannot be overvalued—its lack can easily cause a business's demise.

Customer service can often be improved as a result of computerizing a business. If a customer's request can be handled immediately with the help of a good computer system, two benefits accrue. Time is saved by the staff person in handling the request, and the customer's satisfaction is increased.

Repetitive tasks can often be reduced or eliminated. Valued staff members can devote more time to tasks requiring their imagination and intelligence. When a computerized accounting system has been properly installed and the staff properly trained, this valuable tool can provide increased profits and improved morale for years to come.

Most self-employed businessowners, even those with little ac- counting knowledge, will find that they can use these accounting software packages with DOS, Windows, or Macintosh. The software is categorized as *low-end accounting packages*, as they are designed for accounting novices and yet are robust enough to handle the accounting needs of most small businesses. Still, you may choose to have an accountant help you set up the program.

As for *high-end accounting packages* (retailing for $500 or more per module), these are designed primarily for businesses that need more specific and specialized reports, such as inventory turn by item or group of items; gross profit by inventory item and by customer; the number of times a customer has been charged finance charges; amount of payable discounts taken and discounts lost; and so on.

Self-employed businessowners do not find large-scale financial statements necessary nor do they require an outsider to write their checks. What they do need is a monthly profit/loss statement. This report is a vital tool in determining ongoing financial and operating conditions. It is important to include percentages in all categories to ensure the clarity and meaningfulness of the statement.

Your accounting records should keep you informed of your business's financial situation at any given time—particularly to warn of impending danger. With adequate records you can detect trouble before an irreversible point is reached.

A monthly balance sheet is a necessity—a list of assets, liabilities, and net worth—to preclude the practice of making decisions based solely on how much cash is in the bank on a given day.

In addition, a detailed general ledger that itemizes all expenses listed in the operating statement is important. Bank reconciliations, payroll records, and a record of tax returns filed when due will all contribute to your business intelligence.

Numerous government studies have pointed to financial misman- agement as the most pervasive reason for small-business failure. Accordingly, be keenly aware of the need for accurate and timely financial data.

The programs profiled in detail are extremely flexible and adapt readily to virtually any kind of small or large business. They're designed to arrange accepted, double-entry accounting information into easy-to-comprehend, management-oriented financial reports that you can use to enhance the profitability of your business.

CRITERIA FOR EVALUATING A SMALL BUSINESS COMPUTERIZED ACCOUNTING SYSTEM

Any software should offer the small businessowner increased efficiency and profit. But if the businessowner can't understand how to use the program, all the claims are wasted. Accounting software should meet the following criteria:

1. *Can you understand the system?* This should be your number one test. If you can't understand it, you won't get any of the potential benefits of even the best accounting software.

2. *How much time does it take to enter data?* Do you have to enter any item more than once? Do you have to do any task as tedious as keeping card files on paper or adding long columns of figures? A businessowner's time is too valuable to waste on this kind of work.

3. *Do you get enough useful information?* A good accounting system should work for you, not just for the tax collector. "Good" means that your system not only tells you how much you're making and spending, but also gives you the reasons. However, too much information is as bad as too little, because you won't be able to find the precious nuggets amid all the clutter.

4. *Is the software the right fit?* An accounting system that fits, feels comfortable. Don't get one that is either too large or too small for your needs (allowing for some anticipated expansion).

Use the following guidelines when selecting an accounting system:

1. *Understand the system.* Be sure you understand an accounting program's language before you make a commitment. No matter how highly praised (and richly featured) an accounting program is, you won't get anything out of it unless it speaks the same language you speak.

2. *Start simple—save time.* Nothing is more frustrating than struggling with a system that's just too big for your business. After you've run an easy system for a while, you'll know a lot more about what information you need. You'll also know what types of tasks to automate and what types are easier to do by hand or in some other program, or to farm out. For example, you might find it easier to print invoices from a word processing program than to run complicated accounting software.

3. *Plan ahead.* Think about what information you need—not just to get your tax forms filled out correctly (although that is a first step), but also to chart the future course of your business. Think about whether you might want to organize that information by client, job, region, or property.

4. *Communicate.* Find an accountant you can talk to. The right accountant can help you with many difficulties and technical matters while you manage the recordkeeping on everything else. This can save you the expense of paying a bookkeeper and can give you valuable insight into the financial health of your business. It is strongly recommended that you do the computerized accounting yourself until your business reaches the point when this activity can be delegated.

5. *Get help.* If you really hate keeping the books or find that your time is more profitably spent doing something else, by all means disregard the previous recommendation. You can send the books out to a service or hire a part-timer to enter the data. That way, you'll have up-to-the-minute information without doing something you hate.

6. *Reassess your needs.* Once you have a system that works, keep looking for ways to cut time and improve information. And remember, keep checking for size. If your business is as success-

ful as you want it to be, sooner or later you're going to outgrow today's perfect fit.

ACCOUNTING SOFTWARE AVAILABLE

The accounting software programs that follow have been designed for self-employed businesspeople who have little knowledge of accounting. Each program will handle the most basic accounting needs, such as:

1. General ledger (a listing of the activities for a particular business for a particular accounting period);
2. Accounts payable (the people you owe money to); and
3. Accounts receivable (the people who owe you money).

To that end, they all generate basic financial reports, such as a balance sheet, income statements, and a trial balance. With any of the products included here, it's possible to keep track of the money flowing in and out of your business.

Because these accounting software products are designed for nonaccounting experts, ease of use is key. Many software programs were evaluated and not included in this book because among other factors, user interface was found to be lacking. User interface is a connection between two elements—computer and user—for example. In relation to software it is the manner in which a user enters commands to use the program. Because all the packages conform to DOS, Windows, or Macintosh interface standards, they're all easy to use when compared with character-based accounting systems. You'll be able to find your way around these programs with little effort. Credit the *graphical user interface* (GUI) for that. In these programs, forms look like forms and checks look like checks, so it's much easier to know where to enter information.

One often-overlooked feature is the ability to import data from Intuit's Quicken. Millions of people are using Quicken, and many would like to move on to a more full-featured accounting program.

Unfortunately, some Quicken users will not be able to take their historical accounting data with them, although more software producers plan to have future releases that will enable users to import Quicken data.

Each product offers its own unique features, which makes it hard to say which program is best. They all do the job, although some do it more thoroughly. Some are relatively easy to master, but such ease of use comes at a price. The easier-to-use often offer fewer features than those slightly harder to learn.

All of the accounting software systems analyzed have manuals written in simple English and well organized. (Some include too much accounting jargon.) With each program, someone with virtually no knowledge of accounting has a good chance of understanding how to set up and use the system. If one or more of these programs intrigue you, please write to the listed manufacturer for more information.

CA-Simply Accounting (Version 2.0 reviewed)

Published by: COMPUTER ASSOCIATES INTERNATIONAL, INC.
One Computer Associates Plaza
Islandia, NY 11788-7000
(800) 225-5224 (516) 342-5224

The CA-Simply Accounting (for Windows, DOS, OS/2, and the Macintosh) is an easy-to-use, graphically oriented member of the market-leading Computer Associates family of Accounting Software (ACCPAC). It includes General Ledger, Accounts Receivable, Accounts Payable, Inventory Control, Payroll, and Job Costing modules together in one single integrated solution. Because it has been designed specifically for small businesses, Simply Accounting is easy to learn and easy to use. It features automatic transaction posting, pop-up reference lists for data entry, and full integration among accounting modules. Simply Accounting gives you reports and financial statements that are always as current as the most recent transaction entry.

Computer Associates produces a leading line of "high-end" accounting software with its ACCPAC and ACCPAC PLUS products and adheres to the philosophy that no accounting solution will suit everyone. Complex features and functions were deliberately left out of Simply Accounting because it will be used by computer and accounting novices.

Quick Set-Up. CA-Simply Accounting contains everything you need to be up and running in a flash, allowing you to get on to other things, such as running your business: a primer that walks you through basic accounting principles, understandable documentation, a real-life tutorial with sample data, comprehensive on-line help, and six different modifiable charts of accounts.

CA-Simply Accounting includes an easy-to-learn, consistent menu structure; automatic transaction posting (no more time-consuming month and year-end closing routines to perform); pop-up customer, vendor, employee, job, account, and inventory lists for quick reference during transaction entry; and full integration of functions. Simply Accounting supports both accrual and cash basis accounting methods for your business's data and provides password security to control data entry and prevent unauthorized viewing.

Just click the mouse to produce complete, formatted reports that are always as current as the most recent entry. For the extra flexibility of custom reporting, you can easily export files to word processing and spreadsheet programs. You can also link Simply Accounting data to word processing and spreadsheet documents that support Microsoft Window's dynamic data exchange (DDE).

The General Ledger (GL) produced by Simply Accounting generates a full "audit trail" with unique journal entry numbers. It lets you apply entries to prior periods within the current year. Simply Accounting's GL allows account balances of up to 999 million (talk about the power of positive thinking). It provides for importing general journal entries from other programs.

Accounts Receivable (AR) and Accounts Payable (AP) use the open invoice method and allow for full or partial payments. They also allow entries for one-time customers and vendors. Simply Accounting automatically updates inventory records and the general ledger for sales and purchases. It allows user-definable aging periods. AR and AP will automatically calculate the appropriate sales tax. The Canadian version of sales tax is GST or Goods and Services Tax. Simply Accounting clears paid invoices individually or globally.

Payroll supports both automatic and manual deduction calculations. It retains employee payroll information. Simply Accounting US Payroll handles seven income fields (two user-definable) and 8 deduction fields (three user-definable). It tracks advances. It automatically calculates and accumulates the following payroll taxes and withholdings: U.S. version—FIT, Social Security tax, Medicare tax, FUTA, SIT, SUTA, and SDI; Canadian version—federal and provincial taxes, UI, CPP, QPP, EHT, QHIP, CSST, and WCB. It also tracks vacation pay. This module alone will pay for the software in a short time if you have been using or were planning to use an outside payroll service.

Inventory Control is automatically updated by purchases and sales entries. It maintains current stock levels and values and highlights items to reorder. This module uses the weighted-average costing method. It handles inventory adjustments and transfers, values items using margin or markup calculations, and also expresses prices to four decimals.

Job Costing provides summary or detailed profit-and-loss reports for each project. It tracks revenues and expenses to various jobs, projects, and profit centers, including employer's payroll taxes. Revenues and expenses can be distributed to one or more jobs per line item, by either percentage or amount.

The program capacity is as follows:

- Ledger accounts—5,000;
- Customers/vendors/employees/inventory items/jobs, projects—32,000;
- Actual ledger size and number of transactions are dependent on available memory, and actual number of journal entries is dependent on available disk space.

A software product that experiences long-term success is always backed by a strong company. Computer Associates has annual sales of more than $1 billion, and this financial stability allows it to endure economic hard times, to put money and resources into research and development, marketing, training and support services, and to react quickly to changes in technology and user requirements. Very few companies can make this claim—an extremely important factor that some purchasers overlook when they make their decision on which accounting software to invest in.

No business wants to invest in software developed by a company that may not have the financial stability to keep upgrading and supporting its products. For example, when the Goods and Services Tax was introduced in Canada in 1991, many software developers of accounting products did not have the resources to react quickly to the legislation and update their software. Some abandoned the Canadian market altogether. Many businesses were left with software incapable of meeting government taxation requirements. Computer Associates's accounting software was updated and ready to meet the users' needs on time. This is an example of what can happen in the United States, Canada, or anywhere else, when a manufacturer is unable to meet its client commitments.

DacEasy Instant Accounting
(Version 2.0 with Quicken Import)

Published by: DacEasy, Inc.
17950 Preston Road, Suite 800
Dallas, TX 75252
1-800-DAC-EASY

DacEasy Instant Accounting, designed for the busy manager and entrepreneur, is part of the newest DacEasy family of products—the DacEasy Instant Series for Windows. With powerful accounting features, Instant Accounting helps you manage your business, invoice customers, and pay bills more easily than ever before. Moreover, it instantly puts critical financial information at your fingertips. This powerful system, designed to take the pain out of typical business accounting, also integrates with popular DacEasy Instant Payroll and Instant Rolodex, thus offering a total business solution.

In the dealing with customers, this software product:

- Allows invoicing of customers for products and services;
- Calculates sales tax on customer invoices;
- Allows instant search of customers, products, and services;
- Allows instant search of invoices by customer, invoice number, or date;
- Keeps detailed customer information, including terms and credit limits; and
- Tracks customer purchase activity and credit balance.

In dealing with vendors, this product:

- Allows entry of purchase invoices for payment;
- Tracks purchase activity by vendor;
- Processes returns; and
- Keeps detailed vendor information, including terms and credit limits.

In regard to your products, the program:

- Keeps detailed product information, including pricing and tax information; and
- Allows assignment of product codes up to 14 alphanumeric characters.

For your banking requirements the program:

- Manages an unlimited number of bank accounts;
- Allows checks to be entered on screen and printed;
- Tracks handwritten checks;
- Tracks deposits and withdrawals;
- Allows bank account transactions to be entered using simple "check register";

- Reconciles accounts quickly;
- Features built-in editing, which allows immediate correction of mistakes; and
- Provides a built-in, modifiable business chart of accounts for income and expenses.

For the reports you need the program should:

- Include a variety of predefined reports
  —Budget and budget comparison;
  —Check register;
  —Balance sheet;
  —Sales;
  —Trial balance;
  —Profit and loss;
  —Customer account aging;
  —Customer history;
  —Customer invoice;
  —Audit trail;
- Allow the creation of custom reports;
- Provide WYSIWYG (what you see is what you get) report viewing on screen.

For your communications, this software offers:

- Built-in phone dialer;
- Mail-merge capability for sending letters;
- Compatibility with popular fax software for print-to-fax communication.

The DacEasy Instant Accounting package:

- Features built-in backup and restore capabilities;
- Supports dot-matrix and laser printing;
- Has a full line of DacEasy preprinted forms available; and
- Imports Quicken data.

DacEasy Instant Payroll is a powerful Windows system that can process an entire payroll with a single click of a mouse. This easy-to-use system gives you the power to process employee taxes accurately, maintain important employee information, and take care of all personnel recording and reporting requirements.

Payroll processing:

- Through its AutoPay feature, allows one-step generation of normal payroll;
- Calculates payroll for hourly and salaried employees;
- Calculates earnings and deductions;
- Prints paychecks;
- Allows departmentalization of employee files;
- Allows the creation of an unlimited number of earnings/deductions/liabilities for system;
- Allows five user-defined earnings/deductions/liabilities per employee; and
- Allows user-defined annual limits on earnings, deductions, and liabilities.

Tax calculation and reporting:

- Automatically calculates federal, state, and local taxes;
- Allows multiple local tax tables per employee;
- Creates 941 worksheet;
- Processes and prints W-2s; and
- Prints state quarterly worksheet.

Employee history information:

- Tracks employee tenure and earnings history;
- Allows attachment of memos to employee files; and
- Tracks vacation and sick time.

The system also features:

- Password protection; and
- Built-in backup and restore capabilities.

Since DacEasy first introduced DacEasy Accounting in 1985, DacEasy has become a world leader with more than 1.5 million accounting systems installed across 27 countries and in seven different languages. DacEasy Accounting has received more user and publication awards and nominations than any other accounting package. Among a long list of prestigious awards, DacEasy Accounting has received *PC Magazine's* Editor's Choice Award in 1985 and 1987 and InfoWorld's Product of the Year in 1985, 1987, and 1989. In 1992, DacEasy Accounting received its sixth *PC World's* World Class Award. This is an honor no other accounting software company can claim. With such a proven and consistent record of success for its products, DacEasy is likely to receive many more nominations and awards through the coming years.

DacEasy's operating philosophy, "the customer comes first," provides the main focus in all phases of DacEasy product development, with a commitment to create a full range of quality accounting and business-related software.

DacEasy technical support provides a high level of assistance through one of the largest support staffs in the accounting software industry. Internally trained product specialists are available to answer customer questions promptly and to solve customer problems. A state-of-the-art telephone system quickly channels customers to the appropriate personnel to satisfy their specific product needs. From automated answers and a customer-controlled FaxBack Library, to personal attention from one of DacEasy's support professionals, DacEasy technical support has an option to support almost every user. DacEasy stands behind every product with a commitment to customer satisfaction.

QuickBooks (Version 2.0)

Published by: INTUIT, INC.
155 Linfield Drive
P.O. Box 3014
Menlo Park, CA 94026
(800) 624-8742 (415) 322-0573

QuickBooks 2.0 can do for your business's accounting what Quicken did for managing your checkbook. When you set up the program, you answer a few questions, including the type of business you conduct (retail, service, professional, and so on). QuickBooks then sets up your account structure. You don't have to enter all your previous account information at once—you're free to add previous transactions (or account balances) whenever it's convenient.

The use of familiar business forms (invoices, checkbooks, etc.) for entering information is a comfortable feature. QuickBooks lets you add just about anything (new customers, part numbers, payment terms, even the message printed at the bottom of invoices) on the fly. For example, you can add an invoice for a new customer without first adding the customer to the database.

Many features of Quicken have been retained by QuickBooks. These include:

- Easy account reconciliation;
- Colorful, customizable toolbar;
- Fast reporting;
- Type the first letter or two of a customer's name or account and QuickFill completes the information; and
- The program memorizes recurring transactions.

QuickBooks comes with dozens of predefined reports (from cash flow forecasts to trial balances); you can also create your own by copying and modifying any report in the program. If you're in a preview mode, click on a report line and QuickBooks will zoom in to show you the transactions that comprise the line. Some of the predefined reports let you compare data across years or check actual spending against budget forecasts. The profit-and-loss statements feature an extremely helpful column: percentage of income.

QuickReports lets you create reports from anywhere within the program. Report columns can be instantly resized; you can collapse or expand reports to show totals or details, and all reports allow you to select the transactions you want.

QuickBooks has some very nice touches. If you incur an expense and want to charge the item to your customer, simply enter the expense as you pay it and place the customer's name (and job identifier if you wish) in the expense entry. When you create an invoice for the customer, click on the Expenses button and Quick-Books lists all the expenses you want reimbursed. You can even tell QuickBooks to mark up prices by a fixed amount or by a percentage of the invoice total. When it's time to pay bills, QuickBooks lets you sort outstanding items, then select those you want (or have) to pay. You can pay a portion of your balance, or you can pay in full. The program also displays your ending balance so that you don't overdraw your account.

The invoice module automatically handles sales tax calculations and supports separate bill-to and ship-to addresses. Three formats are available:

- Service industries (hourly rate billing);
- Professionals (fixed-rate billing); and
- Businesses that sell products.

You can print invoices individually or in batches. You can issue credit memos or refund checks. The accounts receivable module can create aging reports and print customer statements (and also offers a print preview mode). QuickBooks can handle cash or credit card transactions, can track and pay sales taxes, and supports depreciation calculations for fixed assets. It can also track the Canadian Goods and Services Tax (GST).

Although you now know the important accounting terms such as debit, credit, ledger, and post, you don't need such knowledge to operate the program. The product makes its double-entry capabilities transparent in that when you make a single entry the appropriate debit and credit are simultaneously entered. However, it does help to know the difference between an income statement and a balance sheet. The user's guide is full of overviews, explanations, guidance, and tips. An on-screen tutorial covers the basics of getting up and running, writing checks, paying bills, running reports, and creating graphs.

However, there are some limitations. QuickBooks has no end-of-period procedures. To ensure that your January balance sheet is unchanged, you can password-protect changes to transactions prior to a user-defined date. QuickBooks can create invoices with line items for inventory items, but there is no inventory module. Software with an inventory module would check to see that the inventory was available and invoice for the inventory to be shipped and create a back-order status for the inventory shortage. Without such a capability, software such as QuickBooks would allow you to invoice for inventory that you don't have. This causes errors in invoicing and requires manual adjustments and could result in customer dissatisfaction. Further, although you can record payroll information, Quick-Books does not calculate taxes and deductions. The check reconciliation module is easy, but it can't scan your data to find errors—such as transposed digits—that may explain why your checkbook doesn't balance. Finally, you can't export your customer list for mail merging.

Otherwise, QuickBooks is a superb program. With its intuitive interface, excellent feature set, and great ease of use, this could be the right program for many small businesses.

Pacioli 2000 (Version 2.0) and Mondial CashBIZ (Home and Cash Business Accounting Software for Nonaccounting People)

Published by: M-USA BUSINESS SYSTEMS, INC.
15806 Midway Road
Dallas, TX 75244
(800) 933-6872 (214) 386-6100

M-USA released the Pacioli 2000 accounting program in 1990. More than 300,000 packages have been sold, making it one of the best-selling accounting software programs on the market. Pacioli 2000, suited for single-user or network environments, combines eight modules in one single system:

- General Ledger;
- Accounts Receivable;
- Accounts Payable;

- Inventory Control;
- Billing;
- Purchasing;
- Budgeting; and
- Auditing.

The Pacioli 2000's unique M2/S2(TM) (multiple module/single system) approach gives you full use of all eight modules without switching between programs. The General Ledger offers:

- Unlimited number of accounts;
- Unlimited number of transactions;
- Up to 36 open accounting periods;
- Sample chart of accounts; and
- Financial statements and automatic recurring entries.

The Accounts Receivable module features:

- Unlimited number of accounts;
- Open item and balance forward;
- Optional monthly financial charges;
- Monthly statements;
- Aging report; and
- Label printing.

Accounts Payable includes:

- Unlimited payable accounts;
- Open item and balance forward;
- Unlimited number of banking accounts;
- Partial payment supported; and
- Aging report and payment program.

Inventory Control:

- Offers five costing systems, including average and true FIFO and LIFO;

- Allows different purchase and sales units;
- Prints labels and count sheets; and
- Prints price lists and alert reports.

Purchasing enables you to:

- Prepare purchase orders;
- Purchase returns and stock receipts;
- Control purchases for any asset or expense—not just stock items; and
- Have automatic recurring purchasing.

Billing lets you:

- Prepare invoices for services, products, or any other sales;
- Prepare sales returns and credit memos;
- Print sales journal; and
- Support three different invoice formats.

Budgeting offers:

- Period-to-date and year-to-date budgeting control;
- Manual and three automatic budgeting calculations; and
- Budget adjustment entries before closing the period.

Auditing:

- Offers electronic "check mark" for any account transaction;
- Helps to prepare bank reconciliation;
- Reports audited and nonaudited balances; and
- Improves audit trail.

Pacioli 2000 has been named *PC World*'s "Best Buy," included in *Compute*'s "Winners Circle" for the Home Office category, and given *Compute*'s Choice Award for "Best Financial Software," *Computer Buyer's Guide and Handbook*'s "Best Buy" award, *PC Computing*'s "Best Value-Accounting Software," *Computer Month-*

ly's "Gold Medal Value" award, and *Personal Computer Magazine's* "Readers Best" award.

In 1991, M-USA released CashBIZ, "accounting software for nonaccounting people." Created to manage personal finances and small cash-basis businesses, CashBIZ offers a checkwriter's simplicity and an abundance of features.

Mondial, released in 1994, contains a Windows-like interface with context-sensitive help; moveable, sizeable screens; easy-to-understand dialog boxes; and full keyboard and mouse control. It also boasts a dual interface that caters to both the computer novice and the computer expert. Those intimidated by accounting and its terminology can just fill in the blanks, as they would on a check or invoice. Mondial does the rest. Those who prefer conventional accounting terms and methods can choose to work within the debit and credit system.

Mondial adequately fits the needs of either inventory-based or service businesses. It provides all the standard modules contained in the most powerful systems, including General Ledger, Billing, Accounts Receivable, Accounts Payable, Purchasing, and Budgeting.

Service-oriented businesses can use its time-billing capabilities, project-tracking control, and cash-basis accounting approach. Mondial simplifies job costing for an incredible variety of businesses, ranging from professional service providers to repair and maintenance shops.

Inventory-based businesses can get organized with sophisticated features designed especially for them. Point-of-sale and multistore control are ideal for retailers. An efficient order-entry system and multiwarehouse support meet the needs of wholesalers and telemarketers. Light duty manufacturers will streamline their operations with Mondial's convenient assembly parts control feature.

Mondial is also effective accounting software for those involved in international trade and NAFTA. Its multicurrency conversion system quickly calculates profit or loss on foreign currency transactions; keeps balances in dollars and foreign currencies; and allows purchasing, billing, checking, and other accounting procedures in different currencies while automatically doing the books in dollars.

Probably the most important feature for small businesses is Mondial's networking capability. Mondial operates efficiently on one computer, then grows as more computers come on-line. Multimodule capabilities, together with multiuser performance, eliminates the hassle and expense of switching to a new program as your business expands.

In tune with M-USA's commitment to get the customer up and running fast, the company provides six months of free technical support for its products. Indicative of M-USA's primary philosophy, "Customer Takes Priority" (CTP), each member of the highly qualified research and development, production, marketing, technical support, customer service, and management team strives to relieve computer intimidation by accommodating the needs of the end user.

BusinessWorks (Version 7.2)

Published by: MANZANITA SOFTWARE SYSTEMS
2130 Professional Drive, Suite #150
Roseville, CA 95661-3751
(800) 447-5700 (916) 781-3880 FAX (916) 781-3814

BusinessWorks is introduced by its developer as an accounting package designed for people who would rather run their businesses than spend time trying to figure out how to use their accounting program. Available in both the DOS and Windows environments, this is a comprehensive double-entry accounting system with exceptional power and flexibility.

If you're looking for an accounting package that just about anyone can use, one that provides extensive reports instantly and can grow with your business, BusinessWorks may be your solution.

BusinessWorks's features include the following:

- Built-in networking capability that supports both single- and multiuser environments;
- Quick access to extensive historical detail;

- Import/export features that make it simple to use spreadsheet and database formats such as Lotus 1-2-3, dBASE, and ASCII;
- Ease in accessing other programs from the BusinessWorks Menu (DOS);
- Convenient lookup windows that provide quick reference to accounts, vendors, customers, invoices, parts, terms, codes, etc.;
- Search file feature that allows quick location of data within certain files;
- Pop-up calendar and calculator for easy date and data input (DOS);
- Comprehensive on-line help that references user manuals for further detail;
- On-screen error identification and instructions for recovery;
- Flexible chart of accounts;
- Twenty-two industry-specific charts of accounts;
- Handy setup feature that makes installation a breeze;
- Number of customers, vendors, parts, and employees limited only by disk storage space;
- Flexible, fully featured reporting;
- Ability to print invoices, statements, orders, quotes, and purchase orders on plain paper or preprinted forms; and
- Ability to accommodate multiple companies and departments.

Manzanita Software Systems designed BusinessWorks to simplify virtually every area of business accounting. The various modules must be purchased separately, but no matter which modules you buy, they're completely integrated to work together. (The required System Manager makes that possible.)

You can purchase modules as stand-alone programs, then add modules later without costly downtime and conversion hassles. You can, however, start with the standard DOS or Windows system that includes the General Ledger, Accounts Payable, and Accounts Receivable modules.

A caveat is necessary at this point. Although BusinessWorks initially costs more than some of the other software included in this chapter, it simply does more than some of them. Many businessowners tried less expensive, all-in-one accounting software packages, only to discover that the products were under-engineered and oversold. Others invested in "high-end" software before realizing they needed an accountant on staff to run the program.

BusinessWorks gives you everything you need from high-priced "high-end" programs, for thousands less and without the need to hire a staff accountant. From networking capabilities to up-to-the-minute sales summaries, its powerful features offer both flexibility and upgradability. Just as important, you won't have to spend a great deal of time installing and learning the program, or training everyone else in the business in how to use it. BusinessWorks was designed from the outset to be easy to install and even easier to use. From the moment you load the program onto your system, it's clear that the people who designed it have firsthand experience in running a business. The management reports you need are built in. Balance sheet and profit-and-loss formats are flexible. Account balances are always up to date. You probably never thought that accounting software could work so seamlessly, so intelligently.

The System Manager:

- Enables users to set up and run BusinessWorks;
- Provides multilevel password protection;
- Features mail message system for communication between users;
- Provides audit report of changes to key BusinessWorks data files; and
- Provides zip code lookup table with user-edit feature.

The General Ledger:

- Provides full financial and management reports, including balance sheets, trial balance reports, income statements and cash flow statements;
- Provides complete audit trails;
- Consolidates multiple companies' financial statements;
- Allows budgeting and variance reports;
- Keeps transaction details for up to two fiscal years;
- Generates profit center or divisional level reports; and
- Allows for recurring entries, as well as correcting entries.

Accounts Payable:

- Tracks money owed to vendors as it provides complete information, such as month-to-date or year-to-date purchases, open credits, and last payment;
- Assigns vendor-specific payment terms so that all discounts can be earned;
- Prints checks using multiple checking accounts and easily handles voided checks;
- Tracks handwritten checks;
- Prints IRS 1099s;
- Allows partial or full payment of invoices;
- Processes recurring payables; and
- Allows printing of checks to any payee through instant check feature.

Accounts Receivable:

- Prepares and tracks all invoices;
- Generates sales analysis reports using multiple categories, such as customer, product, sales representative, etc.;
- Maintains and tracks detailed customer information, including credit limits, credit holds, recurring invoices, outstanding balances, and collections;
- Accepts customer payments, including partial payments and write-offs;
- Allows monitoring of discounts given;
- Calculates finance charges and prints statements;
- Calculates customer aging reports; and
- Processes both balance forward and open-item statements.

Inventory Control:

- Tracks complete inventory, including vendors, transaction history, on-hand parts, and on-order quantities;
- Provides complete purchase order system and supports EOQ (economic order quantity) through order recommendations report;

- Permits classification of inventory parts into subassemblies and product lines;
- Allows up to 15 prices per item and supports sales promotion pricing;
- Simplifies physical inventory by generating inventory count sheets and by tracking shrinkage;
- Provides four costing methods: LIFO (Last-In-First-Out), FIFO (First-In-First-Out), average, and standard; and
- Permits global price changes.

Order Entry:

- Tracks orders from order placement through shipping and invoicing;
- Provides "one button" conversion of quotes to sales orders, sales orders to invoices;
- Updates accounts receivable and inventory automatically;
- Records partial or full shipments;
- Prints pick tickets and packing lists; and
- Checks customer credit status and holds problem orders for credit approval.

Payroll:

- Calculates all federal and state taxes automatically;
- Prints paychecks, tax deposit checks, and W-2s;
- Processes hourly, salaried, commissioned, and piece-rate pay, plus 18 other pay types;
- Allows user-definable deductions, including 401(k) and cafeteria plans;
- Provides 941 report information;
- Tracks complete personnel information, including hire date, review date, advances, sick pay, vacation, and comp time; and
- Updates job cost module automatically.

Job Cost:

- Keeps track of estimated costs, actual costs, and changes in actual and estimated costs for jobs, phases, and job code detail;
- Allows a job bid to easily become a job in progress;
- Sorts reports by job ID number, manager, or customer;
- Allows retainage amounts to be kept for each job;
- Calculates price and cost for jobs and phases automatically;
- Prints job status billings and payment reports; and
- Prints change orders, work completed, and outstanding reports.

Manzanita Software Systems offers three months of free technical assistance when you purchase BusinessWorks. A knowledgeable BusinessWorks consultant will guide you through any steps you're not sure about. This is the kind of responsive and timely support that Manzanita Software Systems is known for. The result of Business-Works is comprehensive software designed for the way you do business—with streamlined steps that make the program easy to use and toll-free technical support that's as accessible as it is responsive. You spend less time doing your books and more time managing your business.

You also get up-to-the-minute reports so that you know where you stand financially at any given time. It helps to know that Manzanita's ongoing commitment to product development means you won't be investing in a software system today that's outdated tomorrow.

BusinessWorks can assist your business to succeed, helping you do what you do best as well as helping you with the accounting activities that you do worst. Manzanita's statement—that building lasting customer relationships is its goal—has been proven.

One-Write Plus (Version 3.0)

Published by: NEBS SOFTWARE, INC.
20 Industrial Park Drive
Nashua, NH 03062
(800) 388-8000 (603) 880-5100 FAX (603) 880-5102

One-Write Plus Accounting is the core of the One-Write Plus product line of small business accounting and financial software. Other One-Write Plus products include One-Write Plus Payroll and One-Write Plus Accounting Works.

Version 3.0 features extensive reporting and budgeting capabilities as well as hassle-free communications and information flow. It offers users flexibility, integration, control, and speed. One-Write Plus, a powerful yet easy-to-use accounting software program, meets the standards of GAAP (generally accepted accounting principles) and is one of the more popular small business accounting programs on the market. Originally published in 1985 (and significantly enhanced each year), it combines the advantages of software automation with the popular accounting format of the manual one-write accounting system used by more than five million small businesses worldwide.

One-Write Plus Accounting is a fully integrated system including General Ledger, Accounts Receivable, and Accounts Payable. It also features Inventory, Job Costing, Bank Reconciliation, and more. Easy-to-fill-in screens are a snap for any small business. Pop-up cards and lists and simple menus help guide you through the program.

General Ledger features include:

- Detail general ledger;
- Variable monthly budgeting;
- Single-column income statements;
- Date and time-stamped reports; and
- Customer, vendor, and general ledger accounts on-the-fly.

Accounts Receivable includes:

- Date-sensitive invoice compress;
- Increase sales tax rates, from 3 to 9 levels.

Accounts Payable:

- Allows printing of credit memos on A/P check stubs; and
- Includes checking account balance on Approve Bills screen.

The One-Write Plus product line was acquired by New England Business Service in January 1993. The acquisition combined two companies whose shared goal is to meet the information-processing needs of small businesses. NEBS Software, Inc. combines the ease-of-use and value of One-Write Plus with NEBS's 40 years of expertise in the small business market.

Accounting for more than 50 percent of today's job growth, the small business market is increasingly recognized as an integral contributor to the nation's economy. For more than 40 years, NEBS has focused exclusively on meeting the business printing needs of this market. With the growth of computer automation, NEBS Software, Inc. has emerged to provide the software applications necessary to manage a small business.

A full staff of professionally trained technical support experts are committed to helping you take full advantage of your accounting software. You automatically receive 30 days of free support with your One-Write Plus purchase. Following the free support, you can select a support plan to fit your specific needs: an annual plan that provides unlimited calls on a toll-free line, priority service, free updates, discounts on upgrades, and more; or a 900-number pay-per-call service with the first minute free.

AccountMate (Version 3.5)

Published by: SourceMate Information Systems, Inc.
20 Sunnyside Avenue
Mill Valley, CA 94941
(800) 877-8896 (415) 381-1011 FAX (415) 381-6902

AccountMate is modifiable accounting software that is different from most other accounting software packages. Written in dBASE III Plus, it is available with free source code or in a Clipper compiled version. The source code version may be compiled using Microsoft FoxBase or Quicksilver compilers. However, do not attempt to modify the software unless you are a competent dBASE programmer.

A primary benefit of dBASE accounting software is that it facilitates the creation of add-on applications by third-party software developers. The SourceMate SourceGuide offers more than 250 software products. Another benefit is that the dBASE-proficient user may modify existing reports or create new reports by sorting the accounting information in different ways.

Such modification, however, does carry a price inasmuch as SourceMate offers free technical support only if the software has not been modified. This support can be valuable, especially for the novice user. The documentation does not include an explanation of the sequence in which the systems should be set up; therefore the user must read through the manuals and make notes of the relationship between files to ensure that they are "loaded" in the appropriate sequence. For example, during the installation process the instructions do not ask the user to make a directory for AccountMate files, even though the installation process stops if a directory cannot be found. A quick call to the technical support line can provide the answers to such difficulties.

The documentation for this software package is extensive. A separate manual for each module includes a table of contents, a list of figures, and a keyword index, which is on the sparse side. One initial difficulty is that the documentation has been organized in the order in which you would use it to perform daily routine functions. This feature is frustrating during the installation process, but useful thereafter.

Creating the chart of accounts is a three-step process. First, if departments are to be used, they are created by assigning numbers and names. Second, the different classifications of the chart of accounts, balance sheet, and income statement are assigned ranges of account numbers. Next, the accounts are created category by category. As accounts are added, they are defined as being either detail accounts or header accounts.

Account balances are added by journal entry. The system will not allow an unbalanced batch to be posted, but does not require that a batch be posted. This ensures that the system will be in balance.

Budgets are handled in a superficial manner. Only expense and revenue budgets can be created and, at the user's option, amounts may be distributed evenly for the year or entered on a month-by-month basis.

All reports can be printed to the screen, the printer, or a disk file. If a report is selected to be displayed on the screen, rerouting for printing—without the need to regenerate the report—is possible as long as the process of displaying the report has not finished.

General Ledger features include:

- A ledger, financial tracking, and reporting system based on a 12- or 13-period cycle;
- Retained budgets for prior and current years;
- Projection of next year's budget by period;
- Multiple transaction batch posting to any prior, current, or future periods of the current fiscal year;
- Safeguards to prevent out-of-balance posting; and
- More than 200 useful management reports, including
    - —Balance sheets;
    - —Income statements;
    - —Statements of cash flows;
    - —Ratio analysis;
    - —Budget variance;
    - —Built-in custom report generator.

The Accounts Payable module offers many features not available in packages costing twice as much. Canceled checks can be recorded so that a bank reconciliation can be performed. The system prints IRS form 1099 and allows for multiple checking accounts. Payments can be sorted by due date or discount date, by reference, or by a general search of open invoices by vendor account. At the time a vendor is added, default account numbers can be assigned for invoice activity against the vendor. These accounts, however, can be overriden.

A useful and time-saving feature of the system is Rapid Lookup, which will search for the closest match if the beginning characters of the vendor name are typed.

Vendor payments and cash management are provided by the Accounts Payable module through these features:

- Records payable invoices and payments to vendors;
- Prints checks;
- Processes handwritten check information;
- Voids checks;
- Records finance charges;
- Processes 1099 independent contractor and other payments and prints 1099 forms;
- Handles prepayments, discounts, credits, and other adjustments;
- Supports up to 10 different checking accounts;
- Reports outstanding checks;
- Provides notepad for each vendor; and
- Prints vendor labels.

AccountMate supports invoicing and allows several different codes to be used for reporting: class, industry, and territory. Salesperson codes are referenced through a separate file. Customers can be added at the time invoices are entered, a convenience when adding past history as a part of system implementation.

Accounts Receivable computerizes inventory, invoicing, and receivables:

- Creates computer, handwritten, and prepaid invoices;
- Handles the posting of credit memos/open credit, cash receipts, and bad debt write-offs;
- Allows multilevel pricing;
- Assesses finance charges;
- Maintains unlimited number of multiple customer shipping addresses;
- Provides customer notepad;
- Prints UPS (United Parcel Service) COD tags;
- Prints more than 200 reports, including

   —Period Analysis Report;
   —Salesperson Sales Quota Report;
   —Cash Refund Report;
- Extensive error-checking system assists inventory management.

AccountMate is a solid accounting software system with a strong focus on functionality. The system is fairly easy to use and offers "lookup" windows when the F4 key is pressed. Technical support is limited, providing only one hour free for the first module and 10 minutes for each additional module.

M.Y.O.B. (Mind Your Own Business—Version 3.0)

Published by: BEST!WARE
One of the Best! Companies
300 Roundhill Drive
Rockaway, NJ 07866
(201) 586-2200 FAX (201) 586-8885

M.Y.O.B. is an award-winning, fully integrated accounting and business management software package for the home and small business marketplaces. The program is available in Macintosh and Windows versions, includes general ledger, accounts payable, accounts receivable, inventory, check writing, and accounting functions. Users may also create 70 comprehensive reports and generate "to-do lists."

Unlike many other accounting software packages that were "downsized" from mainframe and minicomputers, this program was developed from the ground up expressly for the needs of small, independent, and growing businesses. It assumes a minimal level of accounting and computer expertise. It talks to you in simple, plain English and is not a watered-down version of some "high-level" accounting package more appropriate in "corporate America."

Although every businessowner is required to keep track of his or her books, there are few who are interested in the language and procedures of double-entry accounting. For that very reason, M.Y.O.B. handles your most difficult accounting chores behind the scenes and presents simple, intuitive information on the surface. M.Y.O.B. is true double-entry accounting without the jargon. You'll find all the accurate detail you need in a format that is easy to review and analyze.

M.Y.O.B. organizes your work flow by using the Command Center Flow Chart. From this location, you can proceed to any one of seven program areas:

- General ledger;
- Checkbook;
- Sales and receivables;
- Purchases and payables;
- Inventory; and
- Card file.

You can click on the area of your choice and because M.Y.O.B. is organized logically, you'll never have to navigate through multiple menus to get from point A to point B.

Rather than forcing you into a rigid structure, M.Y.O.B. allows you to do whatever you want to do whenever you want to do it. For example, suppose you're looking at a summary of your receivables. Just scan your list of customers and click on one to display a summary of the invoices. To focus on a specific invoice in the list, click again to pull up the original invoice. One more click next to your customer's name takes you to the card file, where you can automatically make a phone call. Then make an entry into M.Y.O.B.'s phone contact log for follow-up.

Learning M.Y.O.B. is very easy. Most windows in M.Y.O.B. are paper look-alikes. The Write Checks screen, for instance, looks just like a paper check—right down to the dollar amount in English, and the user's "signature" in the lower right corner. The same holds true for an invoice, a purchase order, and even a deposit slip.

Your business is more than just its books. The accounting data you enter on a regular basis should be available to you for management decisions. With M.Y.O.B., it is. Use the powerful To-Do List each morning and evening to review an instant summary of every area of your business. Just click an icon to answer questions such as: "Who owes me money?" or "Have any inventory items dropped below my preset order level?" Then take action with another click of the mouse. Your most critical accounting chores are completed in minutes, and you're on to the real business of your business.

Sample business data is built into M.Y.O.B. so you can learn the ropes before you enter your own real-life data. And the easy-to-use, easy-to-understand on-line help or manual should give you a good jump start. In case you need technical assistance, M.Y.O.B. comes with 30 days of free support for all registered users; extended support can also be purchased. If you're moving to M.Y.O.B. from another software package, use M.Y.O.B.'s import feature to capture data from Peachtree, Microsoft Profit, and virtually any other accounting program.

Best!Ware, founded in 1982 in Rockaway, New Jersey, as Teleware, Inc., holds that its mission is to help small businesses run more effectively and profitably. Best!Ware is a wholly owned subsidiary of Best Programs, Inc. of Reston, Virginia, a leader in business and tax-related PC-based software. Founded in 1982, Best develops and markets the FAS line of depreciation and fixed asset management software, as well as the Tax Partner and Master Tax lines of tax preparation software.

If you need full-featured accounting programs but don't understand all the nuances and subtleties of double-entry accounting and accrual-based accounting, M.Y.O.B. is an excellent choice. If you both need and can handle the extra horsepower of more complicated accounting software packages or need features such as payroll or job costing, you will have to look elsewhere.

WORD PROCESSING—THE RIGHT CHOICE FOR THE WRITE STUFF

Selecting word processing software can be like designing the layout of your office. The way to make the right selection is to match your particular requirements to the software and the features offered, at an affordable price.

If you are like most businessowners, you use your word processor more than any other application. You may use it for a variety of demanding jobs—compiling bids and estimates, designing a brochure, preparing a customer or client newsletter—or simply to type business letters. Word processing is the workhorse of most businesses. A look at the features in the most popular word processors reveals the state of the art in document preparation, handling, and production. In addition to basic document creation and editing, many of these products create and manipulate charts and illustrations, perform extensive page layout operations that rival many desktop publishing programs, and create sophisticated work-flow automation routines using built-in programming languages.

Features to Look for in a Word Processor

As a business user, you should look for features that help you generate consistently high-quality correspondence, forms, and other types of documents that adequately reflect your business image and objectives. The ability to create standard stylesheets for your organization and to include logos and graphic images can let even small businesses "look like the big guys."

Certain features are essential to any word processor. The features most people need are easy page setup, templates, drag-and-drop editing, and macros, as well as configurable keyboards, menus, and button bars.

Page setup is your first step in word processing. It should be a simple task that doesn't force you to wade through menus and dialog boxes before you can type your first word. Most word processors have a simplified setup; almost all programs now allow you to specify margins and tabs with your mouse from an on-screen ruler at the top of the editing area, analogous to the way you would set them up on a typewriter. Many word processors provide uncomplicated *stylesheets* and *page templates* that are already formatted for letters, memos, and other documents. You simply open the template and start typing.

Most word processors include a *spellchecker* to help you catch typos and misspelled words, and many programs have a *calculator* to check your math, a *thesaurus* to improve your vocabulary, and *grammar-correction routines*, which won't improve your writing (no matter what their vendors may tell you). However, they can ensure that quotation marks and parentheses are closed, and they can often catch subject/verb and tense agreement problems.

Drag-and-drop editing provides an easy way for you to revise your document. With drag-and-drop, you select a block of text with your mouse and drag it to a new location, eliminating the need to use the cut-and-paste commands in the Edit menu.

If a large portion of your work is repetitive—if you close several letters the same way, type the same paragraph often, or use a number of special characters, for instance, buy a word processor with *macro capabilities*. Macros record keystrokes and mouse movements to automate repetitive tasks. The ability to configure menus, button bars, and the ruler can also ease your work load. For example, you can customize your program by assigning a command to a keystroke, cutting down on the drudgery of repetitive work such as adding bullets. With several programs, you can gain easy access to frequently used menu functions, such as search and replace, by adding them to the button bar.

Many word processing programs help you create *form templates* for filling in preprinted forms that you use regularly. They also aid in addressing envelopes, producing labels in a variety of sizes, and merging names, addresses, and other information from lists or databases to create customized mass mailings. If you handle a wide variety of different documents, look for *document management features* that let you give descriptive titles to your documents, keyword categorizations, and other summary information that will assist you in identifying or retrieving them later.

OLE and DDE (in Windows) offer new ways to share and exchange information between various applications and systems. With word processors that support DDE (*dynamic data exchange*), you can incorporate information from other applications without having to switch to them to get the data. For example, you can query a database program from within your word processor and have the results returned to the document. OLE (*object linking and embedding*) gives you the ability to include information from multiple programs' files to create compound documents.

With OLE, you don't simply insert a snippet of data from another program, you insert a link to the other program that lets you call it up automatically when you need to make changes or revisions. With Windows 3.1 or a later version and a word processor that supports OLE, you can use Sound Recorder to embed voice annotations in word processing documents, or use Clipboard and Paintbrush to embed illustrated screen captions.

Which Word Processor Is Right for You?

No single word processor is right for everyone. Few notebook computer users will need to merge letters with large databases to create a direct mail campaign while on the road. *Mail-merges* combine two files, usually a letter with a mailing list. Most programs perform mail-merges, but their approaches are often quite different. WordPerfect's mail-merge is the simplest of the three major word processors'. It uses merge codes that are easy to understand and insert in documents. You simply insert names, such as Field 1 and Field 2, in the appropriate places in the document. Unlike some other mail-merge procedures, WordPerfect's is quite straightforward. When you reach the end of a record, for example, it clearly states "end of record."

Microsoft's Word uses *comma-delimited procedures*, like those used in programming, which require you to separate fields with commas and quotation marks. If you misspell a field name, or misplace a comma or a quotation mark, the merge executes incorrectly or doesn't work at all.

Feature-rich, high-end word processors often carry a hefty price in terms of hardware resources (some need as much as 35 MB of disk space to fully load the entire program), cost of purchase, and investment of time and effort. If your writing needs don't demand all of the features found in the high-end products, there are plenty of low-end and midrange products from which to choose at significantly lower prices. The Windows' Accessories group includes two word processors: Write and Notepad. Notepad certainly won't serve as a daily word processor, but it's adequate for making notes that you can incorporate into virtually any application that works with text.

Write offers a broader range of features, including support for TrueType fonts, character and paragraph formatting, headers and footers, and OLE, to name a few. Write enables you to create reports, memos, and letters without spending any additional money on word processing software. In addition, it works with other software programs.

If you are setting up your business or moonlighting while working for an employer, you may want or need to use the same applications at home that you use at your primary office. Most software licenses are structured to allow you to use the software on any number of PCs, as long as you use the program on only one PC at a time. This generally means that you can use the software on your PC at your main office and also keep a copy in your home office. You're generally not violating the law by keeping two copies of the software.

However, your employer may have other ideas. Although it may be perfectly legal for you to take software home, many companies are disinclined to let any software be taken off-site, because there is nothing to prevent you from giving a copy to your brother-in-law on the sly or, perish the thought, selling a copy of the program. Very few people actually do such things, but the threat of a lawsuit or heavy fine against the company if a perceived violation is uncovered by the software police often overwhelms an organization's trust in its employees, even when the use of the software at home is completely legitimate.

You should make sure you're adhering to your responsibilities as to the software license for the applications you use and to any corporate policies your company may have in place. If you buy systems with bundled software (included in systems purchases), make sure you get licenses with the software. A set of original manuals and disks is a good indicator that you have a legal copy, but check for a license as well.

Look for a product that meets or exceeds your expected requirements, but don't select one on the basis of price alone. Having extra features available when you need them will save you a lot of time, effort, and a return to the yesteryears of typewriters, carbon paper, and correction fluid. There are several elements to take into account when choosing your word processor. You may want the elaborate macro languages that are provided in Lotus's Ami Pro, Word, and WordPerfect. You can use these languages to create your own dialog boxes, among other things. Even templates become more functional with better macro programming. Consider the extent to which products within one company's suite of software products are compatible.

Complex word processors require comprehensive tutorials. Take time to investigate the tutorial included with the program you are considering; the quality differs widely. Most of the software programs described in this book have demo disks available for you to try out at no cost. WordPerfect ships its product with a workbook-style tutorial of individual lessons covering almost every feature.

You should also investigate a prospective program's support and upgrade policies. WordPerfect provides free support for a limited time and an 800 number for all registered users. Most of the other companies provide support, but the call is on you.

A Shopping List for Word Processors

- *Templates.* Ready-to-go letters, fax forms, memos, and reports with a click of your mouse; just select one and start typing.
- *Drag-and-drop editing.* Move a paragraph from here to there by defining the text and dragging it to a new location.
- *Macros.* Define a repetitious procedure once, assign it to a button or keystroke, and you've got a macro.
- *Configurable keyboards, menus, and button bars.* Do you like buttons better than menus? Reassign menu functions to a button or vice versa. Some programs even let you write your own dialog boxes.

For more information on word processors, you can contact the manufacturers directly at the following addresses:

Ami Pro 3.0
Lotus Word Processing Division
1000 Abernathy Road, N.E.

Atlanta GA 30328
1-800-831-9679
In Canada, call 1-800-GO-LOTUS

Word 6.0
Microsoft Corporation
One Microsoft Way
Redmond, WA 98052-6399
1-800-426-9400

WordPerfect 6.0
WordPerfect Corporation
1555 N. Technology Way
Orem, UT 84057-2399
1-800-451-5151

DATABASE MANAGEMENT

Managing information is one of your most fundamental business activities. You need to track sales, productivity, inventories, customer accounts, and marketing management. You need to be able to do it from your desktop or portable computer without waiting for professional programmers to produce the data for you.

Industry statistics and the leading computer software publications reader surveys show that although almost everyone uses a word processor or a spreadsheet, only one in five uses a database.

History of Databases

The PC database revolution began in the early 1980s with dBASE, a programming language with then state-of-the-art commands that worked well on stand-alone hardware. The solution was good for small-scale application development on dedicated PCs. dBASE was rapidly adopted as a corporate standard in Information Systems (IS) departments for solving current needs. It quickly became apparent, however, that products like dBASE were too difficult for general purpose users.

By the mid-1980s, software vendors attempted to deliver easier-to-use products by incorporating pull-down menus, query-by-example interfaces, and other user-interface elements into products such as Borland's Paradox and dBASE IV. Application development did indeed become easier, and vendors claimed that the same database products were now appropriate for nontechnical users accustomed to word processors and spreadsheets; however, the database market remained relatively small.

With the arrival of PC networking, applications began to share data. *Database management system* (DBMS) vendors met this challenge with the addition of *record-locking* and *file-sharing network models* to their products, allowing multiple users to access the same data at the same time.

At this point, many DBMSs combined improved interfaces with the ability to work over a network. Industry experts suggested that anyone with a PC should now be able to create, manage, analyze, and report on information throughout the business. Despite the broad appeal of this promise, the DBMS market still did not grow, as compared with desktop applications. The Software Publishers Association (SPA) reported that sales of PC spreadsheet units were twice as high as sales of PC database units.

The database solutions of the 1980s failed to penetrate a broad base of users and gain acceptance as a general-purpose business productivity tool for three reasons:

1. Databases were designed primarily for technical users. They originated as programmers' tools, and in order to service their growing installed base of programmers, software designers compromised in favor of their more technical audiences.

2. The market for databases was regarded as one large category, despite their widely varying uses ranging from mission-critical accounting systems to small department mailings. In other categories of software, there was a split between high-end programs for technical users and more approachable software for general

productivity users; with database systems, however, this did not occur. In searching for a single-product database solution, many software vendors ended up compromising the needs of general-purpose business users in order to satisfy the requirements of IS professionals.

3. End-user database solutions were both limited in power and incompatible with existing data format standards. The end-user, flatfile databases that eventually were developed, such as Symantec Q&A and Claris FileMaker Pro for the Macintosh, were incompatible with existing xBase, Paradox, and SQL standards. This left end users locked out of significant amounts of information.

The need for a database solution that addresses these issues and serves as a general-purpose productivity tool has grown as more nontechnical business professionals are required to manage, report on, and update large pools of information.

Currently, the Windows desktop database market can be divided into two segments:

1. Programmable tools such as Access and Paradox, which are appropriate for programmers and the technically astute.

2. End-user databases for general-purpose business users—the same people who buy products such as Lotus 1-2-3 and Word-Perfect. This is a relatively new market segment for the PC and is expected to experience the fastest growth.

The database market segmentation between programmable tools and end-user databases is analogous to the division in the electronic document market between *desktop publishing* packages and traditional *word processors*. Although desktop publishing packages, such as PageMaker, are designed for specialists in their fields, word processors, such as WordPerfect, exist for the broad range of general-purpose users.

Within the two segments of the Windows database market there are five well-known players:

End-User Databases	*Programmers' Tools*
Approach	Access
FileMaker	Pro Paradox
FoxPro	

What Can a Database Do for the Small Businessowner?

Your first question may very well be, "What exactly does a database do?" A database stores data about a common subject. Each piece of information is kept in a field. For example, you can build a database to store a name, address, and phone list. The name is stored in the Name field, the telephone in the Phone field, and so on. Information about a person (all three fields) constitutes a record. Thus, this database stores data about a common subject—people.

Databases are flexible enough to grow and change. You can expand a database to keep facts about birth dates or anniversaries if such data becomes important, by adding fields for this information. Databases can keep track of inventory part numbers and prices or all the information about your contracts and agreements.

The database programs described here all share several features. First, they are designed for the occasional user. The better ones don't take a great deal of time to learn for simple tasks, such as designing and maintaining a list of customers. They are extremely powerful graphical tools. You can build data-entry forms and reports using a screen painter and just a few menu options. You can create your own database from scratch, or you can import your existing data if it uses one of several standard formats. You can export your data for use by other programs, too.

The databases also share these features: You can design reports and input forms graphically, display data in a spreadsheet grid (most let you resize columns by dragging column borders), and search for text or sort records on the fly. When you design a database, each program will create a default data-entry form, usually one field per line. This isn't a glamorous layout, but it's a great way to get started quickly. Most, however, don't provide a default report layout—you'll have to design reports from scratch.

All databases let you use the mouse to click on buttons or choose function names, and you can use the keyboard to build expressions or calculate new values. This is a good idea in theory, but unfortunately, in practice it can lead to problems. It's very easy to click your way to a formula that simply doesn't work. You need software that offers a way to check immediately an expression's syntax.

"Relational" Database Defined

The hot database buzzword is "relational." Talk to a dozen database experts and you'll hear it thrown around and used in heated arguments about just what makes a database relational. Despite the disagreement, there are some generally established concepts and rules. The interest in relational databases stems from the fact that they're widely used on mainframes.

Every database is just a model for structuring, updating, and retrieving information. Unlike many models, a relational database doesn't use addresses, links, or pointers to establish relationships between data sets; instead, it relies on the values in the data. Data is stored in spreadsheetlike tables with rows for each record and columns for each field. All tables have unique names, and any table in which all of the rows (records) are different is mathematically known as a *relation*. A relational database allows users to link separate databases together into a set. Once the databases have been "joined" or "related," fields from any of the databases in the set can be used as though they are all part of one single database. A nonrelational database is known as a *flatfile database*.

The benefits of storing associated information in two or more related databases, instead of using one large, flatfile database, are increased efficiency, data accuracy, and flexibility. The best way to illustrate these benefits is through an example.

Suppose a salesperson for your business has several contact names at each of the customers' locations in his or her territory. If you store this customer and contact information in a flatfile database, you must reenter the customer address each time a new contact is added to the database. If you use a relational database, you can type in the customer address just once, regardless of the number of individual customer contacts, and then display the data as many times as necessary. Because the information is stored only once, disk space requirements are reduced. Moreover, becaues you have to update only one company record when an address changes, it is easier to maintain accurate information.

By organizing data in tables that have values in common, relationships can be established without concern about the order in which data is stored or where it is located. The data entries can be "unordered" and don't have to be in any set position.

Relational databases should also include system tables that define the database structure and provide a systematic method for dealing with missing information (known as null values). There should be support for a well-defined language that allows table definition, data manipulation, integrity checking, access authorization, and transaction processing.

Businessowners use databases to store, update, and report on information. The type of information managed by databases varies widely from customer to customer, ranging from financial data to customer/client addresses and phone numbers.

Lotus Approach 2.1, a relational, end-user database, is powerful, versatile, and very easy to use. Approach enables users to work with data from multiple databases files and database file formats to accomplish important data management tasks such as contact management, invoicing, creating mailings, analyzing business data, and producing sales reports. All of this can be done without writing a single line of code. Unlike Microsoft Access and Borland Paradox, Approach provides the power and functionality computer novice business owners require from a database, without adding the burden of programming.

A key advantage of Approach is that it provides direct access to dBASE, Paradox, FoxPro, Oracle SQL, and SQL Server data through its exclusive PowerKey technology. Approach for Windows is based on client/server technology, allowing users to access and manipulate large databases using the capacity and processing power of a server. The product is 100 percent network-compatible, allowing Approach users to work simultaneously on various files such dBase III and IV, FoxPro, Paradox, Oracle SQL 6.0 and 7.0. SQL Server and other database file types while still within the Approach framework.

Approach for Windows was designed and developed for nontechnical business professionals. Point-and-click macros, relational joins, and advanced functions deliver high levels of power, without requiring any programming knowledge. The software is designed for typical spreadsheet and word processor users who prefer to concentrate on their work, their information, and their businesses—not on programming their software.

Database Marketing Management

Cut to the nuts and bolts of marketing and you arrive at one simple concept: We must match our products and services to the people who will buy them. You already knew that? Not at all surprising, really, because there's no magic to this particular concept; it's no secret to anyone. But understanding the concept is not the problem. Suppose the problem is that you're out of cash and out of ideas.

Help is on the way. Here's an idea that will free up time for selling and add more than 15 percent to your annual sales: Stay in touch with every current customer, past customer, and qualified lead at least once a month. Make them an offer that's valuable and meaningful to them, an offer that can move them to action. It's not difficult. You can do it using information your business generates every day—your information base (database or infobase for short)—to create an ongoing dialog with your market. Database marketing can assist you in generating sales, avoiding pitfalls, promoting a positive business image, capitalizing on "golden opportunities," and accomplishing your other business goals.

Think of yourself as a juggler in your business. Each potential customer is a ball that needs to be contacted and spun. If contact isn't maintained through continual attention, the targets will fall and bounce away, just as they do for the juggler. Your task is to keep all the balls constantly in the air. More time and effort is required to acquire a new customer than to maintain an existing one. Therefore, simple, inexpensive contacts with customers can result in dramatic business growth.

The big question remains: If this is so easy, why hasn't everyone done it? Basically, the answer lies in our tendency to get caught up in the traditional methods of contacting customers and prospects—get a name, give it to sales, and cross your fingers.

As an alternative, let's take a look at the database approach, whereby we concentrate on generating leads, staying in contact for potential sales, and developing a relationship with customers. A model of this approach might look like a pyramid with three distinct levels. Imagine that each level has a specific focus:

- Lead management;
- Contact management; and
- Relationship management.

The *lead management level* at the pyramid's base is where inquiries are generated using various media. This level is characterized by follow-up qualification—generally through phone interviews or a personal visit—to determine whether the potential is high. Each lead is qualified, the buying process outlined, and expectations of consummation defined, in order to determine whether contact should be made.

The *contact management level* in the middle of the pyramid is the process that moves a target through the sale. Once a lead is qualified, it should be followed until it's either sold or disqualified. Contacts can be made by mail, phone, fax, and/or face-to-face visits. Each contact should be tailored to the target's expectations in the form of an offer that moves the process along. This level in the database process is the sales rep's playground—an arena where selling is the preferred mode of activity.

Relationship management at the pyramid's apex, is the process of building dialog models for all customers. Keep in mind, however, that targets that haven't been converted to customers don't have a relationship with your business. Moreover, each customer model should be based on attitudes and emotions, as well as user profiles and demographics.

Relationship management has traditionally been the responsibility of the businessowner. This will have to change. Customer needs must be automated, allowing the right type of contact with the right offer at the right time. Businessowners cannot continue to provide relationship management. As products and services become more complex, an increasing amount of sales time is spent on technical training. This time must be used for selling, not for postsale customer management.

A business's sales reps may be one of the contact options, but they shouldn't be the only ones making contacts. A sales rep is most effective at the contact management level—the level populated by high potential leads and customers that have been regenerated or reconditioned for additional sales. Salespeople must be used for their specialty: selling.

The strategic implications of database management are clear—the business, not just the sales rep, is responsible for leads, contacts, and relationships.

Properly executed, this approach changes the basic foundation of the relationship of a business with its customers and qualified leads. The database marketing management approach converts the sales rep into a form of "media"—albeit one that's highly skilled and capable of moving targets to closings—and assumes information capture and management by the business, which is not at all common in many businesses.

High-tech strategies for sales productivity have emerged to take advantage of the enormous computing power within your PC. Telemarketing and sales force automation are examples; both are having a significant impact on American business, but neither has the potential or peril of database marketing.

The purpose of database marketing is to find customers. Its potential is exponential sales growth. The peril, however, is that there is a finite number of customers, and if a competitor implements database marketing faster and better than you, he or she gets all the rewards.

SPREADSHEETS LET YOU VIEW CASH FLOWS AT A GLANCE

You now know how word processing and database software programs can help you run your small business more efficiently. But there is another program that can prove to be invaluable to you.

At this very minute, in your very city or town, hundreds of small businesspeople are tracking their cash flow with the help of a *spreadsheet*. With its enormous range, from simple list management to persuasive graphics to complex financial modeling, it's no wonder that the spreadsheet was the "killer application" that made the PC an overnight success. Actually, it was the spreadsheet program Visicalc that made the Apple II computer really take off. Until that program appeared, the Apple was considered to be only for hobbyists and computer hackers. Businesspeople bought the Apple so that they could use Visicalc. It was the software that launched an industry. Most of you are probably saying that spreadsheets are for those obsessed "number-crunchers" and not for you. But today's spreadsheet programs are easy to use and can provide you with up-to-the-minute information to help in your decision making.

Choosing your spreadsheet can be compared to selecting a particular Swiss Army knife for the specified functions you rely on. You need a spreadsheet that can handle any problem you enter in it. Choose the right spreadsheet, and it will serve you for years—or at least until the next upgrade that you just can't do without.

The spreadsheet major league has only three entries—Lotus 1-2-3 (Release 4), Microsoft Excel 5.0, and Borland's Quattro Pro for Windows 5.0. They all pack plenty of power. These number crunchers take ease-of-use to new heights. The Windows environment is ideal for spreadsheet work. The Multiple Document Interface means you can load in as many worksheets as will fit into memory, quickly move among them, and even link them together. Window's WYSIWYG (pronounced Whizzy Wig—what you see is what you get) nature makes it easy to create compelling numeric tables, and Windows's DDE (dynamic data exchange) and OLE (object linking and embedding) reduce the frustration usually involved in sharing data between different applications. Working with graphs and charts has never been easier; you might even find that these spreadsheet products are strong enough to meet all of your presentation graphics needs.

Lotus 1-2-3

Lotus 1-2-3 (Release 4) has a user interface that greatly enhances its usability. This is the product of the most extensive user-testing program that Lotus has ever undertaken. It is a vast leap forward in simplicity, usability, and power. First, Lotus improved performance and refined spreadsheet "choreography" to optimize the efficiency of your hand and eye motions. Edit, move, and copy any worksheet element—including charts—right in place. Build formulas and format data in seconds. Create a chart complete with titles, labels, and legends in one step. Powerful analytics include more than 200 @functions, including 120 new @functions, accessible from a handy pull-down menu, and more than 250 new macro commands you can drive from graphical Macro Buttons, menus, and SmartIcons.

Most important, 1-2-3 (Release 4) protects your business's investment in existing data and applications with the best 1-2-3 compatibility you'll find anywhere. There's also Excel compatibility so you can transition to 1-2-3 with confidence.

The features dramatically boost your productivity. Lotus has the following exclusives:

- Context-sensitive interface provides instant access to the menus and SmartIcons appropriate to each task.
- Live status bar provides one-click access to unlimited fonts, formats, mail, and more.
- One-step charting lets you create a chart complete with titles, labels, and legends in a single step. You can make chart edits right in the spreadsheet.
- In-cell editing lets you enter and edit data, formulas, and labels directly in a cell—an easier way to work.
- The @function pull-down menu gives you direct access to more than 120 new @functions (more than 200 total) to help you build

formulas fast. You can promote the @functions you use most to the top of the list.

- The navigator lets you jump to any named range with this handy pull-down tool.
- Clean screen lets you turn off the SmartIcons, scroll bar, and edit panel in one step to see more of your worksheet.
- Designer frames lets you highlight tables, titles, and charts with an array of professionally designed frames.
- Version manager lets individuals and workgroup users track worksheet changes in an instant. You can view contributions by date and author.
- Collaboration using Lotus Notes lets you collaborate on a single file while using Version Manager.
- Data query assistant lets you graphically create database queries right in 1-2-3.

Microsoft Excel 5.0

Excel makes spreadsheet work less taxing. Excel's new Function Wizard provides a dialog box with detailed information about the function in an easy-to-use dialog box. In addition, function help is arranged by function type (such as financial or statistical) so everything is easy to find. Headers and footers now use regular English phrases such as Page, not cryptic codes such as &P.

Excel now makes good use of the right mouse button. Select a cell and then drag it, using the right mouse button, to a new location. Up pops a new menu asking if you want to copy or move the cell, among other options. You no longer have to remember that dragging a cell moves it, whereas pressing Ctrl while you drag the cell copies its contents. Right clicking on the title bar brings up a shortcut menu of the most common tasks for the worksheet, including Save, Save As, Print, and Page Setup. Similarly, right clicking on the worksheet tabs gives you a menu full of shortcuts for inserting, deleting, and moving sheets.

Auditing turns visual in Excel 5.0. An auditing Toolbar provides instant access to tools that use arrows to illustrate relationships between cells, even across worksheets in a workbook.

Excel 5.0 lets you take a list of sales (or any) figures by region, with multiple rows for each region, and inserts a subtotal every time the region changes. The program prompts you to name which column's values change, asks you which field you want, and inserts just what you ask for whenever the selected value changes. Not only can Excel insert subtotals in just the right places and highlight them with outlining, but it can also add a grand total.

Suppose you want to show just the rows with data from the sales department's western region. The AutoFilter command changes the cells in a row to a pull-down list, showing all the values in the cell range. Select the value you want, and Excel shows only those rows that contain the value you've selected. All remaining rows are hidden.

The Chart Wizard uses your data in a chart preview, so creating the right type of chart is easier. You can directly manipulate any item on the chart by clicking on and dragging the legend anywhere you want, or by clicking on any text within the legend and changing it. If you've made a mistake in selecting the values you want to chart, you can invoke the Chart Wizard again to define a new range—or use the Drag and Plot feature. With both the chart and spreadsheet range visible on your screen, simply highlight the new cell range you want to include in the chart and drag this range onto the chart. In a bar chart, for example, Excel is smart enough to know whether it needs to add a new bar for each series, or add a new series.

In-place editing of embedded charts allows you to click on a chart within a spreadsheet and directly edit the chart. No longer do you have to double-click on a chart and open a separate window to make your changes. Charts can be inserted as workbook pages and can be larger than the full screen.

You can add a variety of trend lines to the data you've already plotted, such as moving averages or a polynomial best-fit curve, or you can select the new doughnut chart (similar to pie chart data, displayed in concentric rings) or add drawing objects and pictures to your charts. Drawing objects tell the graphic chip how to construct part of an image on the screen of your computer. These commands break the image into its constituent parts that can be coded digitally to build a shape on the screen.

Excel 5.0 is full of pleasant surprises, such as the Tip Wizard that watches you work and suggests specific time-saving tips or shortcuts. For example, if you use the Autofill feature, the Tip Wizard will remind you that dragging the Autofill handle with the right-mouse button displays a list of fill options. When the Tip Wizard has something to say, it changes the color of a Toolbar icon. Click on the icon to read the tip—and click on another icon to jump to a help topic. It's an amazing spreadsheet and very worthy of your consideration.

Quattro Pro for Windows 5.0

Quattro Pro includes plenty of innovations, such as Experts to guide you through complex procedures, Tutors to teach you how to be efficient, a new workgroup desktop to facilitate data sharing, and stellar graphics.

Quattro Pro handles 3-D worksheets excellently. You get 256 spreadsheet pages, all stored in a single file with easy-to-manipulate tabs to ease navigation. It's also the only program that lets you compile formulas in your spreadsheets for improved speed. Sometimes, however, you may find Quattro Pro overwhelming; the menu choices are lengthy and the number of toolbars displayed can get out of control. The analytical toolkit includes some 300 @functions from @ABS to @ZTEST. Among the scientific, mathematical, and financial functions, about the only one you won't find is @KITCHEN-SINK. It even offers on-line assistance along the way, in the form of its Expert-assisted analysis tools. Overall, it's easy to use and thoroughly impressive. Quattro Pro slices, dices, and purees data, better than most of us ever dreamed possible, with powerful data-analysis tools that are push-button easy.

Spreadsheet data can come from anywhere—a database file, another worksheet, an on-line service, even from the keyboard. Both Lotus 1-2-3 and Microsoft Excel support dynamic data exchange

(DDE) and object linking and embedding (OLE), but Quattro Pro reads and writes every essential file format, including Lotus WK1 and WK3, Excel XLS, and dBASE DBF. It also supports eight common graphics file formats. And if you're connected to a network or an E-mail system, Quattro Pro does much more. Run Borland's Workgroup Desktop, and you'll have instant access to a comprehensive application that lets you share worksheets—all at once or page by page—over a variety of networks and messaging systems. Quattro Pro is the best at gathering data from far-flung sources, and it's unmatched at sending data to the outside world.

Lotus Improv for Windows 2.0

Improv is a dramatic new approach to spreadsheet software, designed for anyone who needs to examine data from many different perspectives. Because Improv is so functional and flexible, it's an excellent tool to build worksheets you can share and expand on over time. Improv is the first dynamic spreadsheet for Windows, and with its exclusive dynamic views it lets you rearrange, hide, show, collapse, and expand the spreadsheet or its components in seconds.

Improv formulas are expressed in plain English—exactly the way you think in business terms. For example, Gross Margin = Revenue − Cost of Sales. It's as simple as that. You can open any Improv worksheet and understand its logic instantly, then use it and build on it, effortlessly. Because Improv formulas are general, they automatically apply to all cells where the same relationships hold true. There's no need to copy formulas, as required by conventional spreadsheets. You save time and effort and ensure greater accuracy.

The intuitive user interface reduces or eliminates the steps needed to perform standard spreadsheet operations. You can even transform your current worksheets into Improv format. Improv reads and writes Lotus 1-2-3 and Microsoft Excel files, so you can turn your existing data on its head—to gain a fresh new perspective. Improv was designed from the start to provide new, integrated capabilities for dynamic on-screen viewing as well as analysis capabilities not found in conventional cell-based spreadsheets. Lotus Improv is a spreadsheet complement, allowing better performance of a new class of spreadsheet tasks.

Spreadsheet Decision Maker

Any good spreadsheet program should let you:

1. Choose the type of spreadsheet you create most often, such as simple lists and worksheets.
2. Choose your most important factor, such as formatting.
3. Use other important spreadsheet features for decision making, such as graphing, sorting, formatting, and database manipulation.
4. Compile financial and data analysis.
5. Compile complex data querying and analysis.

> A verbal agreement isn't worth the paper it's written on.
>
> Samuel Goldwyn

Chapter 8

Proper Forms Management and High-Tech Telecommunications Can Eliminate the "Paper Chase"

FORMS MANAGEMENT CAN INCREASE EFFICIENCY AND REVENUES

The most common tasks in any business are centered around the use of forms. Small businesses or sole operators are no exceptions. Forms serve two purposes in any business:

1. They collect information in a structured manner—a specific piece of data is entered in a particular field; and
2. They communicate that information when the form is submitted to others.

In the paper-based business world, individuals fill out forms by hand and then manually distribute them to their intended recipients. This wastes time and money. In the electronic-based business world, users fill in forms on their PCs and transmit them electronically. This process, once learned by the users, can speed up forms management so that the users can go on to more revenue-producing tasks.

Whether the form is an expense report, purchase order request, mortgage application, engineering change order, or any one of thousands of other form applications, the task it represents is never done in isolation. For example, once an expense form is filled out, it is submitted to a supervisor for approval or sent directly to the accounting department for processing.

One of the biggest hurdles faced by businesses moving from the paper form to the electronic form is that users must learn a new program just to fill in one simple form. It is simply not enough to provide an electronic WYSIWYG (what you see is what you get) representation of the form of users (although it helps) and expect flawless automation to occur as a result. An enormous amount of time must be spent teaching users what functions to use and what steps to take with the application in order to get the form properly filled out and processed. Businesses typically do not have the time and resources available for that kind of intensive training.

Nevertheless, the need to automate paper forms is clear, because the benefits are immense. Businesses want a solution that lends itself to easy implementation and management control. They want something that can be distributed smoothly and requires little attention thereafter—at least, as far as end-user support is concerned.

A second requirement stems from the fact that many businesses have already committed to and invested in certain technologies, such as LANs (Local Area Networks), databases, and electronic mail systems. They have already built the infrastructure; a forms-based workflow solution, therefore, should leverage on that investment by building on the existing infrastructure.

Database and mail vendors that offer forms-based workflow solutions typically do so with their own agenda at the forefront. They want to sell their own database technology or messaging application, not someone else's, which may not be in your best interest. Sometimes, businesses are still in the pilot stage with various electronic mail packages and have not decided on any one particular system. Mail is not yet part of the infrastructure, so they need a solution that is flexible enough to adapt to any mail system.

Another factor specific to mail messaging is the ability to build "rules" upon which a form is routed. Mail vendors are talking about and, in some cases, offering *rule-based routing*. But unless a business has standardized once-and-for-all on that particular mail package, any rule-based routing applications developed with the mail package could not be used in other mail systems. Rule-based connotes a computer system which performs inferences by applying a set of "if-then" rules to a set of facts following given procedures. Again, flexibility is vital for many businesses.

This leads us to two more closely related requirements of a complete forms-based workflow solution. It must be *evolutionary* and *scalable*. Some forms-based workflow offerings require businesses to "dive" into them, in a sort of mass scale reengineering project. However, more prudent businesses want to "wade" into forms-based workflow by reengineering in smaller steps. They prefer an evolutionary rather than revolutionary approach. For example, they may begin by computerizing a series of forms simply for "print-on-demand," add filling "intelligence" some time later, and eventually integrate database links and electronic mail routing in the application, without having to start again from scratch. Moreover, a forms-based solution must be scalable, in the sense that an application can be deployed on a small scale, perhaps within a workgroup or department, and then expanded to the entire business.

One final requirement: if your business has lots of time, money, and many software developers, then a fully customizable, flexible, evolutionary, and scalable forms-based workflow solution can be created using portable high-level languages, such as C. However, if your business doesn't have a lot of time, or money, or many software developers, yours is like most businesses. An enormous application backlog already exists. On top of that, add reengineering and other projects, and you get a sense of why many businesses are outsourcing. Whether a project is addressed internally or farmed out to a third party, businessowners need tools that can accomplish a given task in a relatively short amount of time.

In order to bring about forms-based workflow, there are four "enabling" technologies that must combine and interact:

1. *Intelligent forms processing* to create form applications that automate data entry:

2. *Database technology* to compile and access the information in standard, structured formats;

3. *Electronic mail* (E-mail) to automate the communication or movement of that information; and

4. *Application development* to provide ease of implementation and management control.

The two most common form-management programs are listed here. Please contact the manufacturers for more information.

Delrina FormFlow
Published by: Delrina Corporation
     6830 Via Del Oro, Suite 240
     San Jose, CA 95119
     (800) 268-6082 (408) 363-2345 FAX (408) 363-2340

By Design Portfolio
Published by: Streetwise Software, Inc.
     2116 Wilshire Boulevard, Suite 230
     Santa Monica, CA 90403
     800-743-6765 FAX (310) 828-8258

HIGH-TECH TELECOMMUTING OFFERS SPEED AND FLEXIBILITY FOR SMALL BUSINESSOWNERS

Today's telecommunications technology can eliminate the trip to "work" by moving the work to the workers, instead of moving the workers to work. Instead of commuting, workers are *telecommuting*. Through telecommunications, you and your employees can work just about anywhere, including the following locations:

1. A *home office*—This is the most popular location for work through telecommuting. The employee designates work space at home to conduct business functions.

2. A *satellite office*—This configuration enables multidiscipline employees (i.e., an employee from the accounting department and/or

214

an employee from the data processing department) to work together, sharing office technology. The primary consideration in configuring a satellite office is locating the office in an area where a high concentration of employees live. The employees share the common interest of living in the same general vicinity, as opposed to having similar job functions.

3. *A neighborhood work center*—This configuration builds on the satellite office concept and takes it one step further by housing multicompany employees (i.e., an employee from the ABC Company, an employee from the XYZ Corporation, and/or an employee from QRS Industries), who also share office technology. Again, the employees reside in the general vicinity of the neighborhood work center.

Telecommuting may benefit your business in several different ways. Through the use of telecommunications, your business can experience:

- Increased productivity;
- Decreased turnover;
- Reduced overhead;
- Improved recruiting and retention opportunities;
- Access to new labor pools;
- Preparation for disaster recovery/emergency preparedness plans;
- Compliance with air quality/transportation ordinances, legislation, and regulation.

Your employees and/or you will derive the following benefits:

- Increased productivity;
- Increased flexibility;
- Reduced commute time and cost;
- Reduced stress;
- Increased job opportunities;
- Increased job retention;
- Increased family interaction.

The community also derives a great number of benefits from a telecommunicating system:

- Decreased need for mass transit;
- Reduced fuel consumption;
- Improved air quality;
- Reduced demand on transportation infrastructures;
- Increased employment opportunities for those with limited mobility.

Telecommuting will change the way your business does business. Because you will be changing the way people interact with each other, there are some sensitive issues that you need to be aware of. If you understand these issues from the beginning, you can build solutions to the adjustments before they are a major concern. Everyone needs to understand that by implementing a telecommuting program you will be changing the flow of work in the office. Study how things are done now, before telecommuting is implemented, and then think of everything that could go wrong while the telecommuters aren't in the office. Once you identify the areas of concern, you can put procedures in place to keep the potential trouble areas from becoming major disasters. Careful planning will keep your telecommuting program running smoothly.

The issues you need to be concerned about are:

1. For the telecommuter
   (a) Increased isolation from co-workers;
   (b) Reduced visibility;
   (c) Reduced access to support services;
   (d) Reduction of living space;
   (e) Increase of at-home costs;
   (f) Increased distractions in home environment;
   (g) Increased security responsibility.

2. For the business

(a) Adjustment in philosophy and procedures;

(b) Increased potential for mistrust of employees;

(c) Increased regulatory and legal issues;

(d) Increased start-up and operating costs;

(e) Increased concern regarding security of data;

(f) Increased potential loss of employee loyalty.

3. For the community

(a) Increased potential for abandonment and decay of urban centers;

(b) Increased potential for possible relocation, not reduction, of traffic;

(c) Increased potential spread of urban sprawl;

(d) Increased labor concern over worker alienation and employee abuse;

(e) Increased fear of trend toward an antisocial society.

Telecommuting brings a unique set of challenges to the workplace. Understanding the challenges and implementing methods to manage all circumstances is essential. Address all areas of possible concern and establish contingency plans to keep the workplace running smoothly. Careful monitoring of the program's goals and actual achievements will ensure success.

There is no secret combination of characteristics that will ensure a successful telecommuter. The most important factor in determining who will telecommute is to provide employees with the option of volunteering to participate in the telecommuting program. In professional-level jobs, employees are skilled at self-assessing their potential for telecommuting. In entry level jobs, self-perception is not quite as clear. The most common characteristics of a successful telecommuter are as follows:

• Demonstrates self-motivation;

- Exhibits a positive attitude toward telecommuting;
- Possesses strong time-management skills;
- Maintains a high level of productivity;
- Requires minimal supervision;
- Works well with family members;
- Prefers home environment;
- Is moderately people oriented;
- Possesses a high level of skill and job knowledge;
- Exhibits strong organizational skills.

The telecommuting program must remain flexible enough for employees to use it for their benefit and for meeting the needs of the business. If a telecommuter is experiencing difficulty at home, he or she should have the option of suspending telecommuting until such time as it becomes reasonable to resume telecommuting at home.

The most successful programs recognize flexibility on the part of the telecommuters and the business as necessary to address business problems creatively.

To be a successful telecommuter requires the ability to work with less structure and more freedom in completing your responsibilities. Telecommuting isn't as simple as staying at home and working. It requires careful planning and discipline. The basic tools for working at home and maintaining or increasing your level of productivity and the quality, quantity, and timeliness of your work product are described in the following section.

FIVE STEPS TO SUCCESSFUL TELECOMMUTING

Get Organized

Develop good work habits from the moment you begin telecommuting, and you'll realize how easy it is to complete your work away from the office.

Pick a Work Location

Identify a safe location in your home as your work space. You don't need to devote an entire room to your home office. Some telecommuters have successfully developed a part of an existing room, a garage, an attic, and even a closet for their work stations. Locate your work station away from distractions. Don't try working on the couch in front of the TV or at the dining room table. It doesn't work!

Establish a Routine

Set a work schedule for the days you telecommute and stick to it. Begin and finish working at the same time on telecommuting days. This will help you establish a routine. Replace the ritual of getting ready for the office with another ritual.

As a telecommuter, you'll no longer have the traditional office rituals of morning conversations, coffee, reading the newspaper, or even the long, dreadful commute that symbolizes the beginning of each workday. Establish new rituals for telecommuting days. Some telecommuters actually leave the house, go around the block, return, and begin the workday. Others play a specific kind of music, or begin working after a morning exercise session or bike ride. Find a ritual that will work for you.

Make a To-Do List for Your Work Assignments

Develop a list of goals and assignments for the days you telecommute. At the end of each day, go over the list and see how much you've been able to accomplish. It's beneficial to start the list a couple of days before you're telecommuting to plan for all the resources you'll need to support your activities at home. Schedule your work so that you don't need assistance from others while at home. Remember, you may not have access to a fax machine, a photocopy machine, or even a computer at home. Plan your work accordingly.

Have an End-of-the-Day Ritual

It's a good practice to have a ritual in place to mark the end of the workday. Use imagination. Among the usual signals indicating the end of the workday are the following:

- Turn off the computer and the lights.
- Close the door.
- Turn on the TV.
- Walk around the block.
- Pick up the children from school or day care.
- Change your clothes.
- Sit down with your feet up and relax!

> The wisdom of the wise and the experience of the ages are perpetuated by quotations.
>
> Benjamin Disraeli

Chapter 9

Mastering On-Line Services

WHY SUBSCRIBE TO AN ON-LINE SERVICE?

Have you always wanted to have direct access to sources of information that would provide the background and details of subjects that were of immediate interest and could provide profitable possibilities? Information, in the context of on-line services, runs the gamut from gaining access to economic reports; finding prospective customers in Lexington, Kentucky; downloading the latest version of an antivirus program; getting advice on desktop publishing and design; enrolling in community services business courses; and shopping for hardware, software, and office supplies. Your business can profit immeasurably from the benefits of using one or more of the eight major on-line services: America Online, CompuServe, Delphi, Dialog, Dow Jones News/Retrieval, GEnie, Mead Data Central Nexis/Lexis, and Prodigy.

The operative words of these on-line services are "network accessibility." You can connect with (potentially) millions of other computer users in areas ranging from marketing to materials handling. You'll have access to the publishers and manufacturers of popular software and hardware, including on-line technical support. Downloading shareware and freeware is another advantage of on-line activity—some services are a virtual software candy store. You can access trade industry data, compare notes with others in your line of business but in locations too remote to be competition, send a fax, or even book a seat on your next business flight. If you work from home—running a full-time business, moonlighting, or telecommuting—an on-line service can help you to maximize your information-gathering efforts and to keep on top of your market.

Many on-line services charge by the minute, then tack on surcharges for access to specialized databases, plus extra fees for things like library searches, fax transmissions, and document retrievals. Some charge annual membership fees. Others offer all-you-can-use flat fees—but charge more if you log on during business hours or access certain databases.

Although many on-line services are now trying to simplify their systems by offering graphical, intuitive front-end software, the learning curve can still be steep in some cases—resulting in a rather pricey tuition.

Getting to be king in your field of business requires the ability to access information—on-line, on time, and on budget. It's worth the effort to learn.

The vast amount of information now available makes it possible to predicate marketing planning and strategy on a wealth of information, from world economic trends to demographics for the smallest neighborhood; from industry statistics to details of an individual company that might be targeted as a prospective customer.

AMERICA ONLINE

America Online's mission is to give you the easiest and most pleasurable time on-line. The computing and software department is the flagship of this service, housing forums in business, communications and networking, desktop publishing, development, education, games, graphics, music, utilities, user groups, desk accessories, and more. America Online is easy to use—simply by clicking an icon, you can send off an on-line message, join in a real-time conference session, or download from a choice of more than 70,000 shareware or freeware files. Running into the service's 600,000 other members with similar interests is a possibility each time you go on-line. America Online includes a time-efficient Download Manager that lets you select a group of files, download them all at once, and log off. Members can also exchange messages with CompuServe members through the Internet gateway.

COMPUSERVE

CompuServe provides access to thousands of databases and publications spanning the spheres of finance, business, and government. In addition, CompuServe offers hundreds of special-interest forums where you can leave messages, ask questions, or have live discussions on topics ranging from desktop publishing to working at home. Product support from most major hardware and software vendors is also available. The service's extensive E-mail system makes it easy to upload and download files and to communicate with the service's one million-plus members—as well as those members on America Online and others connected through the Internet gateway.

For a novice, CompuServe's extensive command structure can be difficult to navigate without a graphical front-end program such as CompuServe Information Manager.

DELPHI

Delphi is much lower in price than the other on-line services. One reason for this is that it is not as extensive in features and forums as most of its competitors. Delphi offers a simplified command structure, foreign-language translation services, and a gateway to Latin America through its Delphi/Argentina and Delphi/Miami international services.

Although Delphi does offer stock quotes, commodities prices, and several stock tip newsletters, the service doesn't have much in the way of business databases or bulletin boards, and, unless you tap into Dialog's complex and expensive video text service, there are no newspaper or magazine archives to peruse. Another drawback to

Delphi is its dearth of local access numbers, so long-distance charges can add up, negating its basic cost advantage.

GEnie

GEnie is a full-service resource that resembles a scaled-down CompuServe. Price is one of GEnie's main attractions—as long as you have insomnia and log on at night and don't select anything beyond its basic offerings. GEnie offers a great deal for the business user: investment and business-related bulletin boards, hardware and .software support roundtables, a gateway to Dow Jones News/ Retrieval's wealth of financial information, and all the E-mail you can send.

GEnie is aimed at the consumer market, yet its complex menu structure makes it difficult to navigate without its Aladdin front-end software. It can take a while for the service to move you in and out of the basic, value, and professional service areas. GEnie doesn't offer much business information of its own, forcing users to access Dow Jones News/Retrieval at prices that, during peak hours, can approach $200 an hour.

PRODIGY

Although Prodigy positions itself as a family service, providing education, entertainment, news, weather, sports, personal finance advice, and so on, there are still a variety of business and computing resources to be found. Unlike other on-line services that charge by the minute or tack on surcharges for each specialized database, Prodigy charges a reasonable monthly fee. Designed with the on-line novice in mind, Prodigy's colorful interface and simple on-screen commands make the service easy to master. Prodigy claims more than 1.75 million members.

QUESTIONS TO ASK BEFORE GOING ON-LINE

Before you start dialing for data, you must ask some questions that will make on-line searches painless and cost-effective:

1. *What am I looking for?* Most on-line services charge by the minute and levy additional surcharges for accessing specialized databases; an on-line service is hardly the place to browse

2. *Before you log on, jot down a few notes to remind yourself of what you're going to be looking for.* The more narrowly you can define your search on paper ahead of time, the less time and money you'll end up spending on-screen. For instance, typing the search words "ice cream" and "entrepreneurship" into an on-line database can easily turn up dozens or even thousands of articles, many of which will be irrelevant to your needs. Rather than wasting time and money sifting through a mountain of data, narrow your search. Add a few more words to your search string, such as "competition," "Good Humor," and "Ben and Jerry," and you stand a much better shot at retrieving more specific market information.

3. *How fast do I really need this information?* The faster you want the information, the more it's going to cost you. Many on-line services charge lower rates at night and on weekends when fewer businesspeople use them.

4. *Can I get what I'm looking for off-line too?* This comes down to a question of priorities—your money or your time. If you live in or near a larger city or a university or college, you may find that libraries house much of the same information you can find on-line. You'll have to make a trip to the library(ies), of course, but once you arrive, the information is free and the reference librarians are helpful.

   Many libraries now contain not only printed materials but also information on CD-ROM, such as government census and trade statistics. Many state and federal agencies will send you economic and demographic information at no charge within a week or so—if you can afford to wait that long.

5. *Can I get everything I want from just one on-line service?* Most on-line services overlap when it comes to the more popular business databases such as Disclosure, D&B Dun's Market Identifiers, and ABI/Inform, to name a few. Because there is so much duplication, you can save on annual subscriptions by limiting the number of on-line services you join. Many on-line services offer free software and sign-up plans that let you try before you buy. This enables you to evaluate a service for several hours before the meter starts running.

   Another drawback to signing up for multiple on-line services is that there are numerous small differences that take time to master. For example, typing the letter "m" at a command prompt gets you back to the previous menu on CompuServe, whereas on Dow Jones News/Retrieval, you need to type "/m." Rather than learning a handful of key words in each on-line language, pick one or two services and become fluent in its language.

6. *How much time do I plan to spend on-line each month?* If you plan to spend a lot of time on-line, sign up for a flat-fee plan that won't penalize you for heavy usage. Conversely, if you plan to go on-line only every once in a while, choose the option that lets you pay as you go. Generally speaking, if you plan to spend at least half an hour on-line a month, it pays to invest in a flat-fee plan.

7. *How much money do I want to spend on on-line service?* You have to weigh the cost of going on-line against the potential return on your investment. Although spending several hundred dollars a month on an on-line service may sound like a lot of money, it may actually be a pittance when compared with the cost of photocopying research materials at your local library.

8. *How much time do I want to spend learning about on-line services?* If you're like most businesspeople, the answer is "As little as possible." But if you're planning to rely on on-line services as your primary research tool, it makes sound business sense to devote some time to getting to know the ins and outs of the on-line services you use most often. Not only will your on-line service bills be lower at the end of the month, but you'll also have more time to do what you do best—running your business.

If you don't plan to spend a lot of time on-line, consider signing up for a service that offers pull-down menus and a plain-English command structure even though it may cost you a little more.

9. *What type of information will I need most often?* When choosing which on-line service or services to subscribe to, it's important to know what kind of information you'll need most. Although many of the major on-line services offer access to a wide variety of business and financial databases, it may be worthwhile to subscribe to a specialized service if your business requires it.

If you do business in global markets, think about signing up for Data-Star, which features more than 250 databases offering worldwide financial information on business, medicine, science, pharmaceuticals, and technology. Data-Star also offers Tradstat, a database containing official government import/export information on more than 60,000 commodities from Europe, Japan, Canada, Taiwan, South America, and the United States.

INTERNET—THE KING OF ON-LINE SERVICES

The Internet is a collection of more than 11,000 computer networks—from universities, libraries, museums, supercomputer centers, state and federal government institutions, and businesses—around the world that are linked together. It is not a specific entity (although aspects of it are managed by a volunteer organization called the Internet Society)—it's just the name that has been given to this federation of allied networks, many of which are nonprofit. Even if you don't belong to one of these organizations, you can access the Internet and exchange electronic mail and files with others on the system.

The Internet now counts more than 10 million users in 50 countries and is growing daily. The number of users has been doubling in recent years. A descendant of a network started by the United States Advanced Research Projects Agency in the late 1960s, Internet was further developed by the National Science Foundation (NSF) during the mid-1980s. The NSFnet, in fact, is one of the backbone networks on the Internet. Because of these roots and the number of universities connected, Internet is particularly valuable for scientists, academics, policymakers, market researchers, librarians, and technicians, who can keep in touch with their colleagues around the world and up to date with the latest developments in their fields. Nonetheless, more than half of the groups connected to the Internet are engaged in commerical activity.

In addition to this global community of professionals and scientists, the Internet offers some of the same services as commerical on-line networks: electronic mail to Internet users as well as to millions of subscribers to commercial services; the ability to chat or confer with other Internet users; more than two million files and shareware programs to download; multi-player games; several thousand special-interest groups (called *newsgroups*) whereby you can post and read messages; and access to databases (such as the Library of Congress catalog records, transcripts of electronic conferences, census data, and the Department of Commerce's Economic Bulletin Board). You can download files and access many of these services at no charge.

Electronic mail is the most commonly used application on the Internet. Nearly one-third of respondents to a recent Internet survey said they carried out some kind of collaborative research or work with colleagues via electronic mail. Many people said they used the Internet E-mail as an inexpensive alternative to overnight mail services. Many small businesses use the Internet as their own corporate network. An Internet user can also exchange electronic mail with members of commercial services. An Internet user with a commercial account can access systems from the Internet, which may cut phone costs considerably.

A wealth of information and users is one of the Internet's selling points, but it can also be a drawback. With millions of megabytes of information to choose from and more than 10 million users, you can easily get lost. That is partly because of the Internet's rather unwelcoming and sometimes arcane command-driven interface, in marked contrast to those of commercial services, which are getting more and more graphic. When sending a message from another system to the Internet, you must use the unfriendly Internet address protocol: user name@machine name. For example, the address for the NSFnet InterNIC's information service is info@internic.net. Increasingly, however, Internet sites are offering friendly navigators, which have point-and-click menus in addition to providing the ability to search indexed lists of resources.

Because the Internet isn't a commercial enterprise with standardized fees, you can't call an 800 number and sign up for an Internet account. You set up an account with an organization called a Public-Access Internet Site, which is connected to the Internet, then use your own communications software to sign on. Public-Access Internet Sites are in major cities around the world. Even Delphi, a major commercial on-line service, offers full Internet access.

Most sites charge a mere $1 an hour to access the Internet, no matter the speed of your modem, although you may pay more for some selected databases. With a little patience and practice on your part, the Internet can be the doorway to a new universe of information and resources. At the very least, it's a good way to connect disparate people electronically without incurring big monthly bills.

Internet Resources

The InterNIC Information Services' Referral Desk (800-444-4345) provides a list of groups that offer public access to the Internet; push 1 (registration) at the voice-mail prompt. For help in finding general information or a database on the Internet, push 3 (information services).

Another way to get a list of public access sites is to send E-mail to the Internet from another service and ask for the PDIAL list, which has information about organizations offering Internet accounts for individuals. Address your message to "info-deli-server@netcom.com" on the Internet and include "Send PDIAL" in the subject field.

Internet Business Pages, a free service under development, provides a list of businesses on the Internet. Contact Edward Vielmetti, Msen Inc., 628 Brooks, Ann Arbor, MI 48103; 313-998-4562.

The Internet Business Journal provides ongoing information about business activity and development on the Internet; one year (six regular issues, six supplements) costs $75, small business rate (Strangelove Press, Ottawa, Ontario, Canada; 613-747-6106.) The journal is also available in some libraries.

The *Desktop Internet Reference* is a public-domain hypertext guide to using the Internet, which may be freely copied, $10 for shipping and handling. The Windows requirement signify that the program operates under Windows 3.0 or higher and cannot operate independently. Contact the author: John Buckman, 3520 Connecticut Avenue NW #33, Washington, DC 20008; 301-986-0444, ext. 5841 (daytime).

Appendix

Strategic Resources Guide

ON-LINE SERVICES AND SOFTWARE MANUFACTURERS

AMERICA ONLINE
8619 Westwood Center Drive, Suite 200
Vienna, VA 22182-9806
1-800-827-6364

APPLE COMPUTER, INC.
20525 Mariani Avenue
Cupertino, CA 95014
(408) 996-1010

AVERY-DENNISON
818 Oak Park Road
Covina, CA 91724
1-800-252-8379

BEST!WARE
One of the Best Companies
300 Roundhill Drive
Rockaway, NJ 07866
(201) 586-2200   FAX (201) 586-8885

CAMPBELL SERVICES, INC.
21700 Northwestern Highway
Southfield, MI 48075
(313) 559-5955   FAX (313) 559-1034

CompuServe
P.O. Box 20212

Columbus, OH 43220
1-800-848-8199

COMPUTER ASSOCIATES INTERNATIONAL, INC.
One Computer Associates Plaza
Islandia, NY 11788-7000
1-800-225-5224   (516) 242-5224

DacEasy, Inc.
17950 Preston Road, Suite 800
Dallas, TX 75252
1-800-DAC-EASY

DELPHI
General VideoText Corporation
1030 Massachusetts Avenue
Cambridge, MA 02138
1-800-695-4005   (617) 491-3393

DELRINA CORPORATION
6830 Via Del Oro, Suite 240
San Jose, CA 95119
1-800-268-6082   (408) 363-2345   FAX (408) 363-2340

DIALOG INFORMATION SERVICES, INC.
3460 Hillview Avenue
Palo Alto, CA 94304-1396
1-800-334-2564   (415) 858-3785

GEnie
401 N. Washington Street
Rockville, MD 20850
1-800-638-9636   (301) 340-5397

IMS (INFORMATION MANAGEMENT SERVICES)
P.O. Box 1471
Cary, NC 27512
1-800-298-3674   FAX (407) 339-6520

INTERNET
InterNIC Information Services' Referral Desk
1-800-444-4345

INTUIT
155 Linfield Drive
P.O. Box 3014
Menlo Park, CA 94026
1-800-624-8742   (415) 322-0573

INTUIT
6256 Greenwich Drive, Suite 100
San Diego, CA 92122
(619) 453-4446   FAX (619) 535-0737

LOTUS DEVELOPMENT CORPORATION
55 Cambridge Parkway
Cambridge, MA 02142
1-800-343-5414   (Canada) 1-800-GO-LOTUS
For spreadsheets and all products other than word processing

LOTUS WORD PROCESSING DIVISION
1000 Abernathy Road, N.E.
Atlanta, GA 30328
1-800-831-9679   (Canada) 1-800-GO-LOTUS)

M.-USA BUSINESS SYSTEMS, INC.
15806 Midway Road
Dallas, TX 75244
1-800-933-6872   (214) 386-6100

MANZANITA SOFTWARE SYSTEMS
2130 Professional Drive, Suite 150
Roseville, CA 95661-3751
1-800-447-5700   (916) 781-3880   FAX (916) 781-3814

MICROSOFT CORPORATION
One Microsoft Way
Redmond, WA 98052-9400
1-800-426-9400

NEBS SOFTWARE, INC.
20 Industrial Park Drive
Nashua, NH 03062
1-800-388-8000   (603) 880-5100   FAX (603) 880-5102

POLARIS SOFTWARE, INC.
15175 Innovation Drive

San Diego, CA 92128
(619) 592-7400   FAX (619) 592-7430

PRODIGY INFORMATION SERVICE
445 Hamilton Avenue
White Plains, NY 10601
1-800-776-3449   (914) 993-8000

SERVICEPoint CORPORATION
441 East Bay Boulevard, Suite 200
Provo, UT 84606
(801) 373-3859   FAX (801) 377-8982

SourceMate INFORMATION SYSTEMS, INC.
20 Sunnyside Avenue
Mill Valley, CA 94941
1-800-877-8896   (415) 381-1011   FAX (415) 381-6902

STREETWISE SOFTWARE, INC.
2116 Wilshire Boulevard, Suite 230
Santa Monica, CA 90403
1-800-743-6765   FAX (310) 828-8258

TIMESLIPS CORPORATION
239 Western Avenue
Essex, MA 01929
1-800-285-0999   FAX (508) 768-7660

WordPerfect CORPORATION
1555 N. Technology Way
Orem, UT 84057-2399
1-800-451-5151

BUSINESS ORGANIZATIONS AND SERVICES

NATIONAL ASSOCIATION OF
BLACK WOMEN ENTREPRENEURS
Box 1375
Detroit, MI 48231
(313) 341-7400

Acts as a national support system for black businesswomen to enhance their business, professional, and technical development. Offers educational symposia, workshops, and forums, as well as sharing resources and providing placement services.

NATIONAL ASSOCIATION OF WOMEN BUSINESS OWNERS (NAWBO)
600 S. Federal Street, Suite 400
Chicago, IL 60605
1-800-892-9000 (312) 922-0465

Helps to broaden opportunities for women in business by offering workshops and seminars, providing information and referral services to members, and maintaining a databank of women-owned businesses. Also holds a yearly conference.

SERVICE CORPS OF RETIRED EXECUTIVES (SCORE)

Sponsored by the U.S. Small Business Administration, SCORE is a volunteer, non-profit organization of active and retired businesspeople. SCORE offers free counseling to persons who plan to go into business and those already in business. SCORE counselors provide free, confidential, one-on-one counseling in areas such as business planning, marketing, advertising, personnel management, inventory control, cash and credit management, budgeting, goal setting, bidding, estimating, and international trade.

Management training programs are offered in many cities. Programs cover such topics as starting a business, managing a home-based business, setting your fees, marketing and advertising, basic bookkeeping and financial statements, sales techniques, and developing a business plan.

If you have any questions about SCORE or other SBA programs contact your local SBA office which can be found under the Federal Government section of your telephone white pages. If you are a veteran, some SBA offices have received grants for intensive entrepreneurial training programs and for computer-based business planning programs exclusively for veterans.

Non-SBA Sources

There are many additional sources of small business help available from Federal, State, and local governments and the private sector. Federal agencies and military installations have local Procurement Representatives who can help you sell to the government. They can be contacted by looking up the agency or installation under U.S. Government in the telephone directory. Local field offices of Federal agencies such as the Department of Commerce, the Bureau of Census, and the Department of Agriculture can provide a wide range of statistical data useful for marketing. Most State governments have an Office of Development which can provide detailed business start up information often in the form of a Business Start Up Kit. The kit will cover such areas as permits and licenses, local codes and regulations, state financial assistance, and tax requirements.

Local Chambers of Commerce, colleges and universities, libraries and business development centers also can assist with start up and management information.

Another idea—don't overlook the reference section of your local library. It contains a great many useful publications such as Commerce Business Daily, Catalog of Federal Domestic Assistance, Statistical Abstract of the United States, Statistics of Income, Census of Industry, County Business Patterns, Survey of Current Business, and Business Conditions Digest. These publications provide very useful economic, procurement, grant, and statistical information.

SMALL BUSINESS TAX EDUCATION PROGRAM (STEP)

A cooperative effort to provide business tax education, the Internal Revenue Service's Small Business Tax Education Program is a cooperative effort with local organizations to provide business tax education to the small business owner.

Instructors will teach you:

• The tax advantages and disadvantages of the various forms of business organizations.

- How to use Federal Tax Deposit Coupons and how to fill out other business and employment tax forms.
- The role of the IRS and how to deal effectively with various offices in the IRS.
- What other help is available from the IRS and other federal, state, and local agencies and how to get it when you need it.
- Technical information on a series of selected tax topics pertinent to a small business.

The costs for this program vary. Some courses are offered free as a community service. Courses offered through an educational facility may include costs for course materials in addition to tuition. Still others are offered at a nominal fee to offset administrative costs of sponsoring organizations. For further information, call the IRS at 1-800-829-1040.

U.S. SMALL BUSINESS ADMINISTRATION (SBA)

This independent federal agency is a first resort for entrepreneurs in new and growing businesses. The host of services it offers include classes, one-on-one counseling, publications, and loan guarantees. The SBA also sponsors the Certified Development Company program (also known as the 504 program), the Preferred Lender Program (PLP), the Certified Lender Program (CLP), and the Small Business Investment Company Program (SBIC). The SBA also sponsors the Small Business Person of the Year awards during Small Business Week, the second week in May.

Telephone assistance is available from the Small Business Answer Desk, which takes calls on weekdays from 8:30 AM to 5:30 PM Eastern time. The toll-free number is 1-800-827-5722. SBA also has programs to assist veterans, minorities, and women.

GLOSSARY

Accelerated depreciation A method of depreciation that charges off more of the original cost of the fixed assets in the earlier years than in the later years of the asset's service life.

Accelerator A key or combination of keys that invokes an application-defined function.

Access time The time interval between the instant at which a call for data is initiated and the instant at which the delivery of data is completed.

Account A recording unit used to reflect the changes in assets, liabilities or owner's equity.

Accountant A professional who analyzes financial information, advises management, and interprets trends for a business owner. These services are based on the information in the books and records, both historical and current and on projections of future activity.

Accounting period The period of time over which an income statement summarizes the changes in owners' equity; usually, the period is one year.

Account receivable An amount that is owed to the business, usually by one of its customers, as a result of the ordinary extension of credit.

Accrual basis The measurement of revenues and expenses, as contrasted with receipts and expenditures.

Accrued expense Expense that has been incurred during the accounting period but has neither been paid nor recorded. An example is unpaid employees' salaries.

Accrued revenue Revenue that has been earned during the accounting period but has neither been collected or recorded. An example is uncollected interest.

Accumulated depreciation An account showing the total amount of depreciation of an asset that has been accumulated to date.

Acid-test ratio The ratio obtained by dividing quick assets by current liabilities.

Actives Customers on a list who have made purchases within a prescribed time period—usually not more than a year.

Activity driven All of the functions and processes and their interdependencies with a computer software program.

Address Your online code name or number to which others send messages and files. Each service either assigns each member an online name or series of numbers and letters, or allows you to select your own.

Adjusting entries Journal entries made at the end of an accounting period to bring the revenue and expense account balances up to date and to show the correct ending balances in the asset and liability accounts.

Aging receivables A schedule of accounts receivable according to the length of time they have been outstanding.

A.I.D.A. The most popular formula for preparing direct-mail copy. The letters stand for get Attention, arouse Interest, stimulate Desire, ask for Action.

Allowance for doubtful accounts The amount of estimated bad debts that is subtracted from accounts receivable on the balance sheet.

Amortization The process of writing off the cost of intangible assets; similar to depreciation.

Application swap file A temporary disk file used by Windows to store some or all of the information used by a non-Windows application when you switch away from that application.

Archive attribute One of four markers that MS-DOS can use to classify a disk file. The archive attribute indicates that a file has been modified since it was last backed up.

Asset An item which is owned by the business and has a value that can be measured objectively.

Auditing A review of accounting records by independent, outside public accountants.

Audit trail The documentation of transactions that allows an auditor or accountant to verify the accuracy of information contained in the books and records of the business. The trail follows a source document through the system of journal entries, then to the general ledger.

Back end   Activities necessary to complete a mail-order transaction once an order has been received; measurement of a buyer's performance after he or she has ordered the first item in a series offering.

Bad debts   The estimated amount of credit sales that will not be collected.

Balance of an account   The difference between the totals of the two sides of an account.

Balance sheet   A financial statement which reports the assets and equities of a company at one point in time. Assets are listed on the left and equities and liabilities on the right.

BASIC   Refers to Beginner's All-purpose Symbolic Instruction Code. A higher-level language developed to allow the user to formulate a problem in a more convenient and efficient manner than machine language

Baud (or bps)   The unit of measurement for the speed at which a modem transmits and receives information. The higher the number, the faster the modem.

Bingo card   A reply card inserted in a publication and used by readers to request literature from companies whose products and services are either advertised or mentioned elsewhere in the publication.

Bond   A written promise to repay money furnished the business, with interest, at some future date, usually five or more years hence.

Books of original entry   One of several journals in the accounting system. All information in the general ledger is posted from the receipts, disbursements, and general journals, or from subsidiary journals representing one of the three books of original entry.

Book value   The cost of a depreciable asset less its related accumulated depreciation. Also called carrying value.

Boot   To start or restart your computer. Loading the MS-DOS operating system from your hard disk or floppy disk.

Bounce back   An offer enclosed with a mailing sent to a customer in fulfillment of an offer.

Broadcasting   Having the capability to send one document or file to two or more recipients.

Bulletin boards (BBS)   In the context of online services, a section within forums where members voice opinions, and ask and answer questions. They are sometimes referred to as message boards.

Bus   Common channel (pathway) between hardware devices either internally between components in a computer, or externally between stations in a communications network.

Capital   The invested value of ownership in a business. Capitalization may consist of both equity (capital investment of the owners) and debt (borrowed money).

Capital stock   A balance sheet account showing the amount that was assigned to the shares of stock at the time they were originally issued.

Capital turnover   A ratio obtained by dividing annual sales by investment.

Cash basis accounting   An accounting system that does not use the accrual basis.

Cash receipts journal   A book of original entry in which cash receipts and sales are posted. May include accounts receivable information.

Catalog sales   Products with their specifications and applications are displayed in a catalog that is mailed to end users. This may be done by the manufacturer or a reseller.

Central processing unit (CPU)   The control section of a computer.

Cheshire label   Specially prepared paper (rolls, fanfold, or accordian fold) on which names and addresses are printed to be mechanically affixed, one at a time, to a mailing piece.

Closing entries   The entries to transfer the balance from one account to another account.

Common stock   Stock whose owners are not entitled to preferential treatment with regard to dividends or to the distribution of assets in the event of liquidation; usually, common stockholders control the corporation.

Communications software   The software necessary for your computer to communicate with a modem to access on-line services and other computers.

Compiled list   Names and addresses—derived from directories, newspapers, public records, retail sales, trade show registrations, or other sources—that identify groups of customers or prospects with something in common.

Comparability   A financial presentation in which the current balances of accounts are shown in comparison to a previous period.

Complex instruction set computing (CISC)   Traditional computer architecture that uses microcode to execute very comprehensive instructions.

Configuration   A textfile that contains configuration commands used when you start your computer. Commands in the CONFIG.SYS file enable or disable system features, set limits on resources, and extend the operating system functionality by loading device drivers.

Connect time   The amount of time you are logged on to an online service, and is the usual basis for online service billing—usually measured in fractions of an hour.

Continuity program   Products or services bought as a series of small purchases, rather than all at one time. Generally based on a common theme and shipped at regular intervals.

Contra account   Account whose balance is subtracted from another related account to determine a resulting amount. An example is accumulated depreciation.

Co-op mailing   A mailing of two or more offers included in the same envelope or other carrier, with each participating mailer sharing mailing costs according to a predetermined formula.

Cost accounting   The process of identifying manufacturing costs and assigning them to inventory in the manufacturing process.

Cost concept   Assets are ordinarily valued at the price paid to acquire them.

Cost of goods sold   The cost of merchandise sold to customers.

Credit   The right-hand side of an account or an amount entered on the right-hand side of an account.

Creditor   A person or company who lends money or extends credit to a business.

Crossfooting   Combining the amount of an account with debit or credit adjustment to the account on a worksheet. Horizontal addition or subtraction. (Confined to manual accounting systems).

Current assets   Assets which are either currently in the form of cash or are expected to be converted into cash within a short period of time (usually one year).

Current liabilities   Obligations which become due within a short period of time (usually one year).

Current ratio   The ratio obtained by dividing the total of the current assets by the total of the current liabilities.

Database   The structure for storing and controlling information about the relationship between a business and its customers. In direct marketing, a database may provide a means to contact a group of prospects, measure respondents to a direct marketing effort, measure purchasers, and maintain continuing communications.

Database management systems (DBMS)   A computer-based system for defining, creating, manipulating, controlling, managing, and using data-bases.

Days' receivables   The number of days of sales that are tied up in accounts receivable.

Deadbeat   One who has ordered a product or service and, without cause, hasn't paid. "No-Pay", "Uncollectible", and "Delinquent" are often used to describe the same person.

Debit entry   A left-sided entry in the double-entry accounting system.

Debt capital   The capital raised by the issuance of bonds.

Debt ratio   The ratio obtained by dividing debt capital by total capital.

Decoy   A name especially inserted in a mailing list for verifying usage.

Deferred revenue   The liability that arises when a customer pays a business in advance for a service or product. It is a liability because the business has an obligation to render the service or deliver the product.

Depletion   The process of writing off the cost of a wasting asset.

Depreciable assets   Long-term physical assets whose expected economic benefits expire over the useful life of the assets. The related costs must be apportioned as depreciation expense in the accounting periods during which the assets are used.

Depreciation   The process of recognizing a portion of the cost of an asset as an expense during each year of its estimated service life.

Depreciation expense   The part of the cost of a long-term physical asset allocated as an expense to each accounting period in the asset's useful life.

Desktop internet reference   The screen background for Internet on which windows, icons, and dialog boxes appear.

Desktop publishing   Electronic publishing using a microcomputer small enough to fit on a desk.

Dimensional mailing   A mailing of packages or fat letters that stand a good chance of being put on top of a prospect's pile of mail.

Discriminant function (DIF) system scores   The IRS frequently uses a computerized program to determine the potential of a return for examination. Based on IRS experience in examining other returns, the discriminant function (DIF) system scores are assigned to returns as they are processed. Those containing higher potential for a tax adjustment are considered for examination.

DJN/R   Dow Jones News Retrieval is an online news service specializing in financial events and stock market prices.

Direct labor or material   The labor or material that is used directly in the manufacture or fabrication of a product.

Direct marketing   An organized and planned system of contacts, using a variety of media, seeking to acquire or maintain a customer. It requires the development and maintenance of an information base to control targeting, manage the offer, and maintain continuous contact.

Direct marketing or inside sales   An inside sales group that is employed by the manufacturer that sells to end users and resellers via telemarketing and direct mail. This is one of the least expensive ways for a manufacturer to sell a product.

Direct sales   A sales group that is employed by the manufacturer that sells to end users. This is the best type of sales channel but is also the most expensive.

Disk compression   To save storage space by eliminating gaps, empty fields, redundancy, or unnecessary data to shorten the length of records or files.

Distributor   Distributors typically stock a manufacturer's product and resell it to end users. They also typically provide some level of customer support and service.

Dividend   The funds generated by profitable operations that are distributed to the shareholders.

Document management features   Whatever you create with an application, including information you type, edit, view, or save. A document may be a business report, a spreadsheet, a picture, or a letter, and is stored as a file on a disk.

Domain   The set of a field's valid values. For example, a date field can't contain the word "yorkshire."

Double-declining balance method   An accelerated method of depreciation.

Double-entry system   A characteristic of accounting in which each transaction recorded causes at least two changes in the account.

Downloading   The act of retrieving a file from the online services's computer and saving the file to your computer's disk.

Drag-and-drop editing   To move an item on the screen by selecting the item and then pressing and holding down the mouse button while moving the mouse.

Dual-aspect concept   The accounting concept which assumes that the total assets of a company always equal the total equities and liabilities.

Dynamic data exchange (DDE)   A set of conventions that allows information to be transferred automatically between certain Windows applications.

Earnings   Another term for net income.

Earnings per share   A ratio obtained by dividing the total earnings for a given period by the number of shares of common stock outstanding.

E-Mail   Private messages sent back and forth among onl-ine service members.

Employer identification numbers (EIN)   IRS identifies business accounts by assigning a unique nine-digit employer identification number (EIN). Requests for EINS are made on Form SS-4, "Application for Employer Identification Number", available from IRS. A business should have only one number. If a taxpayer has more than one number and is unsure which is the valid number, he or she should check with the Internal Revenue Service center where their returns are filed. A taxpayer, or properly authorized representative, can now call the service center to obtain an EIN using Tele-Tin. Service center personnel can provide the number immediately. Form SS-4 is still required to be mailed to the service center.

End user   The organization or individual that buys and uses the product.

End user database   A group of people, devices, programs, or computer systems that utilize a computer network for the purpose of data processing and information exchange.

Entity concept   The accounting concept which assumes that accounts are kept for business entities, rather than for the persons who own, operate, or are otherwise associated with the business.

Entry   The accounting record made for a single transaction.

Equities   Claims against assets that are held by owners or by creditors.

Equity capital   The capital raised from owners.

Expanded memory   Memory in addition to conventional memory that some non-Windows applications use. Expanded memory is an older standard being replace by the use of extended memory.

Expenditure   An amount arising from the acquisition of an asset.

Expense   A decrease in owners' equity result from operations.

Extended memory   Memory beyond 1 megabyte (MB) in 80286, 80386 and 80486 computers. Windows uses extended memory to manage and run applications.

External cache   An area of memory used to hold data recently read from a hard disk. A cache improves the performance of your system by reducing the number of times Windows has to read your hard disk.

Fair market value   The amount for which an asset can be sold in the marketplace.

Field   A group of associated characters stored in a table's column. Fields are usually classified by data type—character, numeric, date, currency.

FIFO   The first-in, first-out inventory method which assumes that the goods that enter the inventory first are the first to be sold.

File sharing   A structure for file requests (open, read, write, close, etc.) between stations in a network.

Fixed assets   The tangible properties of relatively long life that are generally used in the production of goods and services, rather than being held for resale.

Fixed disk   A disk that is permanently mounted in its drive. Also known as a hard disk.

Flatfile database   A one-dimensional or two-dimensional array: A list or table of items.

Floppy drive   A drive into which a disk can be inserted and removed.

Foot   To total a vertical column of a worksheet. (Applicable to manual systems).

Foreign key   A column or combination of table columns whose values match those in the domain of another table's primary key. Foreign key values need not be, and usually are not, unique.

Forums   Departments of specialized interest usually run by experts in that particular field, where members can exchange messages, questions, and answers; download and upload related software; and sometimes "meet" in live, electronic conferences, or chats. Also referred to as round-tables, special-interest forums, and special-interest groups (SIGs).

Front end   Activities performed to produce responses to a direct-marketing program; the measurement of those activities.

Fulfillment   Delivering the offer made in direct marketing promotion.

Gateway   A service used as a connection between two different on-line services. For example, America Online and CompuServe utilize the gateway function of Internet to allow the members of each to exchange e-mail.

General journal   A journal used for recording adjustments, non-cash transactions, and other entries not appropriate to the receipts or disbursements journals.

General ledger   The book of final entry in the accounting system, where all transactions are summarized for each month, and ending balances are used to prepare financial statements.

Generally accepted accounting principles (GAAP)   Promulgated by the American Institute of Certified Public Accountants (AICPA) and the Securities and Exchange Commission (SEC) to provide more consistency in accounting. The accounting treatment that should be followed in meeting specific accounting problems through certain rules, regulations and opinions.

Going-concern concept   The accounting concept which assumes that a business will continue to operate indefinitely.

Goodwill   An intangible asset; an amount paid for a favorable location or reputation.

Grammar-correction routines   A program that checks documents for usage according to standards established by the U.S. Government Printing Office, Army writing programs and other civilian and military guides.

Graphical user interface (GUI)   A type of computer interface consisting of a visual metaphor of a realworld scene, often of a desktop. Within that scene are icons, representing actual objects, that the user can access and manipulate with a pointing device.

Gross margin   The difference between sales revenue and cost of goods sold.

Hierarchial directories   A data model whose data are nodes of a tree structure.

House list   Any list of names—owned by a business as a result of compilation, inquiry or buyer action, or acquisition—used to promote the business's products or services.

IBM clones   A clone functions like the original, but does not necessarily look identical. It implies 100% IBM compatibility.

Income statement   A statement of revenues and expenses for a given period.

Indirect sales   A small sales group that is employed by the manufacturer that sells to resellers. This is less expensive than direct sales and maintains vendor control.

Industry standard architecture (ISA)   Refers to the original PC Bus architecture, specifically the 16-bit AT bus.

Information management strategy   The functions of controlling the acquisition, analysis, retention, retrieval, and distribution of information.

Input-oriented principles   The input/output section of a computer is an interface between the computer and the outside world.

Intelligent forms processing   Data entry application that provides help screens and low levels of artificial intelligence (AI) in aiding the user to enter the correct data.

Interactive   Pertaining to a program or system that alternately accepts input and then responds.

Interest   Amount charged for the use of money. For an interest-bearing note the interest is computed by multiplying the principal times the annual interest rate for the length of time the note has been issued.

Interest rate   Rate of interest charged on the principal of a note. Expressed as an annual percentage.

Interim financial statements   Financial statements prepared for a period of less than one year.

Internet   A service through which many other online services exchange messages. It is a wide area network connecting thousands of disparate networks in industry, education, government, and research. The Internet network uses TCP/IP as the standard for transmitting information.

Inventories   Goods being held for sale, and material and partially finished products which will be sold upon completion.

Inventory turnover   Tells how many times inventory was totally replaced during the year; calculated by dividing the average inventory into cost of goods sold.

Investments   Securities that are held for a relatively long period-of-time and are purchased for reasons other than the temporary use of excess cash. They are noncurrent assets.

Join   The resulting rows showing columns of information from all tables that are selected by matching the values of related columns in two or more tables.

Journal A record in which entries are recorded in chronological order.

Keyboard Typewriter or teletype terminal. It is the peripheral equipment connected to the input/output section of the computer.

Keyword or jumpword Shorthand names used to quickly access forums and other services. For example, on CompuServe, you type "Go OAG" at the prompt to access to the Official Airline Guide.

Lease An agreement under which the owner of property permits someone else to use it.

Ledger A group of accounts

Liability The equity or claim of a creditor.

Library The department within forums where shareware and freeware files are stored, and to and from which these files are uploaded and downloaded.

LIFO The last-in, first-out inventory method which assumes that the last goods purchased are the first to be sold.

Liquid assets Cash and assets which are easily converted into cash.

Liquidity ratios The relationship of obligations soon coming due to assets which should provide the cash for meeting these obligations.

List broker A specialist who arranges for one business to use the list(s) of another. A broker's services may include list research, selection, recommendation, and subsequent evaluation.

List manager One who, as an employee of a list owner or as an outside agent, is responsible for the use, by others, of a specific mailing list or lists. The list manager generally serves the owner by providing list maintenance, promotion, clearance and recordkeeping, and collection of fees for use of the list by others.

List owner One who, by promotional activity or compilation, has developed a list of names having something in common; one who has purchased (as opposed to rented, reproduced, or used on a one-time basis) such a list from the developer.

Log on The act of connecting to another computer via modem.

Macros In the recorder section of a program, a series of recorded actions.

You can use recorder to create macros. When you run a macro, recorder carries out all the recorded actions.

Mail-merges   To combine the items of two or more sets that are each in the same given order into one set in that order. For example, commonly used to combine the names and addresses of letters and envelopes and incorporating the name into the body of the appropriate document.

Major or minor revision number   In an information resource dictionary, a nonnegative integer that is a component of the version identifier of the access name of an entity and that is assigned consecutively to each change that affects the entity.

Manufacturing overhead   All manufacturing costs that are not direct material or direct labor.

Manufacturer's representative (Rep)   A Rep acts as an agent of the manufacturer and typically has a defined territory or vertical market.

Marketable securities   Securities that are expected to be converted into cash within a year; a current asset.

Master directory   Information stored on disk that describes system characteristics. For example, system data format disk capacity, and main storage capacity.

Matching concept   Costs are matched against the revenue of a period.

Materiality concept   Disregard trivial matters; disclose all important matters.

Messaging API's   A system that manages electronic messaging of application program interfaces.

Money measurement concept   Accounting records show only facts that can be expressed in monetary terms.

Monitor   The cathode ray tube (CRT), which is a television screen, component of the computer.

Mortgage   A pledge of real estate as security for a loan.

Multitasking   Simultaneous processing of two or more applications.

Net book value   The difference between the cost of a fixed asset and its accumulated depreciation.

Net income   The amount by which total revenues exceed total expenses for a given period. Also known as Net Earnings and Net Profit.

Net loss   The amount by which total expenses exceed total revenues for a given period.

Network   A group of computers connected by cables or other means and using software that enables them to share equipment (such as printers and disk drives) and exchange information.

Nixie   A mailing piece returned to a mailer (under proper authorization) by the postal service because of an incorrect or undeliverable name and address.

Node   In a network, a point at which one or more functional units connect channels or data circuits.

Nominal account   An income statement account that is closed at the end of the period to a balance sheet account.

Noncurrent liability   A claim which does not fall due within one year.

Normalization   The separation of data elements into naturally associated groups and defining the correct or right relationships among them—one of the first and most crucial steps in the design of an effective relational database.

Note (notes receivable or payable)   An amount owed that is evidenced by a promissory note.

Notes to financial statements   Pertain to an AICPA rule that "departures from Board opinions must be disclosed in footnotes to the financial statements or in independent auditor's reports when the effect of the departure on the financial statements is material."

Null value   A missing or inapplicable data value as opposed to a blank string or zero numeric value.

Object linking and embedding (OLE)   A way to transfer and share information between applications.

Obsolescence   A loss in the usefulness of an asset because of the development of improved equipment, changes in style, or other causes not related to the physical condition of the asset.

Offer   The terms promoting a specific product or service; the proposition made to customers or prospects to elicit an action.

Office automation   The integration of office activities by means of an information processing system. The term includes in particular the processing and communication of text, images, and voice.

Operating expenses   Costs associated with sales and administrative activities as distinct from those associated with production of goods or services.

Original equipment manufacturer (OEM)   An OEM private labels a vendor's product and resells it as their product. This typically requires a label or nameplate change to match the reseller's other products. Software and operator's manual changes may be required to display the OEM's name.

OS/2   Single user, multitasking PC operating system for 286s computers and up. The 16-bit versions have been developed by Microsoft Corporation and IBM. The 32-bit versions are being developed independently.

Outer join   A join of information from tables that includes information from rows where a null value in the specified common column of one table does not match any value in the common column of the other table.

Output-oriented principles   Messages and other output data, printed or displayed on output devices by an operating system or a processing program.

Overhead rate   A rate used to allocate overhead costs to products.

Owners' equity   The claims of owners against the assets of a business.

Page set-up   The electronic representation of a single-sided physical page.

Paid in capital   An amount in excess of the par or stated value of stock that is paid by investors.

Partition   A fixed-size division of storage.

Par value   The specific amount printed on the face of a stock certificate.

Partnership   An unincorporated business with two or more owners.

PC-DOS   A disk operating system based on MS-DOS that operates with all IBM and IBM compatible computers.

PC Magazine Aimed at relatively experienced and sophisticated end user audience. Published 22 issues per year.

PC World Bimonthly magazine devoted to multimedia computing.

Peripheral Device Any device that can communicate with a particular computer.

Per inquiry (P.I.) A payment method where a marketer agrees to pay for services on a per-inquiry basis.

Period costs Costs associated with general sales and administrative activities.

Physical inventory The counting of all merchandise currently on hand.

Piggy-back An offer that hitches a free ride with another offer.

Posting To add, or upload a message to an online service bulletin board. Also in accounting, the process of transferring transactions from the journal to the ledger.

Preferred stock Stock whose owners receive preferential treatment with regard to dividends or with regard to the distribution of assets in the event of liquidation.

Prepaid expenses Services and certain intangibles purchased prior to the period during which their benefits are received; treated as assets until they are consumed.

Price-earnings ratio A ratio obtained by dividing the average market price of the stock by the earnings per share.

Primary key A field in a table that contains a unique value for each record to identify each row. Tables with primary keys are mathematically known as relations.

Principal Amount of a note.

Printer An output unit that produces a hard copy record of data mainly in the form of a sequence of discrete graphic characters that belong to one or more predetermined character sets.

Product costs Costs associated with the manufacture of products.

Profit margin   Net income expressed as a percentage of net sales.

Programming language   An artificial language for expressing computer programs.

Proprietorship   An unincorporated business with a single owner.

Protocol   The settings that determine how two computers will communicate.

Purge   The process of eliminating duplicates and/or unwanted names and addresses from one or more lists.

Query   A string of statements that when executed returns a data set from one or more tables. For example, a query could locate all customers in a particular state that have a yes in a certain field.

Quick assets   Current assets other than inventory and prepaid expenses.

Random access memory (RAM)   The memory that can be used by applications to perform necessary tasks while the computer is on. When you turn the computer off, all information in RAM is lost.

Real account   An account with a balance after the closing process has been completed; it appears on the balance sheet.

Realization concept   An accounting concept which assumes that revenue is recognized when goods are delivered or services are performed, in an amount that is reasonably certain to be realized.

Recency   The latest purchase or other activity recorded for an individual or company on a specific customer list.

Recognize   The act of recording a revenue or expense item in a given accounting period.

Record   A group of related fields (all the columns) stared in a row of a database table.

Record lock   A lock that prevents some or all of a file from being written to or read.

Records management   Creation, retention, and scheduled destruction of an organization's paper and film documents.

Reduced instruction set computing (RISC)   A computer that uses a small simplified set of frequently used instructions for rapid execution.

Referential integrity   A database characteristic that assures that no entry in a child table can exist if its foreign key does not match a value in the domain of a parent's primary key.

Relation   A database table where each row is different from all other rows; all rows are distinct. Relations have primary keys.

Remainder   In a division operation, the number or quantity that is the undivided part of the dividend, having an absolute value less than the absolute value of the divisor, and that is one of the results of a division operation.

Residual value   The amount for which a compnay expects to be able to sell a fixed asset at the end of its service life.

Response rate   Percentage of returns or inquiries from a mailing.

Retained earnings   The increase in the shareholders' equity as a result of profitable company operations.

Return   The amount earned on invested funds during a period.

Return on shareholders' investment   A ratio obtained by dividing the return by the average amount of shareholders' investment for the period.

Revenue   An increase in owners' equity resulting from operations.

Reversing entry   Journal entry that is the exact reverse (both account titles and amounts) of an adjusting entry. Dated the first day of the new accounting period. It is optional and used to simplify the recording of a later transaction related to the adjusting entry.

Root directory   The top-level directory of a disk. The root directory is created when you format the disk. From the root directory, you can create files and other directories.

Roundtables   See forums.

Rule-based routing   A computer system which performs inferences by applying a set of if then rules to a set of facts following given procedures.

Salting   Deliberate placing of decoy or dummy names in a list to trace usage and delivery.

Security   An instrument such as a stock or bond.

Seek time   The time required for the access arm of a direct access storage device to be positioned on the appropriate track.

Service life   The period of time over which an asset is estimated to be of service to the company.

Shareholders   The owners of an incorporated business.

Software   The set of instructions that make computer hardware perform tasks. Programs, operating systems, device drivers, and applications are all software.

Solvency   The ability to meet long-term obligations.

Sound card   In multimedia, an add-on adapter card that incorporates a synthesizer without a musical keyboard and has audio output jacks for the sound created.

Source code   The input to a compiler or assembler, written in a source language.

Special-interest forums   See forums.

Special-interest groups (SIGs)   See forums.

Spelling checker   A computer program in a text processing system that verifies the spelling of words in text by means of a stored dictionary.

Spreadsheet   A worksheet arranged in rows and columns, in which a change in the contents of one cell can cause electronic recomputation of one or more cells, based on user-defined relations among the cells.

SQL Structured query language (pronounced "sequel").   A language for expressing and presenting information requests, for updating contents and for creating/altering the structure of relational databases. ANSI/ISO SQL standards have been published and is considered the language of choice for relational databases. The SQL SELECT command is universally used to query relational databases.

Standard industrial classification code (SIC)   A uniform coding sytem set up by the United States government to classify businesses and professions. It is also used by the Internal Revenue Service for classification of business taxpayers.

Stated value   The amount that the directors decide is the value of no-par stock.

Statement of cash flows   This shows where cash came from (profits, capital invested, sale of assets, or loan proceeds, for example), where it was spent (to buy equipment or reduce a loan balance, for example), and how much your working capital increased or decreased during the year. You always use the same closing date for financial statements that are prepared together.

Statement of changes in financial position A financial statement explaining the changes that have occurred in asset, liability, and owners' equity items in an accounting period.

Statement of income Also called the profit and loss statement, this reports the income, costs, expenses and net profit for a specified period.

Statement stuffer A small, printed piece designed to be inserted in an envelope to carry a customer's statement of account, such as the bill sent by a credit card company.

Straight-line Method of depreciation that records an equal portion of the cost of an asset as depreciation expense in each accounting period in which the asset is used.

Style sheet A file that contains layout settings for a particular category of document. Style sheets include such settings as margins, tabs, headers and footers, columns and fonts.

Sub-chapter S corporation A corporation which has elected under sub-chapter S of the IRS tax code (by unanimous consent of its shareholders) not to pay any corporate tax on its income and, instead, to have the shareholders pay taxes on it, even though it is not distributed. In many respects, sub-chapter S permits a corporation to behave for tax purposes as a proprietorship or partnership.

Sub-distributor A smaller reseller that works for a distributor. They may or may not stock product and provide support.

Support Training and assistance with technical problems.

System integrator An SI usually provides a large turnkey system to an end user that includes multiple vendors' products. SIs are especially geared to work with government agency purchasers.

System memory All of the addressable storage space in a processing unit and other internal storage devices that is used to execute instructions.

System processor The logic that contains the processor function to translate and process the computer's control language commands and programming language statements.

Table A row-and-column structure or arrangement of data values; typically composed of fields (columns) and records (rows). The central organizing element in a relational database. Rows may be and usually are unordered.

Target market Businesses or individuals identified as the type who will buy a particular product or service; in business-to-business marketing, companies are identified by such characteristics as number of employees, annual sales, SIC code, etc.

Taxable income The amount of income subject to income tax, computed according to the rules of the Internal Revenue Service.

Taxpayer compliance measurement program (TCMP) TCMP is a random selection system to determine the correct tax liability. The results of these thorough examinations are used to measure and evaluate taxpayer compliance characteristics and also to calculate discriminant function (DIF) system scores which are used to evaluate returns for potential examination.

Tax year Every business must compute taxable income and file a tax return on the basis of a period of time called a tax year. A tax year is usually twelve consecutive months. It can be either a calendar year (from January 1 to December 31) or a fiscal year (any period of fifty-two to fifty-three weeks). The tax year under certain conditions can be shorter than twelve months, but never longer.

Template A pattern to help the user identify the location of keys on a keyboard, functions assigned to keys on a keyboard, or switches and lights on a control panel.

Tower Floor-standing cabinet taller than it is wide. Desktop computers can be made into towers by turning them on their side and inserting them into a floor-mounted base.

Transaction A business event that is recorded in the accounting records.

Transistor A small solid-state semiconducting device that can perform nearly all the functions of an electronic tube, including amplification and rectification.

Treasury stock Previously issued stock that has been bought back by the company.

Tree structure   A data structure that represents entities in nodes, with at most one parent node for each node, and with only one root node.

Trial balance   A worksheet summarizing and proving the balances of all accounts in the general ledger. A preliminary step to the preparation of financial statements.

Unearned income   Advance receipt for goods or services to be provided in the future. Recorded as a liability at the time of receipt. An example is unearned rent.

Universe   Total number of individuals who might be included on a mailing list; individuals who fit a single set of specifications.

Uploading   The act of sending a file to the online service's computer for one or more other members to access.

User interface   Hardware, software, or both that allows a user to interact with and perform operations on a system, program, or device.

Validity checking   The process of assuring that all values entered for a field fall within an allowable domain of values. For example, a typical validity check would make sure that only numerical digits are entered in a social security number field.

Value added reseller (VAR)   A VAR provides enhanced product offerings. They take the vendor's product and add additional value. This may be accomplished through the use of hardware, software or service.

Version number   Identification of a release of software.

Video electronics standards association (VESA)   Organization of major PC graphics vendors devoted to improving graphics standards. It is involved with video controller, monitor and multimedia standards.

Video text   An interactive text-retrieval service.

View   Literally, a view to table information returned by a query. A view can include data from multiple tables.

White mail   Incoming mail that isn't on a form sent by the advertiser; all mail other than orders and payments.

Word processor   A desktop or portable device into which text can be entered and stored along with format control and characters. Stored text can be moved, copied, deleted, altered, added to, displayed and printed, usually in various formats and fonts.

Worksheet A large columnar accounting paper for initially preparing the trial balance, adjustments, adjusted trial balance, income statement, and balance sheet at the end of an accounting period. With computerized accounting this is all provided electronically.

Write down To reduce the cost of an item, especially inventory, to its market value.

ABOUT THE AUTHOR

Jack Fox is President of Jack Fox Associates/Accounting Resources Group, in San Diego, California. This is a consulting firm specializing in the accounting and recordkeeping needs of the self-employed and equipping their solution providers to fulfill those needs.

He earned a Bachelor's Degree, in Business Administration from the City College of the City University of New York, and an M.B.A. from the Bernard M. Baruch College of the City University of New York. During the last twenty five years, he has assisted thousands of newly and established self-employed business owners improve their financial abilities and profitability. It is the lessons from these experiences as well as from the failures and successes of his own business ventures that formed the basis for this book.

Mr. Fox has been devoted to the development of marketing, accounting, and data management skills with a keen focus on the self-employed. As an accomplished speaker, seminar leader, and marketing consultant, he provides a wide range of resources for individuals, business, nonprofit, and educational organizations. Jack Fox is noted for his individually crafted presentations and self-employment focused practical approach to consulting, made even more effective by an engaging sense of humor. As a speaker and consultant, he has helped self-employed business people of diverse fields and executives at some of the country's top companies understand and form strategic partnerships. Fully customized on-site keynote presentations and seminar and workshop programs are offered.

ABOUT THE AUTHOR

Jack Fox, keynote speaker, seminar leader and consultant is available upon request in your area. Mr. Fox's presentations, which he has given for associations, colleges and community colleges, *VarBusiness* magazine, county governments, and *The New York Times*, are known for their practical information, results and humor.

For further information, inquiries, comments and availabilities of open dates for live appearances . . . please call or write:

JACK FOX
Accounting Resources Group
6115 Gullstrand Street
San Diego, CA 92122-3823
(619) 452-8403

INDEX

T

INDEX